Strange Son

Strange Son

TWO MOTHERS, TWO SONS, AND THE QUEST
TO UNLOCK THE HIDDEN WORLD OF AUTISM

PORTIA IVERSEN

RIVERHEAD BOOKS

a member of Penguin Group (USA) Inc.

New York

2006

RIVERHEAD BOOKS
Published by the Penguin Group
Penguin Group (USA) Inc., 375 Hudson Street, New York, New York 10014,
USA • Penguin Group (Canada), 90 Eglinton Avenue East, Suite 700, Toronto,
Ontario M4P 2Y3, Canada (a division of Pearson Penguin Canada Inc.) • Penguin
Books Ltd, 80 Strand, London WC2R 0RL, England • Penguin Ireland,
25 St Stephen's Green, Dublin 2, Ireland (a division of Penguin Books Ltd) • Penguin
Group (Australia), 250 Camberwell Road, Camberwell, Victoria 3124, Australia
(a division of Pearson Australia Group Pty Ltd) • Penguin Books India Pvt Ltd,
11 Community Centre, Panchsheel Park, New Delhi–110 017, India • Penguin
Group (NZ), Cnr Airborne and Rosedale Roads, Albany, Auckland 1310, New
Zealand (a division of Pearson New Zealand Ltd) • Penguin Books (South Africa)
(Pty) Ltd, 24 Sturdee Avenue, Rosebank, Johannesburg 2196, South Africa

Penguin Books Ltd, Registered Offices:
80 Strand, London WC2R 0RL, England

ISBN-13: 978-1-57322-311-9
ISBN-10: 1-57322-311-5

Printed in the United States of America
1   3   5   7   9   10   8   6   4   2

Book design by Amanda Dewey

While the author has made every effort to provide accurate telephone numbers and Internet
addresses at the time of publication, neither the publisher nor the author assumes any
responsibility for errors, or for changes that occur after publication. Further, the publisher
does not have any control over and does not assume any responsibility for author or third-
party websites or their content.

To Dov

CONTENTS

I have begotten a strange son. He is not like an ordinary human being, but he looks like the children of the angels of heaven to me, his form is different, and he is not like us. . . . It does not seem to me that he is of me, but of the angels. . . .

—Lamech, from the Book of Noah

Preface

It was his mind they came for. They came to steal his mind.

Before anyone gave it a name, even before I knew what it was, I knew it was in our house. I can't say exactly how I knew. Except that I could feel it. Not that I wanted to. Believe me. They were very, very dark things. And there was no way to get rid of them.

Sometimes I could hear them, late at night, when the house was very quiet; a creaking sound, an inexplicable hiss, a miniscule pop, a whistle out of nowhere. And when I closed my eyes, I felt their shadows passing over me as they floated through the house and drifted invisibly with the smoke, up the fireplace chimney, out into space, back to God knows where. I didn't like to think about where they came from or where they were going. It was too frightening. Dov was only a baby and something was trying to steal him away. Sooner or later, I knew I would catch them swirling above his crib. I knew that was what they did whenever I accidentally fell asleep.

A violent thudding jolted my senses awake. My heart was banging like two fists in my chest. How long had I been sleeping? My eyes darted over to the crib I was supposed to be watching. He was still there. I could see him through the white wooden bars. Asleep. His small body gently rising and falling with each little breath.

Night after night, I sat beside his crib. I knew he was slipping away from us, away from our world. And there was nothing I could do to stop it from happening. There was nothing anybody could do, they told me. So I did the only thing I could. I guarded him, although I knew it would do no good, because I could not guard his mind.

And then one day, it had happened. He was gone.

1.

Departure of the Mind

There is a small group of people in this world to whom an event so devastating has occurred that they may even have stopped believing in God. Yet the one characteristic those struck by lightning share is a deep and persistent vulnerability to the possibility of miracles. The very fact that something so impossibly terrible could have happened makes the chance of a miracle seem just as possible. Although I didn't recognize it in myself, I am certain it was this vulnerability to miracles that was at work when I first heard of Tito Mukhopadhyay.

It happened on a rainy spring day in 1999 at Rutgers University in New Jersey where I was attending a conference called Attention and Arousal in Autism that I had organized for the Cure Autism Now foundation. Our son Dov was seven years old.

"There's a boy I think you should know about," Francesca Happe began, gesturing for me to sit down. "His name is Tito." The renowned psychologist from England, whose specialty was autism, continued: "He's eleven years old and he lives in India. He's quite autistic, but he can read and write and he's very intelligent."

She smiled at me and paused before going on, as if to gauge my reaction.

"Tito is a wonderful poet as well," she continued. "He's even published a book, an autobiography with some of his poetry in it."

"And he's autistic?" I asked in disbelief, thinking I must have misunderstood.

"Yes, he is definitely autistic."

Francesca's colleagues in England had heard about this severely autistic boy in India whose mother had taught him to communicate by pointing at letters on a board. Of course they didn't believe he could really be autistic, since a profound deficit in the ability to communicate was a hallmark of the disorder. So they invited Tito and his mother to England to be tested by experts and settle the question of his autism once and for all. To their astonishment, Tito fulfilled the diagnostic criteria for autism beyond a doubt.

"Do you think there could be other autistic people like Tito?" I asked Francesca, trying not to sound too hopeful.

"There is only one Tito in this world, and no one else like him. He is his own disorder," she replied with certainty.

I knew that no one had ever heard of such a severely autistic person being able to write and communicate independently. But wasn't there even a remote chance that there could be others who looked and acted just like Tito but couldn't communicate? At the very least, couldn't Tito provide an extraordinary window into the most severe kind of autism?

As soon as the New Jersey conference was over, I began e-mailing Francesca in England. I had to find Tito. To my dismay, Francesca no longer had their correct address and said her attempts to locate Tito and his mother Soma in India had failed. She said they kept moving because people were superstitious about Tito and afraid of him. But I might be able to get a copy of Tito's book if I contacted the National Autism Society of the United Kingdom, she suggested. The BBC had made a documentary about Tito when he was visiting England, although it was hard to find.

Francesca did not understand. Finding Tito was not optional. Finding Tito was a matter of life and death. Or perhaps I should say it was like being told that maybe, just maybe, you could bring someone back from the dead.

Before Dov became autistic I used to be a sitcom writer and before that I was an art director and a set decorator. And, nearly twenty years ago, when I first arrived in Hollywood in a pickup truck with my six-year-old son Billy, escaping a midwestern winter and a lousy marriage, I dreamed of becoming a filmmaker.

Being the land of dreams, it wasn't long before I landed my first job in Hollywood. It was called craft services, a term I soon learned meant serving coffee and cleaning up after the crew fourteen hours a day.

And it wasn't long before I met the man of my dreams, a Jewish matinee-idol-handsome man on whom I would have a crush for seven miserable years, before his deeply neurotic indecisiveness allowed him to choose me as the dreaded "friend for life." This term struck a chord of fear in his heart and cruelly cut short his unrealized dreams of a sex-crazed bachelor lifestyle, which he'd always been waiting for, not that he had ever had one or ever would. Still, it was the idea that he could, that I robbed him of, by marrying him. By the time we actually did get married, Jonathan was a struggling but mostly working movie producer, I had won an Emmy for art direction on the *Tracey Ullman Show*, Billy was thirteen years old, and I was five months pregnant.

After our honeymoon, we moved into the lower unit of a Spanish-style duplex in the mid-Wilshire district of L.A. Jon and I spent our weekends window shopping for the furniture we wished we could afford and driving around town dreaming of the house we would buy someday. We became even happier when our extraordinarily beautiful baby boy Dov was born.

That summer, we met Jon's parents at the Jersey Shore for our vacation. We walked along the beach holding hands with our little baby riding in a pack on Jon's shoulders while Billy ran alongside us, drawing in the sand with a stick, and we were happy. Jon and I talked about all the things we wanted to do in life, about our careers and decorating our house, about traveling and how many children we wanted to have, imagining our idyllic future with an optimism reserved for those who have never experienced tragedy.

It's hard to say exactly when we first suspected something was wrong.

Babies do get fevers and babies can seem irritable or lethargic after an immunization, it's true. But as Dov lay in his crib, looking quiet and gray for the next three days, I could hardly get him to nurse at all. "Just a common reaction to the vaccination," Dr. Fleiss said over the phone reassuringly. But Dov was never the same. He stopped gaining weight and every time he nursed, he would writhe and cry, flailing his skinny little arms as if nursing hurt his stomach, and I often spent my afternoons sitting in the doctor's office. I knew something was wrong with Dov and so did Dr. Fleiss. But no one knew what it was or what to do.

By four months old, although Dov was still breast-feeding, I could hardly get him to nurse for more than a few minutes at a time. I tried to get him to take a bottle, but he refused. He was barely gaining weight and his stomach problems seemed to be growing worse by the day. Then one day, to my surprise, he suddenly chugged down a whole bottle of soy formula. The next thing I knew, his face turned gray, he projectile-vomited and lost consciousness. It was the weekend, and luckily Jon was at home when it happened. I couldn't tell if Dov was breathing as I held his limp little body in my arms on the way to the hospital. I'd never been inside Children's Hospital of Los

Angeles before. I had no idea what a familiar place it was going to become.

"What did you give him?" a resident bellowed at us as we carried him into the emergency room. Dov's white blood cell count was sky high. He'd had a near-fatal reaction to something. *But what?* They hooked his tiny body up to a hundred tubes and cords and a big light shone down on him. But no one knew what was wrong, no one could figure out what had happened to him. And no one ever did. After a while he regained consciousness and they moved him to a room. We stayed at the hospital for the next three days. The thought that these events could have anything to do with a developmental disorder never crossed our minds.

What little impression I had of autism when Dov was a baby came from a picture I'd glimpsed on the cover of a magazine years earlier. It was a picture of a boy who rocked in the corner all day, a boy who had withdrawn into himself completely—a condition they called autism, which doctors mistakenly thought was caused by bad parenting—a belief that tragically persisted for over fifty years, devastating parents and preventing any kind of advocacy or scientific research from getting under way.

Jon was worried about Dov's development long before I was and I was angry at him for imagining such terrible things, much less saying them out loud. Why was he so being so negative?

Jon was a first-time dad. He needed to relax. Hadn't we heard a hundred times over that every child is different? We needed to give Dov a chance to be who he was and not compare him to other kids. We needed to stop worrying so much.

Still, at night, after Jon was asleep, because I didn't want him to know, I pored through the baby books, looking for things I saw Dov doing, or not doing, that were beginning to worry me. But I couldn't find any descriptions that matched Dov's behavior. Maybe that meant they were insignificant, silly, hysterical-parent worries, not even worthy of mention in the Dr. Spock and Brazelton bibles of baby and toddler development. Or maybe it meant they were not so common—serious, devastating things that were too terrible to be listed. No, I told myself, snapping the last book shut, I wasn't going down that path.

Ever since we were kids, my sister Sarah had an intense fascination with Helen Keller and Annie Sullivan, so when she told me she thought we should get Dov's hearing checked, I was alarmed. But I also knew that Sarah could sometimes overreact and make a big deal out of things.

Besides, Dov was not deaf. In fact, certain sounds seemed to frighten him badly, like the vacuum cleaner or the blender. But there *was* something strange about his hearing lately. It seemed to have changed. Loud sounds like pot lids banging didn't seem to startle him at all and sometimes he didn't seem to hear his name being called.

For the first time in months, I was actually looking forward to seeing Dr. Fleiss. It was Dov's twelve-month checkup and by now most of his early health problems had cleared up and he seemed stable.

I felt optimistic as I entered the craftsman-style bungalow, with its rainbow-painted windows and waiting room filled with mothers on corduroy couches breast-feeding their babies. Dr. Fleiss's practice was a friendly, '60s-style place. Just being there made you feel like if you ate your veggies and breast-fed, everything would be all right. I loved hearing Dr. Fleiss's reassuring voice as he counseled his smallest patients: "I'm your doctor, I make you feel all better."

I set Dov down in the small examination room and watched as he careened around, chattering away in high-pitched sounds, to no one in particular. He was wearing blue checked shorts that day and his blond hair was cut in a bowl shape that swung to and fro as he inspected every object in that tiny room. As I sat there waiting, I tried to make a mental checklist of the things that I was worried about and the things Jon wanted me to ask Dr. Fleiss.

Dov had started shaking his head back and forth a lot lately. And we'd noticed his cheeks turning red. He was opening and closing the kitchen cabinets over and over. It was harder to get his attention. He seemed to have odd reactions to sounds. I kept replaying the list in my mind to keep it from going blank with nervousness.

At last, Dr. Fleiss came in to see us. I'd been coming to him since Billy was a kid, his shaggy hair and wire-rimmed glasses had probably not changed since college. We talked for a few minutes as he observed Dov and jotted down some notes.

"Jon is worried about Dov," I started out. "I was hoping you could reassure him that everything's okay." Fleiss just kept writing, looking up over his glasses at Dov and writing some more. I didn't like how much he was writing. And I didn't like how long he was taking to answer me.

Dr. Fleiss got down on his hands and knees and started talking to Dov. But Dov didn't seem to notice Dr. Fleiss. He just kept running from toy to toy, jabbering away and making high-pitched noises. Dr. Fleiss followed Dov around the small room on all fours, trying to get his attention, calling his name, offering him a ball, even tickling him. I wished Dov would just look at Dr. Fleiss, I wished he would turn his head when Dr. Fleiss said his name.

Dr. Fleiss stood up. "I think you should see a specialist," he said.

"What kind of a specialist?" I blurted out, in shock.

"A developmental psychologist."

"But why? What do you think is wrong?"

Fleiss thought for a moment. "He might have some kind of a personality disorder."

"What do you mean?" I asked, stricken.

Dr. Fleiss looked away. He seemed to be considering his words carefully. "Sometimes we see these things. The way he's running around, making those sounds, not connecting with people."

"But isn't that the way all one-year-olds act?" I said defensively, suddenly knowing that it was not.

I left the little craftsman house that had once been my refuge in the storm, shaken, with a small scrap of paper in my hand. The number of a specialist to call.

It was the Friday morning of Memorial Day weekend. Four days during which all offices would be closed and all experts, specialists, and other highly paid miracle workers would not be available. But this was an emergency.

I knew I should call Jon. But I couldn't do it. I would wait until he came home from work. I would let him have a few more precious hours of not knowing. I felt a sudden wave of relief. I had won a few more hours before Dr. Fleiss's dreadful pronouncement would have to be shared with anyone. Before it would spread and grow beyond the containment of my own private fearful knowledge, to invade every part of our lives, as I sensed it would.

I was so afraid. I needed to talk to someone. My sister Lenore was a child psychiatrist. She would know what to do. Lenore listened quietly as I told her what Fleiss had said. How I wished she would argue with me, say that Fleiss was out of his league, out of his mind, anything but just listen quietly. Lenore said she knew some specialists at UCLA and she would try to get us in to see them as soon as possible.

I looked down at my lap and saw that I was still clutching the scrap of paper Fleiss had handed me, with that terrible, damning name and number that irreversibly linked us to those tragic worlds I did not want to know about. But it was too late now, the damage was done. This unlucky slip of paper with its dreadful implications had already cast a shadow across our lives and Dov's future. How could he have handed it to me so blithely, not thinking of the consequences, the pain and suffering it would cause? I hated Dr. Fleiss now.

Then slowly, as if someone else were prying open my hand, I allowed the damp, crumpled piece of paper to unfurl in my open palm, and, like a small bird, gave it one last chance to fly away. And when it did not alight, when it would not vanish or burst into flames or blow away in a sudden gust of wind, only then did I do the only thing left to do. I smoothed it out, releasing the black hex that was embedded in those words and numbers, and I dialed Dr. Arthur Rosenberg, the developmental psychologist.

We were lucky to get a phone appointment with Dr. Rosenberg over the holiday weekend, his receptionist told me. But I did not feel lucky at all. The call was set for Saturday afternoon, the next day.

I broke the news to Jon that night. We couldn't stop talking because the silence scared us. We worried and argued, we agreed and disagreed, we panicked and soothed, we fought and made up, we did and said everything we could think of until we ran dry and just sat there, watching Dov sleep in his sweet one-year-old unknowingness.

The next afternoon, we called Dr. Rosenberg. A nondescript voice answered at the other end of the line. A generic picture snapped into my mind—tweed jacket, brown hair, fiftyish—more than I needed to know. We thanked Dr. Rosenberg for talking to us and immediately launched into all the things we had discussed endlessly through the long night, cataloging what worried us about Dov. We talked on top of each other, we interrupted each other, we finished each other's sentences. Breathless and intent, all the while hoping we were being complete idiots, we exhausted every worry, paired with every explanation, that we could produce for the doctor in the course of one phone call, until at last there was nothing left to say.

"It sounds like autism," Dr. Rosenberg said finally.

"What do we do about that?" Jon blurted out, incredulous.

Dr. Rosenberg cleared his throat and answered slowly, deliberately, without emotion, as if he were prescribing an ordinary painkiller, which I suppose he was: "Just hold on to each other and cry. Get on with your lives."

Hold on to each other? We weren't even in the same room, for God's sake. Didn't he realize we were on separate phones? And, although I could not see him, I knew Jon was crying. And I was sure he knew that I was crying too, although our tears were the quiet kind. I was glad we couldn't see each other because it was too sad and it wouldn't help us to see each other falling apart this way. We were going to have to be strong, stronger than we had ever been in our lives, and we both knew it.

Later that night, we did hold on to each other as tightly as we could, and for a long time we clung to each other and just stood there. But no matter what, we were not going to take that doctor's advice. Maybe we would cry, it was so hard not to, but we would not just get on with our lives.

The first person we went to see was Dr. Shelly, an elegant and kindly white-haired woman, recommended by an analyst we knew. She was a developmental psychologist who recommended play therapy. Jon began taking afternoons off work and we drove across town to the Palisades where Dov had play therapy twice a week. Dr. Shelly had a room full of toys that were supposed to make children get better: teapots for the pretend play that Dov wasn't doing and little dolls for the social behavior that was not emerging. She told us to hold off on going to UCLA for a diagnosis. Maybe Dov would start to get better. We liked the sound of that; it was hopeful and reassuring. But as the months passed, Dov didn't seem to be getting better. In fact he was getting worse. He no longer turned when we called his name and instead of running to Jon, he preferred to stare at the specks of dust suspended in the shaft of light that came through the door when his father came home.

We saw a developmental pediatrician, a child psychiatrist, a pediatric neurologist, a metabolic geneticist, a chiropractor, and a naturopath. Dov had blood tests and an EEG.

But no one knew what to do and no one was quite as certain that Dov was autistic as Dr. Rosenberg had been on that first phone call.

As the weeks grew into months we were sucked into a gray tunnel of time, waiting for some kind of pronouncement that would end our unbearable state of not knowing; waiting for those few words of advice that could either lift the curse off our lives or bring our world crashing down. This was not normal sequential time, it was the painful, agonizing, slowed-down kind of time that occurs when panic intersects with endless waiting.

Every day Jon got up and went to work and tried to do his job. And every day I took care of Dov and played with him and tried to get his attention and hoped that he would get better. I dreaded the ringing of the phone because I could not explain to anyone what was happening to us. Yet somehow life went on and although we didn't know it, I was already pregnant with our daughter, Miriam.

Dov was eighteen months old when we finally went in for a diagnostic workup at UCLA. It was dark and hot in the tiny room where I stood and watched from behind a one-way mirror as they tested Dov. Jon was in there with him, sitting on a tiny child's chair, holding on to Dov as they tried to test him. They had been testing him for more than two hours when I saw they were letting Dov out of the room and I knew they were done. Jon stood up and scooped up Dov, and he stared for a moment at the mirror, where he knew I was watching.

"Autism," the doctor finally said.

"Autism?" I repeated. I wanted to scream at them: "That's impossible. Einstein didn't talk until he was five. Thomas Edison didn't either, and they were both geniuses. Most boys talk late, everyone says that. Dov's grandfather is an accomplished attorney, the stoic type, always reading briefs or writing them in his head, not that sociable, it could just be a personality trait that runs in the family. Big deal." But I said nothing.

"What should we do?" Jon asked, breaking the silence.

"There are special schools," the doctor replied.

"Isn't there anything else we could do?" Jon persisted. "Special diets, vitamins, therapies?"

"We don't usually tell parents to do those things," the doctor said. "We don't want to give you false hope."

Outside in the brightness of the hospital hallway, I broke down and wept on Jon's shoulder while Dov ran up and down the corridor, making high-pitched shrieking sounds, never tiring. "If he had cancer," I sobbed, "at least we would know what to do."

The day after our visit to the UCLA clinic, I carried Dov into the Cheerful Helpers group for the last time. Cheerful Helpers was a Mommy and Me group where a few "at-risk" toddlers were included to be carefully watched by specialists for signs of developmental delay. I'd been taking Dov to the group for about six months and now, for the first time, I allowed myself to admit that he wasn't doing the same things as the other children. He wasn't playing purposefully with toys, or pointing to things, and he wasn't coming to me for help. He made lots of sounds but he never said "Mama," or anything else that resembled a word. I didn't know that his failure to point or wave were classic signs of autism.

I hoped the group had forgotten that Dov's evaluation was yesterday. At last, the hour passed and everyone was starting to clean up. The moment I had been avoiding all morning hadn't happened. I was sitting on the edge of one of those big cement planters, zipping up Dov's sky blue windbreaker, when the program director, the cheerfulest helper of all, with the pink lipstick and the degree in psychology and the three normal children, asked, "How did it go?"

Instinctively, I picked up Dov. "They said . . ." I started out, hoping I could stay calm. I would not let this woman see me fall apart. And yet how could I say it and not fall to pieces? "They said he has something, he has a pervasive developmental disorder." The Cheerful Helper gazed sadly at me and said nothing.

"It's not autism," I said quickly, instantly regretting it, but unable to stop myself from continuing, "It's . . . well, a lot of kids have it these days."

The Cheerful Helper pursed her lips in a half smile, or a half frown, I couldn't tell which. Her perfectly shaped eyebrows gathered slightly in the middle, in an expression that said, *Sorry to hear that, What a shame, Too bad,* better than any words ever could.

"They say there are therapies, special schools." I added urgently. But I could not go on. I had started to cry and I hated it when people saw me crying. Especially here, holding Dov. They must know by now, just by looking at me, what had happened yesterday. I looked at the faces that had already started to gather around, then I looked at the blue sky and the medical towers and the clouds that were not moving, and I ran out of there.

After the diagnosis, I did what I always did when I was in trouble— I turned to books. I have a lot of faith in books of every kind. If the library was a sanctuary in my childhood, the bookstore was a church. For it was there, my mother taught me, that you could turn for help in your darkest moments, reaching out to the almighty pyramid-shaped displays of self-help paperbacks whose titles changed weekly. It was there that my mother, who was widowed at thirty-one with four children under the age of seven, never failed to find answers to just about everything in life.

Autism, I discovered, would be a different story. For the first time in my life, I could not find the answers I needed in any book.

"So I guess autism is when you can't do anything?" Billy asked as much as said one day when he was fourteen. Billy was trying to understand the terrible thing that had turned our household and our lives upside down; the thing that had stolen away the baby brother he used to know. "They don't really know what it is," I said miserably, wishing I had a better explanation.

In the first few years that followed Dov's diagnosis at UCLA, the Spanish duplex we lived in became filled to the limit with new life and with autism. Billy's room was crammed with teenage stuff like mannequins and music posters, and the rest of the place was bursting with baby furniture, toys, and books. Autism-related paperwork covered the dining room and kitchen tables and every other surface in the house. Therapeutic toys and special swings and a minitrampoline crowded Dov's room and spilled out into the hallway, and an endless stream of therapists, baby-sitters, and housekeepers came and went all day long. By the time Dov was diagnosed, his sister, Miriam, was born, followed by Gabriel, three years later. Billy moved out as soon as he was old enough to get his own apartment. I can't say I blame him; our lives were one big emergency with no end in sight.

When Dov was eight years old, we bought the wonderful old house we live in now. It had been a convent for fifty years before we moved in, and I secretly hoped that all the praying that took place there might hasten the miracles we were working and praying for now. There is a sun porch that joins our bedroom and Dov's room; the walls are painted an intensely bright color called mango. This is where I have spent much of my time these past several years, surrounded by books and scientific journals, at my computer, searching through databases and across the Internet for the right molecules, the right genes, the right concepts, but most of all trying to find the researchers who will figure out autism. And yet I am certain that if I had not met Soma and Tito, I would never have found Dov.

Just about the time Dov was born, Soma must have been dragging Tito from doctor to doctor in India, in search of a diagnosis. And probably, just as I was taking Dov from specialist to specialist, Soma must have just begun to succeed at getting Tito to communicate. And probably, just as I might have been eating a mango at my kitchen table, Soma may have visited her childhood home and sat in the courtyard shaded by the mango trees, real mango trees—the

Alfanso type, not Langra mangos like we have here, according to Soma.

Probably just as I was selecting this very color for these very walls, Soma could have been standing under a mango tree, waiting for a bus, in India, with her son Tito, carrying a sheaf of his poetry under her arm. And probably Tito must have written "Mutilated Spirit" right before we met each other.

Mutilated spirit still breathes in
Moment by moment
Mutilated spirit still breathes out
Event after event.
Every event gets counted within
One and two and three
As the moments pass unstill
Under the mango tree.

—From the poem: "Mutilated Spirit,"
  by Tito Mukhopadhyay

2.

Listening
to Sand

There is a famous picture of two Victorian women having tea, which if it is pointed out to you can be seen instead as the image of a huge menacing skull. The most amazing thing about it is that once you have seen the hidden skull, you can never go back to *not* seeing it. In much the same way, after Dov's diagnosis at twenty-one months old, autism invaded every photograph we'd ever taken of him.

Like most new parents, we took a lot of pictures. And like most amateur photographers, some pictures turned out better than others. But just as the word *autism* had invaded our vocabulary and our lives, so did a kind of invisible scourge creep into Dov's photographs, racing through our photo albums like a fast-spreading virus, destroying any remnants of happiness that might try to take refuge between those pages. And just as autism was stealing his future, it reached back with its long dark fingers and took away all the joy of the past. Adorable moments captured by the camera were transformed into signs and symptoms, as the last remaining fragments of joy metamorphosed into sorrow.

It is impossible to say which is harder to look at, a picture of Dov before he became autistic or after.

"Before" pictures are embedded with missed clues, lost opportunities, failed detection, ignorant bliss, and the premonition of a terrible loss. "Look at that smile—right into the camera!" Where did it go? Did we miss something? Is there something we could have done? You're sure you could have saved him when you look at "before" pictures—if only you'd known how.

"After" pictures look abnormal, disturbed, lost, tragic.

There really is no picture that does not make you want to cry.

Not too long after we met Soma and Tito, Soma showed me her photo albums. There were three of them. These albums, segmented with plastic pages, milky and scratched with wear, protected the precious fading photos. Soma told me Tito loved these photo albums. Sometimes he would flip through them hundreds of times a day and sometimes he even slept with them at night. Tito was thirteen years old when I first met him, and he did not want these photo albums to be taken out of the house.

The photographs were displayed in chronological order. They told a story. In the first album, there were pictures of a pretty young woman with a long black braid, in a bright blue sari, surrounded by female relatives, holding a little baby and glowing with the pride of new motherhood. Tito was the cutest baby there ever was, with his big brown eyes, dark curls, and chubby cheeks.

The second album had lots of birthday celebration pictures of a mother and father happily holding their one-year-old, standing in a doorway decorated with paper garlands. There were a few more pictures of Tito, up to about age two, then suddenly they tapered off dramatically, as if the camera had been lost or broken. After the age of two, there were only scattered pictures of Tito, further apart in time. A two-year-old staring at the calendar. A four-year-old doing a puzzle. The figure in the pictures became smaller and the backgrounds grew larger as the boy in the photographs seemed to be getting farther and farther away over time.

By the age of five, only one badly faded picture depicted the boy seated on a chair holding a book in his lap. It would not have seemed so strange had it not been one of the only pictures taken of him that year, as if sitting and holding a book were an important occasion. After that, there were only a few more pictures of Tito, all of which were taken at a great distance, making details impossible to see.

Most of the remaining pictures in the third album were long shots of three small figures in the distance, standing in front of some national treasure, some historic monument, or some wonder of the world. A man, with a dark, expressionless face, in traditional Indian garb, a white Nehru shirt and baggy pants. A wife, small and demure, always wearing a colorful silk sari, smiling shyly and squinting at the ground, even on a sunless day. And a boy, held in place by the shoulders; a very sweet-looking, handsome boy wearing shorts and an intense expression, which grew more disturbed with each passing year until by the time he was ten his eyes had the look of a madman.

A dozen years earlier, Soma and her husband, R.G. Mukhopadhyay, had been living in the northeast of India where R.G. worked as an engineer, holding a coveted government job at a nuclear power plant. Soma had already earned a master's degree in inorganic chemistry. Their marriage had been arranged by Soma's parents, who identified R.G. as her husband-to-be with the help of an astrologist. Soma was not resentful of this in the least, even though her younger brother was allowed to choose his own spouse. Soma thought she and R.G. were a good match and she believed in astrology.

Soma told me her father had wanted her to become a physician, but her empathy for people was too great and her sensitivity to their pain and suffering would have made being a doctor unbearable. Inorganic chemistry suited her much better, and by the time Tito was born, she was in the midst of getting her advanced degree in education.

Life was good, if ordinary, for Soma and R.G. But Tito was no ordinary child, even as a tiny infant. When he was four months old,
Soma thought she noticed Tito stiffening and arching his body with
displeasure whenever she substituted a wrong word in a familiar
song. Could he really understand the words she was singing enough
to realize when she substituted an incorrect one? She tried it again,
this time using a different word, and later trying it in a different part
of the song. Each time, Tito responded in the same way. Soma was
ecstatic. She kept her observation to herself and quietly gloated: She
must have a genius on her hands.

In 1995, when Dov was three, we went back to the Jersey Shore for
the last time. We laid down blankets on the sand, set up beach chairs
and umbrellas, and sipped cold drinks. Miriam was eighteen months
old and jabbering away. I watched her playing, in her little red-and-
white polka-dot bathing suit, her dark hair pulled up in a bow. How
normal she looked, pretending to drink from a little toy cup, digging
in the sand with her shovel and filling her bucket, excitedly pointing
at a seagull and looking back at me to see if I was watching. Thank
God, she was developing typically,

Although Dov was three he still wasn't talking; he wasn't even
pointing. I could not get his attention. All he wanted to do was feel
the smoothness of the pebbles, and repetitively splash the surface
of a puddle, or run his hands through the sand. Everything was
one big sensory experience. He flipped over the toy truck his grandfather had given him, and gazed intently at the wheels as he set
them spinning. By now I knew this was called stimming, a word that
was used for the odd repetitive behaviors often displayed by autistic
children. He didn't seem to know how to play like a typical three-
year-old.

I cannot recall the board games he played that summer or the
house that we rented. In fact the only thing that sticks in my mind

are the miles and miles of wet sand beach stretching out in either direction and that Dov put his ear to the sand and listened to the
ground for the entire ten days.

During this time Jon and I argued about everything. Why hadn't
Dov started talking when some other autistic children had? Was he
seeing the right speech therapist? Was he stimming more? Was his
preschool a total waste of time? Did the baby-sitter know enough
about his therapies? We fought about Dov's diet, his vitamins, his
medications, about which doctor to see, what expert to believe.
Why were other autistic kids getting better and not Dov? Weren't
we doing enough? Weren't we doing everything we could think of?
Everything possible? What were we doing wrong?

While I willed myself to see some modicum of progress, Jon could
only see the gulf between Dov's autism and the prospect of becoming
normal growing wider. If Dov learned to stack two blocks, Jon wanted
to know why he couldn't do a puzzle. If Dov learned to make the
sound "ba," why wasn't he saying "Hi, Dad"? The one thing we could
agree on was that the gluten-free diet did seem to be helping; he had
stopped biting himself and drooling and he was sleeping better.

I used to sing to Dov in the car and talk to him while we drove
all over town to his therapies. I told him stories and jokes, riddles
and their answers, facts and fiction, anything I could think of. I
didn't know if he could understand a word I was saying, but there
was always a chance he could—wasn't there? "He may *not* understand you," his speech therapist said one day, suggesting that I not
bother to sing or talk to him on these long car rides anymore.

It was starting to look as though Dov might be *severely* autistic. If
he didn't talk by now, the speech therapist said, it was unlikely that
he ever would. "I haven't seen too many cases this severe," another
therapist remarked, causing my hands to go cold and my body to feel
shaky. Then one day, after an hour of spinning Dov on a swing while

handing him plastic rings, the occupational therapist said that there was nothing more she could do for him. He simply was not responding to therapy and there was no reason for him to continue, she told me at the end of his session. "Look," she said defensively, her big eyes bugging out from beneath her wavy black bangs, "I've been doing this for a year with him and there's no progress. There are a lot of other kids on the waiting list."

To me there is nothing much sadder than giving up on a three-year-old. If Dov wasn't making progress, it wasn't his fault. He was only three and he had autism. It was her job to help him get better, wasn't it?

But we had not run out of things to try—not yet. There was still Applied Behavioral Analysis.[1] We'd read that this kind of behavior modification program, if applied forty hours per week, could sometimes even return children to mainstream schools, eventually training them right out of their diagnostic category. This was the very therapy we had been warned against in the beginning by the play therapist, who told us it turned autistic children into little robots instead of real, fully developed human beings. We'd also heard that, in the 1960s, aversion reinforcement was used on autistic children in behavioral research and even in behavioral therapies, but the practice had been abandoned years ago.

Ivar Lovaas was the first to use Applied Behavioral Analysis in the treatment of autism, and he was a genuis and a hero in the eyes of many parents. In the early '60s, when authorities advised parents to put their autistic children into state mental institutions for the rest of their lives, and the scientific community and medical profession resolutely proclaimed that bad parenting was the cause of autism, Ivar Lovaas was a psychology student studying Skinnerian behavioral theory.

While observing autistic patients locked away in the state mental institution, Lovaas began to wonder if behavioral theory could be applied to autistics to alter their behavior. This made Ivar Lovaas the first person to suggest that autistic people were capable of learning. Over the next ten years, Lovaas developed a behavioral intervention program for autistics based on Skinner's behavioral paradigm. For the first time, people saw that autistics' behavior could be altered.

The good news for us was that Ivar Lovaas was a professor at UCLA.

I pulled every string I could think of to get to Ivar Lovaas. I made sure he knew that I'd read every research paper he'd ever written, except for the first few which I could not find. By the time we met at a restaurant near UCLA, Dov was almost four. A tall, thin, angular-looking Norwegian, Lovaas claimed that 47 percent of the children who received his behavioral treatment had recovered from autism. I knew there was a lot of controversy surrounding this pronouncement, but I wanted to believe him. The fact was Applied Behavioral Analysis was the only therapy that existed for autism that had been studied at all.

While eating our salads, I asked Lovaas how he'd gotten involved in autism research. His light blue eyes lit up as he began to describe what autism was like in the early '60s. "You would walk into one of those state institutions and they were all there. Banging their heads, blood dripping down their faces. Nobody thought you could help these kinds of people. They were the worst kind." Unable to eat another bite, I was determined to keep the conversation going. By the end of lunch, Lovaas had agreed to help set up a home-based behavior modification program for Dov. As he stood up to leave, Lovaas handed me a packet—these were his earliest research papers, he said, the ones you couldn't get ahold of anymore. I felt honored.

That night I got into bed and put on my reading glasses, eager to read Lovaas's earliest published research. What I read drained the blood from my hands, and flooded my entire being with an over-whelming sense of disbelief, regret, and despair.

The title of the paper was "Building Social Behavior in Autistic Children by Use of Electric Shock." It described a research project that took place in 1965; twin five-year-old autistic boys were brought to the University of California, Los Angeles, to participte in the experiment, which was funded by the National Institute of Health. Before the horror of what I was reading had fully registered, I had already read too much:

> In the present study, pain was induced by means of an electrical grid on the floor upon which the children stood. The shock was turned on immediately following pathological behaviors. It was turned off or withheld when the children came to the adults who were present.

How could anyone have done this to them? How could their parents have allowed it? Almost as if an afterthought, the paper stated that although the children were completely trained, meaning that they understood what to do and what would happen if they did not, the children would sometimes, for no apparent reason, and begin to flap their hands, even though they knew that by doing so they would receive an electrical shock to their bare feet.

This was extraordinary. I couldn't think of any animal experiment where fear conditioning with electric shock would not work to pre-dictably shape behavior, except for the cocaine-addicted rat. Were the children's flapping behaviors so highly self-reinforcing that they overrode the conditioned fear response the same way cocaine ad-diction could override the conditioned fear response in an animal model? Or were these small children simply so anxious, so afraid of being shocked again, that their need to regulate their nervous system, their need to flap, overcame them and stopped them in their tracks?

Suddenly, a thought crystallized in my mind. I wrote it down: Was flapping the only thing they knew how to do to regulate their own nervous system—and was this behavior so terribly necessary that it got in the way of all other behavior? Maybe that's what autism was.

Modern-day Applied Behavioral Analysis was different, of course. Only positive reinforcement, like candy and hugs, was used to shape behavior. For the next several years, Dov received Applied Behavioral Analysis therapy from ten to thirty hours a week. Dozens of cheerful young therapists supplied by local university psychology departments spent hundreds of hours working with him. People we hardly knew inhabited our house throughout the day and regularly saw us in our pajamas, sometimes even in our underwear; they saw us with bad hair, fighting, crying, and sick. But we didn't care because maybe Dov would get better. Maybe he would be a *responder*.

Lovaas believed that learning to imitate was the greatest indicator of a good prognosis for autistic children. Years later, research would confirm his hypothesis when studies showed decreased mirror neuron activity (the neurons involved in imitation)[2] in autistic subjects. Lovaas thought autistics needed to have behavior broken down and taught in the tiniest components possible in order to learn how to imitate. A therapist would sit across from Dov at the little table in his bedroom and produce two identical sets of blocks. "Do this!" she'd say in a loud, flat voice, demonstrating an action such as moving one block next to another. Then the therapist would model the action hand over hand with Dov. Then she would repeat the whole thing, the objective being that Dov would eventually begin to imitate her actions. If an autistic child could learn to imitate at this very basic level, it was thought that more complex behaviors could be constructed on this foundation.

In the end, Applied Behavioral Analysis therapy didn't really work for Dov either, at least not in the big way that we'd hoped it would. Not that it didn't work for lots of other autistic children, because it did. It just didn't help Dov that much.

Jon and I were burning out. What time I did not spend driving Dov around town to therapy sessions those days was spent doing endless paperwork and making phone calls, fighting with our health insurance company, the state's early-intervention program, and the school district—fighting to get services for Dov. These institutions had a limitless capacity to generate red tape and delays, a battle I knew we would never be able to win, no matter how right we were. And even when we did succeed in getting some services, there were one- and two-year waiting lists for appointments with the best therapists. And then there was the cost. The cost of all these therapies was bankrupting us. We were getting worn out and demoralized before we'd gotten very far at all. Something had to change because autism wasn't going away anytime soon and the one thing we'd heard over and over was that time was not on our side. The term *early intervention* was just another way of saying that if Dov didn't get better now, he never would.

There was nothing unusual about the night that it happened. Jon was trying to read the newspaper for as long as he could keep his eyes open and I was sitting at the end of the bed folding laundry. We didn't talk much at night anymore because we both knew that autism was the only thing on our minds and we didn't want to talk about it before going to sleep.

"We have to start a research foundation," Jon announced, looking up from his paper to see my reaction. "I've been thinking about it for a while," he said. "It's what we have to do if we want to help Dov."

This kind of thinking was typical of Jon; he always came up with ideas that most people would consider totally out of reach. This was something I loved about him.

"We have to get the government to give money to autism research," he continued, as if I knew what that meant. Of course the government gave money to diseases, I thought. Of course they were working on autism—weren't they? They had to be. Jon had been getting up at 5:00 A.M. lately to talk to people in Washington at the National Institutes of Health. There were no good figures on how much was being spent by the government on autism research and the only way he could come up with an estimate was to get the lowliest accountants on the phone and go through each institute's budget line by line. There were four institutes that were supposed to be funding autism research and he had added up their figures. Autism was getting around $5 million a year for research, he told me. "Let me put it into perspective for you," he continued. "Alzheimer's—sixty million a year. Breast Cancer—six hundred million. AIDS—nine hundred million."

"But they *must* be working on autism," I said, shocked.

"There is no *they*," he said, carefully enunciating each word with an equal measure of wrath.

We sat there for what seemed like a very long time as this information fully took root in my mind. I had never seen Jon like this before. He was *fervent*, like some age-old rabbinical fire had been ignited in his soul. I could feel fate descending upon us. It was in the air, palpable and alive.

"Get on with your lives," the doctors had told us—and now at last we could. Because now we knew what to do. The year was 1995; we were starting the Cure Autism Now (CAN) foundation, and we would devote ourselves to finding treatment and a cure for autism from this moment on.

And so Jon and I held on to the dream of a better life for Dov, or perhaps it was just stubborn insistence, that Dov could and would get well, someday, somehow. I am sure our unrelenting insistence on a better life for Dov seemed absurd to many people. We were accused of giving "false hope" to parents when we chose the name Cure Autism Now for our foundation. We were stunned by the resistance we met from professionals in the field, but even more so by the unexpected bitter resentment we encountered from some parents whose autistic children had already grown up. They had been disappointed too many times already; they preferred not to open old wounds or rekindle the painful spark of hope that had finally been dampened in their hearts. If there was ever going to be a magic bullet, it was too late for their children and they didn't want to know about it, long for it, or hope for it ever again.

When people tell you to give up on your child, they'd better have a damn good reason—they'd better have proof—evidence that their dire advice is supported by indisputable scientific evidence.

I learned quickly that almost no research had been done on autism at all. The future of autism research was a blank slate at a time when headlines proclaimed the discovery of new treatments and cures for other diseases every day. We now knew more about the brain, developmental biology, biochemistry, genetics, and virtually every area of science than we could even imagine was possible just a decade ago. There had never been a more optimal time in the history of science and medicine to set out to discover the causes and treatments of a disease. This was especially true for autism, which was an untapped field, poised for discovery. The more I learned and understood, the less I could understand why I had been advised to give up on my autistic child.

The traditional model for advocate-supported research foundations goes something like this: Raise money, turn it over to a higher power (scientists), and don't ask questions. This was not a model I could devote my life to.

For one thing, it was these very scientists who told us Dov was retarded, that he was unreachable and that we should give up on him. It hardly seemed promising to throw our support behind a group of experts whose scientific conceptualization of autism could be summed up by the word *incurable*.

. . .

I knew that if we were going to fight this battle, I needed to gain a deep understanding of the limitations and the possibilities that science had to offer for figuring out autism. I could not take anyone's word for it.

Jon and I immediately gravitated to two separate areas of CAN; he took on the politics, and, although I had no background in it, I took on the science. There was no need for discussion, we worked together seamlessly because we were driven by the same all-consuming goal: to help Dov get well.

Making the government spend more money on autism meant Jon was going to be away in Washington a lot from now on. Besides earning a living, and being a dad and a husband, Jon was now a lobbyist. He spent much of his time talking to senators and congressmen, he brought in busloads of parents and their autistic children to hold court in their representative's offices, and he enlisted his Hollywood celebrity friends to testify before Congress about the need for more autism research. Jon now regularly attended political fund-raisers and rallies and was even seen on a golf course; at night he would call from his hotel room where he was holed up waiting with nervous enthusiasm to meet a congressman he would never have voted for.

In Washington, in Congress, at the National Institutes of Health, Jon was a constant menace, the squeaky wheel that would not shut up—and he loved it. The political pressure on the autism front grew exponentially and eventually Arlen Specter's former chief of staff and professional lobbyist, Craig Snyder, joined Jon and CAN in Washington. In 2001, the Pediatric Health Act would be signed into law, bringing millions of new federal dollars into autism research.

The first thing I learned about starting a research foundation was that my tiny one-room writing office two blocks from our Spanish duplex was going to become Cure Autism Now headquarters.

I began spending my time at the UCLA and USC medical libraries searching the stacks and making copies of articles from research journals. I collected quarters as though my life depended on it because copying articles on those clunky old coin-operated machines was the only way I could carry information out of there. I read anything and everything that seemed in any way related to autism research. This was 1995 and there was only one journal that published autism research. Unfortunately, it was not stocked in university medical libraries.

Reading and understanding research papers began to take over my life. It seemed as if every other word was a term I had never seen before and did not understand. I went to the medical school bookstore and bought textbooks and reference books. Sometimes it took me days or even weeks to grasp the contents of a single research paper. I carried them around with me until they were dog-eared and almost every sentence had been highlighted and underlined, and the margins were filled with my questions and notes. The process grew easier and faster as my new vocabulary increased. And although I was making progress, I soon realized that I was going to have to go all the way back and start at the beginning. I could no longer get away with not knowing what a molecule was. I knew that if I were to have any chance of getting to the bottom of autism, I would have to know this stuff in my sleep.

But I had no time to go back to school. It felt like time was running out for Dov. If science was ever going to help him, the field of autisim research was going to have to move ahead quickly.

Unfortunately, I had been an utter failure at math and science my whole life. I was good at art and it was my sister Lenore who was good at math and science; in fact, she was a doctor now, a child psychiatrist. A smile crept across my face when the thought occurred to me and I hatched my plot: Lenore must have learned everything I now needed to know, back when she attended medical school. Fortunately, she had recently moved to Los Angeles.

Suppressing any residual tendencies toward sibling rivalry, I coaxed Lenore, with promises of donuts and coffee, to meet me every Sunday and tutor me on the basics of science, the stuff I should have learned in high school biology class had I not dropped out to celebrate the '60s. Over a period of weeks, with repeated exposure to cinnamon rolls and lattes, molecules, atoms, electrons, and neutrons and eventually neurons and synapses, I gained a kind of hierarchical understanding of the systems that make up the physical world. But I was learning these systems out of context. I still didn't know the difference between a digestive enzyme and a catalytic enzyme, I couldn't distinguish the differences in scale between signal modification systems such as prenylation, ubiquination, glycosylation, or phosphorylation. Nor did I understand at what levels any of these systems interacted. I didn't know how to think about a polymorphism in the context of a gene or a chromosome. But I forgave myself these transgressions, since it wasn't that long ago that the only kind of protein folding I knew about was beating egg whites into meringue. And the last science class I'd taken was in seventh grade.

To get to the next level, I knew I would have to find a tutor in molecular biology. Tony was his name and he was a postdoctoral student at UCLA. We met once a week in the evening, in a cramped little conference room where he drew diagrams on the whiteboard walls and patiently explained molecular genetics and second messenger systems to me. These tutoring sessions were the high point of my week because each new level of understanding I gained felt like a triumph and fueled a sense of empowerment leading toward understanding autism. This was my version of a support group. As long as I was doing something about autism, I could survive.

It's hard to believe that not long ago, computers still had glowing green text on black screens and it took hours to download a single research paper using antiquated programs like Gopher or Fetch-it.

Desperate for information, I hired a teenage hacker named Karl, and with his indispensable assistance I began to painstakingly piece together a picture of the state of autism research. If there was a God, if miracles were possible, this was one: Within a year after my initial foray into autism research, Netscape came on the scene, ending my hacker days, and not too long after that, the National Library of Medicine launched Pubmed, a free, searchable database, available to everyone, containing the electronic version of every major peer-reviewed scientific journal there was.[3]

Using the Pubmed database I soon made my first discovery: there was a small group of genetic studies from the '70s and '80s, done in different labs in different parts of the country, on different groups of patients, which, when considered together, were startling. These studies showed that if autism was found in identical twins, it affected both twins in the majority of cases. This meant genes were somehow involved in autism. It was the first solid lead I had come across. Under the auspices of CAN, we called together a small group of scientists and asked them what we could do to speed up the pace of autism research. "Become the data," they said. "CAN should start a gene bank," they advised. "It's the only way you can make sure everyone has access to the data."

At the time there were only a handful of scientists studying autism genetics and each had their own collection of blood samples from "multiplex" families (families with more than one member who had autism). Each of these collections was small and none of the researchers pooled their samples. The result was that no one had a large enough sample size to do any meaningful research. But, to our dismay, we found that these scientists were in no hurry. They did not have a child with autism. They could wait however long it took to collect enough families to do the research, however long it took to make their discovery, however long it took to earn tenure or their Nobel Prize. We, on the other hand, could not in good conscience wait another day. And so it was that we took on the most daunting project of our lives and started the Autism Genetic Resource Exchange (AGRE), CAN's autism gene bank.[4]

Shortly thereafter Jon and I traveled to the National Institute of Mental Health to attend the first-ever meeting on autism genetics. If there was solid evidence that genes were involved in autism, why wasn't the research further along? That was the question we put forth to this rather defensive group. The problem, they said, was that there weren't enough multiplex families to go around. Their studies required larger numbers of DNA samples to gain sufficient statistical power to do the research. Each group that was represented seemed to have a surprisingly small collection of DNA samples, which they had taken years to recruit and collect.

At this point, Jon stood up and proudly announced that CAN was going to establish an open-access gene bank for autism research. We would recruit multiplex families, store their DNA in a repository along with high-quality clinical data, and make everything available to the entire scientific community. Instead of the encouragement we expected to receive, a wall of silence rose in the wake of our announcement. "You mean you would just *give* the samples to anyone?" one scientist finally blurted out, furious. "Are you saying you'd let a pharmaceutical company just take the samples and go off and find the genes?" another outraged researcher accused. I looked over at Jon and saw a strange expression developing on his face—it was a perfect blend of disbelief and fury. "Listen," another researcher threatened, "if you make samples available to just anybody, we'll get out of the field!"

I watched Jon to see what he would say next. What was he doing? He was getting a photo out of his wallet. It was of Dov, of course.

He handed Dov's picture to the indignant scientist sitting next to him and instructed him to pass it around. As the photo began to make its way around the table, Jon began to speak.

"There are six of you," he said quietly, "and five hundred thousand of him. What do you think we should do?"

As it turns out, there were not 500,000 autistic people in the United States. There were actually a million and a half. And by the time CAN was ten years old, 1 in 166 children was being diagnosed with autism.[5]

Not too long after CAN was established and the Autism Genetic Resource Exchange gene bank was getting under way, I heard about the Society for Neuroscience, the largest meeting of its kind in the world. Once a year neuroscientists from around the globe congregated in what was doubtless the largest collection of brain cells ever to assemble in one physical location. Never had I felt so stylish in my life as when I arrived in a city that had been overrun by thirty thousand nerds. Merely wearing a black leather coat turned heads and put me into the glamorous category. The fact that I was six months pregnant with Gabriel seemed to make no difference.

This was 1996 and the first year we set up a Cure Autism Now booth at the Society for Neuroscience and we behaved like barkers at a carnival, a bunch of desperate parents hawking our grants, trying to lure researchers into our field with hand-painted signs that read Free Money. We were so much younger then, we had less gray hair and more untapped reserves and our children were still small enough to be carried; it seems like a hundred years ago.

Over time, my role at CAN evolved and I became a kind of talent scout for autism research, recruiting top researchers from related fields, lab by lab, across the country and around the world. I had learned to speak their language, but I could also tell them straight from the heart what it was like to have a son like Dov.

By 1999, Dov was seven years old and CAN had more research grant applications coming in than we could fund; the number had quadrupled in just a few years and the caliber of scientists who were getting involved was spectacular. CAN was now the leading source of nonfederal funding for autism research and CAN's Autism Genetic Research Exchange had become the world's largest autism gene bank, allowing hundreds of new scientists to join the ranks of autism research. And although everything seemed excruciatingly slow to us, scientists and politicians told us that the field of autism research was growing faster than anything they'd ever seen before.

And yet in spite of the monumental achievements of CAN and the fact that I had become well versed in matters of science, I found myself confronted by something I was entirely unprepared to understand: a boy named Tito Mukhopadhyay.

The book Francesca Happe told me Tito had written was nearly impossible to track down. *Beyond the Silence: My Life, the World and Autism*, had apparently been self-published by the National Autistic Society of the United Kingdom, whose director of services, Richard Mills, had been so moved by Tito that he took it upon himself to personally edit Tito's book and finance getting a small run of the book printed.

After a number of weeks passed, a hand-addressed envelope containing a thin paperback book with a handsome boy staring out from its cover arrived. I tore it open and began to read.

Men and women are puzzled by everything I do. My parents and those who love me, are embarrassed and worried. Doctors use different terminologies to describe me. I just wonder.

Could Tito really have written this? I flipped to the Editor's Note on the title page.

To retain the integrity of Tito's writing, very little has been changed. The Voice of Silence was written when Tito was eight years old, and Beyond the Silence *was written when he was eleven years old.*

I checked the back cover.

Tito is an eleven-year-old boy from south India with a special talent. Although almost completely nonverbal, he can communicate his thoughts and feelings through remarkable prose and poetry, written in fluent English.

I returned to the first page and continued to read.

The thoughts are bigger than my expressions to get a shape. Every move that I make interprets my helpless way to show how trapped I feel in the continuous flow of cause and effect. The happenings occur in a way that shows the continuity of cause and effect. The effect of a cause becomes the cause of another effect. And I wonder.

That is not just wonder alone but also a reason for my worry. I think of the little boy who had a way of expressing himself, not through speech but through a frustrated temper tantrum.

The language was known but it did not relate to anything.

How could someone who was severely autistic write like this? It seemed impossible. Either Tito was not actually autistic or Francesca Happe had grossly exaggerated how low functioning he was.

As if in answer to my question, about a week later another package arrived. It was a videotape, the 2000 BBC documentary about Tito, which had been even more difficult to find than Tito's book.

I sat down and played the tape.

Tito did behave a lot like Dov. He spent most of his time engaging in repetitive behaviors like hand flapping and body rocking or flicking a pencil in front of his eyes. And like Dov, Tito tried to speak, but his words could not be understood. But that is where the resemblance ended, for Tito could communicate. I watched as Tito pointed at letters on a hand-drawn alphabet board to form words and sentences as his mother read them aloud. And Tito could hand-write. His penmanship was barely legible, but it was decipherable. There could be no doubt that the letters Tito so painstakingly formed were his own words.

How had his mother taught him this?

Up until this moment there had been no shred of evidence to suggest that someone whose behavior was as abnormal as Dov's could possibly possess real intelligence.

As I watched the documentary, more scenes unfolded: Tito being diagnosed by British psychiatrists, Tito expressing his worries to his therapist that people would perceive him as a "madman," Tito at home in their tiny apartment in Bangalore, writing his daily essay under the strict supervision of his mother, Soma, Tito rocking beneath the ceiling fan, mesmerized by its spinning blades. . . .

Everything Francesca had told me about Tito was true.

That meant that Tito could be a window into autism such as the world has never seen. And if that were true, how could they have sent him back to India without studying him.

3.

The Indian Poet

Not long after watching the BBC video I received an e-mail from the National Autistic Society of the U.K. saying that Soma had contacted them again. It turned out that Tito and his mother had established a Yahoo account and could be reached at the Internet cafés of Bangalore, India.

I e-mailed Soma immediately and, to my utter joy and amazement, she replied. I could barely keep my excitement from bursting through in those first short, awkward e-mails, but I didn't want to overwhelm Soma with my wild enthusiasm. I didn't want her to know that I thought her son could be the Rosetta Stone for autism. At least not yet.

Because in reality, I had no idea how I was going to make any of this happen. I had stumbled upon a gold mine, a hidden treasure, a person who was capable of communicating in great detail exactly what it was like to be nonverbal and severely autistic.

Sometimes an idea just pops into your head so suddenly that you don't even know where it came from. This is what seems to have happened when, in my next e-mail, I found myself inviting Tito, an autistic boy who did not speak, to be the keynote speaker at CAN's

Innovative Technology for Autism (ITA) conference that was to be held in Silicon Valley in the fall of 2000.

I had started the ITA initiative at CAN a year earlier because I believed that if scientists could use technology to make a blind man see and a deaf man hear, they should be challenged to turn their efforts toward the seemingly impossible problems presented by autism. These were children who could not sit still, could not speak, or even point—how could you teach *them* to type? I knew it was going to take more than some high-tech keyboard. Yet I also knew that many of these children were inexplicably drawn to computers, like a moth to a flame. And some autistic children even mysteriously started to read and write when they were still toddlers, without any instruction at all. Why couldn't we bring all that glitzy technology that had been developed for Palm Pilots and Game Boys to bear upon the lives of people with autism?

Soma and Tito were ecstatic. They had never been to the United States. In fact, they had never been outside India except for their trip to England when Tito was eleven.

The day of the ITA conference, Jon and I flew from Los Angeles to Walnut Creek in northern California. I felt as if I were in a dream or a fairy tale; it was too good to be true. I was finally going to meet Tito and Soma in person. But Jon was worried. What if Tito freaked out and could do nothing at all. He was the keynote speaker! I had the videotape of the BBC documentary, I reassured him. If nothing else, I would show the tape. What if Tito wasn't for real, what if it was all a hoax? Jon wanted to know. How would it reflect on CAN?

Our cab pulled up in front of the Oracle building and I jumped out, leaving Jon to pay the driver. Inside, I was greeted by CAN staffers who tried to update me on the meeting. But their words barely registered as I scanned the lobby looking for Soma and Tito. They had not arrived yet. Attendance was good, it was mostly therapists and parents, but there were also some Silicon Valley intelligentsia types and a handful of neuroscientists from UC San Francisco.

Finally, it was just minutes before the meeting was scheduled to begin and Soma and Tito still hadn't arrived. I entered the auditorium. I would introduce the second speaker and hope that Tito and Soma would show up. There were at least two hundred people seated in the auditorium. Would Tito freak out, start flapping, and run away? I began to worry. Was I asking too much of him? Would the "experts" in the audience wonder what in the world I was hoping to accomplish with this poor soul? I stepped up onto the stage and stood at the podium, looking out over the sea of expectant faces. Maybe Jon was right.

Suddenly, I saw them. A small Indian lady with a short dark bob wearing a sari and an Alpine ski sweater was heading down the aisle straight toward me, almost running as she ushered her son ahead of her. Tito looked bigger and older than the picture on his book cover; in fact, he was taller than Soma now. He was flicking his fingers at the sides of his face as they advanced toward the podium.

The room fell absolutely quiet as Soma maneuvered Tito onto the stage, where for a moment he stood frozen as if spellbound by the lights. Soma nudged him to sit down and then sat down beside him, smiling broadly out at the audience. I welcomed our special guests and started describing Tito as "the brilliant young man from India who was nonverbal and severely affected by autism and yet was an eloquent writer and had an IQ of 185." I looked over and saw that Tito's eyes were bugging out of his head as he rocked fiercely to and fro, rattling the frame of his metal folding chair. Meanwhile, Soma was scribbling out the alphabet on a piece of cardboard, which she handed to me. I placed the handmade alphabet board under the glare of the overhead projector bulb where it was beamed onto the giant screen that loomed overhead. Tito's eyes were now crossed as if he were staring at something mesmerizing inside his own brain. His rocking and flapping had accelerated so much that it looked like he might levitate at any moment. Soma seemed to take no notice of this and continued to stare politely out toward the audience with her unwavering smile. I felt awkward interrupting Tito with my first question but forged ahead. "Tito, is there anything you would like to say to the audience?"

Tito just kept rocking and flapping his hands and staring ahead as if he hadn't heard me at all. I thought of the BBC documentary I had waiting in the wings if everything fell apart, as it now seemed it might.

"C'mon!" Soma shouted suddenly. Her voice rang shrill and loud, startling the audience and momentarily snapping Tito out of his rocking and flapping frenzy. Tito began to point at a series of letters on the alphabet board as the silent room watched on the screen above. *"Hello"* was all Tito had to tap out before the audience was on their feet in thunderous applause. Witnessing a person like Tito simply communicating in any way at all was nothing short of a total Helen Keller miracle unfolding before our eyes.

Tito stared blindly into the stage lights and began to twiddle a pencil at great speed in front of his eyes before pausing long enough to tap out *"I am honored to be here"* on the alphabet board.

A microphone was passed into the audience. One mother stood up to speak. "My son is nineteen," she began, then faltering. "I always knew he was in there. . . ." her voice trailed off as she choked back tears. "What should I say to him?"

"What can you tell us, about our children?" another parent asked Tito.

"Believe in your children," Tito typed out.

A scientist in the back asked: "For those of us who are researchers, Tito, what can we do for you?" Without hesitation, Tito pounded out: *"I need an artificial voice."* And when another asked: "What are your hopes for the future?" *"Get me a publisher,"* was Tito's reply. As I was to learn, nothing in the world meant more to Tito than publishing his poetry.

For the next half hour, the audience plied Tito with questions, and except for once when his beloved pencil flew out of his hand into the gutter of the stage where he could not be persuaded to abandon it, Tito held himself together and handled the questions with wit and humor and compassion.

I had never witnessed anything like this before and I knew that no one else had either. My mind flooded with questions—I wanted to ask Tito everything I had ever wondered about autism, and everything I had only dreamed of being able to ask Dov.

When their time was up, Soma and Tito descended the stairs of the stage to a standing ovation. I watched as they hurried down the aisle in much the same way they had arrived. It took all my self-control not to run after them. Instead I introduced the next speaker and made my way toward the speakers' area. That's when I saw Mike Merzenich.

Quietly observing from the back of the dim room, illuminated by the blue light of his ever-open laptop, was a kind-looking man wearing a rumpled shirt and glasses. His unassuming appearance and friendly manner revealed no outward evidence that he was one of the most accomplished, respected, and well-known researchers in the world of neuroscience. I was amazed and delighted when Mike Merzenich agreed to speak at our conference and I was now even more surprised to find him sitting there, actually watching the other presentations.

I sat down beside him, introduced myself. I thanked Mike for coming and then, as I often do, nervous upon meeting a scientist I am in awe of, I blurted out my latest hypothesis about autism. "If you deprive a litter of mice of food, they will live longer than if you deprive them of touch. Perhaps in autism, there is a peripheral neuropathy in infancy. Perhaps it disrupts development. It could be the Merkle cells, or maybe the Pacian cells" (pressure-sensing mechanoreceptors found in the skin). I caught my breath, instantly regretting everything I'd just said. I should have been trying to show Mike

Merzenich that I'd read all of his research papers and that maybe I even sort of understood some of them. But instead I sounded like a fool and painted myself into a conversational corner I couldn't get out of. Why couldn't I just shut up and listen when I was in the presence of a brilliant mind like Mike Merzenich's? He was the guy we needed to work on neural retraining in autism, and I was doing anything but impressing him.

An amused smile crept across Mike Merzenich's lips, revealing a friendly gap between his front teeth. He leaned back and let his glasses slide down his nose as if to get a better look at me. I felt my eyebrows knit together involuntarily—I knew I had been too weird. After a long moment he said, "I don't think I've ever heard a civilian use the term *Merkle cell* before."

Mike stayed the whole day. He was just about the smartest person I'd ever met. The trouble was autism wasn't Mike Merzenich's field at all, though I thought it should be after I heard him speak at a symposium on neural plasticity at the Society for Neuroscience a year earlier. Merzenich was a pioneer in the new field of brain plasticity—how the brain can change and learn in response to the environment.[6] He had already translated his research into a successful computer-based neural retraining tool to remedy dyslexia. Every advocacy group that involved a brain disorder was pursuing him. He'd been kind enough to take my call when I contacted him after the Society for Neuroscience symposium, but Mike Merzenich was also brutally honest. His next big thing was fixing cognitive decline in aging, he told me. He didn't have time to get involved in anything else, much less something as complicated and misunderstood as autism.

Even though he'd already said no once, I realized that there might never be another chance to try to get Mike Merzenich on board. Didn't he realize that his work was absolutely the most promising thing we had for developing treatments and training tools for autism? He was putting his papers away and closing up his laptop when he looked up and answered me. "Autism seems impossible," he explained patiently. "No one even knows where to start working on something like autism." I held my breath and smiled as I felt myself catapulting from despair to fury to dogged determination, all in one split second. "I'll be in touch with you very soon," I said, trying to sound confident as I shook his hand good-bye.

Outside in the lobby, parents were still lined up to ask Tito for answers to the questions they could never ask their own children. My mind flooded with questions about Dov. But before I had a chance to ask Tito anything, I saw that Jon had staked out a place at the head of the line. "Why do you flap and rock?" Jon wanted to know. *"I get a scattered feeling when I cannot feel my body. I need to flap to feel my body,"* Tito replied. The flicker of doubt I'd detected earlier in Jon's eyes was gone and in its place I saw a look of fascination, as if Jon were realizing that Tito could be a doorway into his own son's mind.

It was believed that people with autism lacked emotion, empathy, and the desire for social interaction, that they were unable to understand the minds and feelings of others. But if what Tito was telling us was true, the current beliefs about autism were probably wrong.

Tearful parents continued to surround Tito and his mother, overwhelming them with endless questions: "How did Tito learn to write?" "Does Tito know how to read?" "What are your hopes for the future, Tito?" "Do you think other autistics are intelligent?" "Do you think my son can understand what I am saying to him?"

For the next week, I spent as much time as possible with Soma and Tito. I questioned Tito endlessly about his behaviors, about his feelings, and about how his mind worked. And I asked as many questions of Soma: how she had taught Tito to communicate? What was Tito like as a younger child? All the while, of course, I was hoping that Dov might be a little bit like Tito. Anyone with an autistic child couldn't help but secretly harbor this hope in their heart, once they had met Tito.

All too soon the day had come for Tito and Soma to return to India. As I drove them to Los Angeles Airport, I found myself screaming at Tito, who was trying to unlock the back door of my van and jump out as we drove down the freeway. It was hard to know how to relate to Tito—what was my role or my relationship with him? One moment we were discussing existentialism and the next I was yelling at him as if he were a two-year-old child. I felt bad when that happened, but I didn't know what else to do. It was as if Tito were a thirteen-year-old and a two-year-old, all in one body. As we pulled into the airport, we were discussing the origins of names. *Soma* meant "moon" in Bengali. Tito said something from the backseat, which I made out to be "Yours is from *The Merchant of Venice.*" It was true, my name, Portia, was from this play. How did Tito know about *The Merchant of Venice?* Had he read it? Had it been read to him? I asked Soma. "No, he's just heard about it," she replied. I supposed it made sense that anyone who was literate might have heard of it. But I simply could not reconcile the impulsive, out-of-control Tito with this other Tito who knew that my name came from a Shakespeare play. And if he had such a brain, I didn't see why Tito couldn't attend college with an aide and have a real life. At least now, for the first time, Tito had a keyboard; CAN had presented him with a laptop computer at the ITA conference.

Inside the Los Angeles Airport international terminal, Tito and Soma blended into the pool of humanity from everyplace on the globe. It was hard to concentrate because I was growing sadder by the moment. I felt a sense of impending loss, the way one does when you know someone is leaving you forever. I had been giddy and exhilarated while I had the chance to communicate with Tito. But now what? Would Tito disappear back into the landscape of India, to live out his days as an autistic poet savant? The bigger question that weighed on my mind was: How could I bring all that Tito represented—the possibilities, the knowledge, the information, the hope he let us glimpse—into the world of autism research?

As I drove home down the dark freeway, my mood was as black as the road ahead. My ability to imagine a hopeful future for Dov or any autistic child returned to its former state, out of my reach. I felt a strange, deep sense of loneliness for Dov, because Tito was gone. I made up my mind that somehow, I was going to bring them back to the U.S. I would bring Tito to the scientists, and somehow we would begin to figure out autism through Tito.

Nothing had changed, yet everything had changed.

Dov was still the same nonverbal, severely autistic boy who could hardly point or nod his head to show what he meant. Yet I saw him differently now.

All of Dov's short life, no matter where I turned, I was told I was a dreamer, unrealistic, even destructive, in my determination to help him, to change him, to make him better. There was no chance for Dov, they told me over and over. Absolutely none. No reason to believe in any kind of a future for him. He was retarded. I shouldn't wreck my marriage and destroy my other children's lives for his sake, when doing so was utterly and completely useless. Dov was born without a chance in life and he would never get one as long as he lived, so we might as well get used to it and the sooner the better— for everyone, including Dov.

But now, for the first time, in meeting Tito, I had glimpsed one solid piece of evidence that a person could look and act like Dov, yet in spite of that could still have an intact mind, feelings, and thoughts. Everyone had said that such a paradox was impossible and yet now I had witnessed the existence of just such a paradox in real life, with my own eyes and I now knew that it *was* at least possible.

The experts in England agreed that Tito was severely autistic and that yet he possessed some sort of remarkable intelligence, but they spared no words in warning parents like myself that Tito was most certainly "one in a million," admonishing us not to get our hopes up that our own children might also have hidden intelligence. Yet if Tito met all criteria for the diagnosis of autism, why shouldn't we get our hopes up? Tito was living evidence that against all odds, there was at least a chance that our children might have intelligence too; that they might be reachable after all.

Because it is generally accepted that severely autistic people are retarded and can't communicate, when a severely autistic person comes along who can communicate, think, and feel, it's easy to understand why experts would think Tito must be one in a million. Yet it was Soma who taught Tito to read and write, to do math, to think and communicate—maybe it was Soma who was one in a million. Maybe there was a lot more people in the world like Tito. Wasn't it at least possible?

But there seemed to be no tolerance for this to be considered even a remote possibility. Was it simply unthinkable to imagine that the experts might have wrongly proclaimed thousands of autistic children as hopelessly retarded and advised their parents to give up on them, as the child stood there, if there was even the remotest chance that the child could have been listening, understanding, thinking, and feeling all the while? It would be a very terrible thing to have done for so many years, *if* they were wrong.

Maybe they were so adamant about Tito being one in a million because his very existence meant they *could* be wrong.

More than anything else, I wondered what Tito could tell us about autism. The inexplicable enigma that Tito was merely fueled my desire to learn more about him. I wanted to discover everything I could about him, I wanted to get to know Tito, I wanted to understand how his mind worked, how he experienced life, how he existed. I wanted to know how he thought, how he felt emotions, what his sensory perception was like, how did he compose his poems and stories, what was it like to be autistic? I would travel into his world as far as he would allow me to. I knew that this was the opportunity of a lifetime to find out what autism was.

All the years Jon and I had been working for CAN and praying for Dov, we never wavered in our mission to find treatment and a cure for autism. But we had the same fear that is in the back of every parent's mind: What if the magic bullet is discovered too late for my child? How many years can go by without meeting early milestones, much less cognitive and academic markers, before the damage has become permanent? How will he ever catch up, when he's had to adapt to the world all his life with an autistic brain? Will he ever be able to recover? Is it already too late?

But now I knew there was Tito. A living being whose very existence suggested it was actually possible that Dov and others might have far more potential than anyone had ever suspected. And that meant there was a chance that they might be able to get better.

When I contemplated Tito and then thought about Dov, silent all these years, unable to express himself, I was reminded of a story that had dominated the national news some years ago. A small child had fallen down a well and was thought to be dead. Rescue workers struggled around the clock to save the child, on the one-in-a-million chance that they could. Against all odds, in a kind of a living miracle, they did save her. I imagined Dov as a one-year-old, falling down a deep well, believed to be dead. And then years later, a light shone down that dark shaft and I could see him there, *somehow still alive*. The shock, the amazement, the sheer joy, and the sheer horror of finding him there, alive after all those years—it was almost more than I could bear to imagine. And we would lift him ever so slowly, ever so carefully, up and up and up until at last he would emerge from the darkness of that deep well, into the light he had not seen for so very, very long. A miracle.

After encountering Tito, I was flooded with hope and the kind of energy that allows you to lift a car off a loved one pinned after a crash. I didn't need sleep, food, or anything else. I just needed to know what to do next.

But in spite of this, precious months passed and I was making very little headway in trying to get Soma and Tito back to the U.S. My belief that Tito was an incredibly valuable and unique window into autism, one that might never be found again, met with resistance everywhere I turned, from the CAN board to the scientists I knew. No one seemed to understand how important Tito was.

I could think of a thousand questions I wanted the scientists to ask about Tito, but there was one that pressed most heavily on my own mind was, why was Tito's behavior still so severely autistic in spite of his language ability and all the cognitive gains he'd made? In fact, Tito's mind and body seemed to be living separate lives. How was this possible?

Finally I hatched a plan. All I needed was one really big-name scientist to agree to study Tito. Then I could present a proposal to the CAN board requesting a stipend for Soma and Tito to return to the U.S. for a number of months so that Tito could be studied. I wracked my brain. Merzenich would have been perfect, if he hadn't already rejected me outright twice.

Over the next few months, as I contacted scientists, I also began to correspond with Soma and Tito by e-mail. Soma seemed strangely familiar to me, like I'd known her for a very long time. In reality, Soma and I didn't have much in common except for two very important things—each of us had a severely autistic son, and we shared a philosophy that Soma stated so eloquently, shortly after we first met: "If you want something very much and constantly allow yourself to want it, the whole universe conspires to allow you to have it."

Yet I knew there were some things in life that no amount of willpower or determination could fix, like when my father died when I was seven. But autism was different. Dov was alive, he was here, now, living, he was with us. If there was life, there was hope. I knew that too.

Whether our hopes and dreams for our sons were realistic, logical, or even remotely possible did not—could not—factor into the equation. How two such logical people as Soma and I had become such stubborn and willful, rampant dreamers remains a mystery to me even now.

Soma began writing to me as if to a diary, as if we were sitting in the same room over a cup of tea. We were becoming friends.

She seemed so lonely, so isolated, and there was something else going on. Apparently, Tito was starting to hit adolescence with a resounding crash. He was becoming aggressive, even violent with her. And he was now a full head taller than his mother. I was worried about them. Soma could not get any help or medication to manage Tito's aggressive behavior. To make matters worse, there was a severe water shortage in Bangalore and Soma, by herself with Tito, who needed constant supervision, had to carry all their daily water up flights of stairs each morning before dawn. Soma was desperate to return to the U.S., and she wrote e-mails to me almost daily expressing this.

Tito also began to correspond with me. The waiting was impossible for him, the not knowing if they would be able to return to the United States, torturous. I began to worry that the very possibility of returning might be making things worse for Soma and Tito.

. . .

By early spring, Soma's e-mails were verging on hysteria. In the latest incident, Tito, in a fit of blinding rage, had tried to push her out of a moving motorized rickshaw. If people saw his violent behavior toward her in public, Tito could be taken away from her for good, she explained. And yet roaming the streets of Bangalore was their only escape from the tiny apartment in which they otherwise must spend all their time. No wonder Tito was becoming unbearably anxious and depressed.

> *April comes tomorrow again*
> *Wonder Portia what could happen*
> *Will the world get Bubbled like a soap*
> *And get burst up like a breaking hope*
> *April comes tomorrow again*
> *Yet I know that things will be the same*
> *Portia tell me how to welcome it*
> *April looks so Autistic*
>
> *Tito*

Although Soma and Tito were foremost in my thoughts, there were a thousand other things going on in my life. Jon and I were traveling constantly for CAN. We tried never to travel together, so that our children would always have one parent at home.

In fact, by the time Miriam and Gabriel entered school, CAN had completely taken over our lives. It was hard being a family. There were too many people in our house; it felt like we had subcontracted out every fragmented piece of our existence just so we could keep going. We needed help to get the kids to school, help to make sure they had clean clothes, and still the army of therapists for Dov, while Jon traveled to Washington and I was getting CAN's autism gene bank up and running. Our lives were a financial and emotional sinkhole.

Once again, I found myself preparing to leave town. I was booked on an early-morning flight to New York where I was scheduled to meet with some of the investigators CAN was funding at Columbia University. It was after midnight and a car would be picking me up in only a few hours to take me to the airport. I emptied out my worn suitcase that was still filled with clothes and research papers and business cards scrawled with handwritten notes that I hadn't sorted through from my last trip. I wasn't even sure there were any clean black socks in my drawer to pack. My fashion repertoire had been reduced to one remaining icon and that was black socks; they had become a symbol for me. Being out of clean black socks was the last straw that meant my life was out of control. The littlest thing can throw you into despair when you live your life on the edge of it.

In my office, too tired to be productive, I slumped in my chair and stared at the unopened e-mails on my computer screen. I'd become accustomed to staying up all night at least once a week to try to catch up on things, and I was sleeping on average three or four hours a night the rest of the time. I felt as if I was aging in light-years, and on the rare occasion when I looked in the mirror, my reflection confirmed this. And while I was getting older, so was Dov, and he was still as autistic as ever.

Suddenly it flashed into my mind—who else to study Tito but the king of consciousness himself, Rodolfo Llinás? He practically invented consciousness. I had discovered Llinás in a *New York Times* article by Sandra Blakeslee entitled "How the Brain Might Work: A New Theory of Consciousness." I would call him the minute I arrived in New York. Who knew what incredible insights a man like Rodolfo Llinás might have about someone like Tito?

In the few hours I had on the flight to New York, all I could think about was "the binding problem," which was to say, pretty much the sum total of what I knew about consciousness. The binding problem asked what makes us experience life as we do? What holds together all the bits and pieces of sensory information that our brains perceive? How do we experience consciousness as one smooth, flowing experience, when what we see, hear, feel, smell, and taste enters our brains in a million separate fragments of perception?

When I awoke in New York, the city had fallen silent, buried by a heavy snow that fell during the night. I opened my window, letting in a stream of frozen air that could only thrill a Californian. I watched out the window of my hotel room as a few brave souls ventured out and children began to drag their sleds into Central Park.

It was a snow day, the radio announced. Schools were closed, trains were delayed, much of the city was shut down. My heart sank. Rodolfo Llinás would probably not be in his office on a snow day but I called anyway. I was not actually prepared to speak to a human being, expecting at most that I would leave a recorded message. I certainly didn't expect Llinás to answer the phone himself. Apparently these wise men of consciousness were more intrepid than postmen and no mere blizzard could keep them from their pursuit of the meaning of it.

Not more than an hour later, I found myself sweating from the brisk walk through deep snow that landed me in a chair across from Rodolfo Llinás himself. I was in awe. Not wasting any time, we were already deep into the center of the brain. I felt like the Incredible Shrinking Man, delving ever deeper into the unknowable core of consciousness with this man who seemed entirely unafraid of it. Llinás not only had an explanation for consciousness but he held steadfastly to the conviction that his idea, the so-called binding problem, was an absolute fact.

What happened in that room, while blizzards whirled around outside blasting up and down the avenues of New York, I cannot exactly say, except that a journey took place. It was more like a dream than a dream could ever be, filled with unusual sights and sounds of the kind one never sees during normal waking states.

For one thing, rarely had I heard the word "thalamus" used so frequently. According to Llinás, signals emitted by projections from the thalamus sweep across the cortex at a frequency of forty cycles per second, activating neurons in a synchronous pattern that binds together all the bits and pieces of perception much as the frames of a movie are held together in time when they pass before the lantern of the projector, giving the illusion of smooth continuous motion and a coherent reality.

Llinás explained that the brain perceives the environment in tiny fragments that when bound together in time can make up the apparently seamless perception of the world we experience. These perceptual fragments are the result of individual neurons specializing in specific features, such as orientation, edge, color, shape, texture, motion, and many others. Llinás's theories readily explained how all these seemingly fragmented pieces of perception could be bound together.

For the first time, I was to hear the term "bottom-up processing." This, I soon found out, simply meant that lower-level bits and pieces from perception were being sorted, organized, and bound together at higher levels of the brain. It seemed hard to imagine that this could all happen so quickly and result in what we experience as consciousness.

I was not wearing a watch, and Llinás had nothing so mundane as a clock in his office, so I was surprised when a guard came by to tell us the building would be locking up in half an hour. It was time. Now or never. I had to tell Llinás why I'd come to see him. I had to tell him about Tito. I had to ask him how it was possible that someone like Tito, whose mind and behavior were split apart, could exist, for surely this master of the subject of consciousness would have some insight, a way of explaining the possibility of it. I drew in a breath and started talking about Tito.

"Impossible," Llinás declared, cutting me off. "An elaborate smoke and mirrors."

Disappointment swelled in my throat and I could not speak. Where was the brilliant imagination, the intellectual panache, the daring curiosity he was famous for? But I was so in awe of Llinás that I could not argue with him. I knew he was wrong about Tito. But still, he'd given me so much of himself in these few snowbound hours. He'd thrown open a door into consciousness that I had not known before our meeting, a door that would help me understand Tito, even if Llinás himself could not entertain the possibility of a consciousness as different from ours as Tito's must surely be, even if Llinás thought Tito was a fake and was not interested in meeting him.

A feeling of warmth and enormous relief flooded my body and mind as the revolving glass doors delivered me into the spacious lobby of the hotel. A friendly doorman greeted me with a nod and a smile softening my crash landing back on Earth. I was coming down.

The old hotel room radiators clanked and shook in some concert to the heat gods. The room was stuffily warm, yet pleasant, like a greenhouse. All I really wanted was to read the newspaper in bed and order a bowl of oatmeal from room service, but I couldn't get Llinás's last words out of my mind. "I feel terrible when I harm an in-sect," he had said, his voice burdened with compassion and existen-tial angst, brimming with the heart-rending inevitability that we are destined to harm one another in spite of the miraculous nature of our existence, "because we live in the same temporal processing stream." The way he said it, I knew it contained everything he knew, everything he thought, everything he was. And yet, though Llinás could feel compassion toward the lowly insect because he believed it shared some form of awareness, the thing he called qualia, still he could not believe that a human being who behaved like Tito could possess a consciousness similar to our own.

By the next day, the sun came out and the snow began to melt, and over the next few days I met with the researchers I'd planned to visit and everywhere I went there was good news—good news on the genetic front, good news on the neuroimaging front, and good news on the bioinformatics front. But I couldn't help feeling discouraged by my meeting with Llinás.

I'd planned to convince Llinás that autism might be the first disorder of consciousness ever to be described. But, in the presence of his genius, I'd forgotten to mention the idea.

And I had failed to bring all that Tito had to offer any closer to being taken seriously.

4.

Acting As If

I can appreciate a flower, but the beauty is revealed to me more when it is described to me.

—*Tito*

t was a typically bright and sunny Southern California afternoon when I arrived back from New York and at last trudged up the massive stairs to the second floor. I unpacked and threw yet another round of laundry over the bannister. A few hundred e-mails greeted me when I turned on my computer. The regular mail was heaped on my desk along with some faxes and the dozens of phone messages that were skewered on a spindle that was about to topple over. I stared out the window, paralyzed with exhaustion. I was deeply tired. I wanted to garden, to go shopping, to take a walk, anything but more CAN work. I wanted to have a life again.

The time was rapidly approaching when I would have to present my case for bringing Soma and Tito back to the U.S. to the CAN board. Maybe it wasn't going to work out after all. I felt angry and helpless. My eyes were not focusing as I sat unable to move from my chair. Maybe it was time for one of those really good cries, the kind you used to have when you were a kid and your mom would just hold you and pat your back and whisper, "Good, good. Let it all out." The kids were still in school and Jon was at work. No one was in the house. It was as good a time as any. I cut loose and cried my eyes out for I don't know how long, and after a while, as it always did, the despair, like the blizzard in New York City, eventually blew over.

I could barely see by the time I checked the clock. The kids would be home from school any minute. I breathed deeply. I felt better. That's when I spotted the e-mail from Tito, titled: *"Answer to your question."*

Tito was a poet of such prolific output that every thought expanded into ripples of metaphor. At first, one can only be astonished and delighted by the torrent of words that pour forth from a person who outwardly appears to have no comprehension of language. Like interpreting a dream, I dwelled upon his long strings of words, searching for their meaning. But these endless stanzas, beautiful as they were, did not tell me what I wanted to know: What was it like to be autistic? How did Tito actually experience the environment? How did he see, hear, and feel? Again and again, I wrote to Tito, asking him to describe just one small incident and how he experienced it. I asked him to write about one single moment in as much detail as possible. Short poems and short stories and chapters of his many short books, stanzas of long poems and even essays arrived in my electronic mailbox. Even the most practical correspondence, the answers to which could have been simple and straightforward, elicited from Tito an outpouring of mysterious, cryptic verse, the actual meaning of which was as undecipherable as a Japanese haiku might be in answer to the question, "How do you like your new computer?"

At first I thought this was another amazing and complex piece of prose from the labyrinth of Tito's mysterious mind, but this e-mail was different. Suddenly I was no longer tired. My brain came back to life. I read this e-mail over and over as if to prove to myself that what I was reading was really there. Yes, this was it, this was what I'd been wishing, hoping, and praying for, for months. Here it was at last, Tito's attempt to describe in exact detail one single moment of his existence.

Dear Portia,

Autism, as I have learnt from my experience, and my observation of other autistic people, is a state of a total chaos.

Chaos in the sense, that we perceive the things in a way which gives us an incomplete information of the whole situation. Here I am giving the collective 'we' because I have generalised my experiences. And I may be wrong. But I may be correct also.

To clarify my statement, let me give an example of a simple situation.

'Water running down a tap, and filling a blue bucket.'

How many nouns do I have to concentrate on and then link with each other? Three. Water, bucket and tap. The movable item is water, which is linking the tap and the blue bucket. Water is transferred from the tap to the bucket, which is blue.

A very simple situation.

Now this situation also has a sound associated with it. The sound of water.

The situation also has a background. Where is the tap? Garden? Basin?

Now I concentrate on the sound of water falling and recognise it because I am more sensitive to sounds.

I understand that the water is certainly not filling something small like a tumbler but the bucket and realise then that the blue colour was the property of the bucket.

Now, by the time I try to understand the whole situation, the bucket is already filled and the tap is closed.

The closed tap, the silence and the filled blue bucket becomes another situation. This again needs a closer study.

The close analysis of each and every situation, gets too overwhelming.

The result is that, each Autistic person tends to develop one particular sense organ through which he tries to perceive the situation. I have developed my hearing better than my other senses. I have learnt to be comfortable that way because trying to use all the senses turns into a total chaos.

If I am asked to close my eyes and pick potatoes from a mixture of potatoes and onions, I would not be able to do so because my sense of touch is poor. So I do not mind people hugging me like Tom, who is tactile sensitive. My tactile sensitivity is limited to textures of fabric. I do not like wool.

Again I shall recognise you from your voice rather than your features.

The world has a separate picture for you and a separate picture for me.

You call it 'terrible' and I call it a 'gift of nature'. And gifts can come in any way.

Tito

Yes, this was it. Tito first described *seeing* water running from a tap into a blue bucket. But then a moment later he pronounces: *"There is also a sound."* He goes on to wonder, as he listens to it— what is the water flowing into, where is all this taking place?

Yet didn't he just a moment ago describe the color of the bucket while he was looking at it?

I read Tito's description again. My heart was pounding. Tito was revealing something no one had ever heard of, thought of, or even dreamed of before. In fact, it had absolutely nothing at all to do with what people believed about autism. It had nothing to do with the absence of normal human drives like sociability, empathy, "theory of mind."

Tito was telling us he could not see and hear at the same time. At least not when he was concentrating on something.

Without narrowing his senses down to one channel, Tito says that the world *"turns into a total chaos."*

What's more, Tito suspects that each autistic individual tends to develop one sense more than the others—because concentrating on one sense is a way to get better information from the environment—a chance to make more sense of the world.

Question after question entered my mind. Was Tito born like this? Or did he become this way by adapting, trying to understand the world as best he could? Could Tito only *pay attention* to one sensory modality at a time? And what exactly was this "total chaos"?

But most of all I wondered: Were there other autistic people like Tito? Over the months that followed, I corresponded with Tito nearly every day. It was one of the most exciting times of my life. I woke up each morning feeling like an archeologist who'd just struck the layer in which an undiscovered civilization lay buried.

I returned to Tito's book *Beyond the Silence* and read it again with new eyes. I saw now that the pages were filled with descriptions of Tito's single-modality sensory processing. Until now, I had not understood.

THE MIND TREE

Maybe it is night
Maybe it is day
I can't be sure
Because I'm not yet feeling the heat of the sun
I am the mind tree
When I had been gifted this mind of mine
I recall his voice very clearly
To you I have given this mind
And you shall be the only kind
No one ever will like you be
And I name you the mind tree

I can't see or talk
Yet I can imagine
I can hope and I can expect
I am able to feel pain but I cannot cry
So I just be and wait for the pain to subside
I can do nothing but wait
My concerns and worries
Are trapped within me somewhere in my depths
Maybe in my roots
Maybe in my bark
When he comes next who gifted me my mind
I shall ask him for the gift of sight
I doubt his return and
Yet I hope for it
Maybe he will
Maybe he will not

—From *Beyond the Silence*,
   by Tito Mukhopadhyay

That night, I looked at Dov as I sat next to him on his bed. His eyes were aimed at some corner of the ceiling; his mouth was open, with one hand limp at his side and the other clutching a favorite rock he could not live without that day. The pale yellow walls, the therapeutic games, toys, and books; Dov's room had become imprinted in my mind forever during the thousands of unbearable moments I experienced as we tried new therapies that failed and during all the hours I spent sitting beside him, not knowing if he was having a toothache or a bad dream.

As I looked at him now, tall and skinny, delicate and fragile, I had to admit that in some respects he was worse than he'd ever been. When I allowed myself to let down my guard, to lapse into the terrible despair that was always lurking just below the surface I would cry for hours and hours, to deplete myself of the sadness. It was hard to find a place to do this because I could not let anyone see me cry. I was the optimist, the stubborn one who never gave up. If I gave in to despair, who would hope for Dov?

When a brain goes off the track of normal development early in life it does not mean that development stops. The child continues to adapt, to develop, as best he can, but as each new stage unfolds and the child interacts with the environment, the original deviation is amplified. Think of a marble rolling down a gully in the side of a mountain. The gully is where most marbles will roll down the mountain. When a brain goes off the track of normal development, it's as if the marble falls outside the gully and begins to take a different path. The more time that passes and the farther down the mountain it rolls, the farther off the normal course it will go. And so it is with autism. The abnormally developing brain also has to adapt and interact with the environment and so the circuitry weaves a pattern that is more and more out of the ordinary.

I had been spending less time with Dov as the years went by. It was just too painful. I didn't know what to do when we were together. None of the therapies were working. Yet I still found new things to try. I made up my own therapies, and during those periods I spent more time with Dov, fueled by even the most remote chance that something might work for him. But as the years slid by, nothing worked. And yet I could not accept that this was his life, that this was all there could ever be for him. I loved him so much I could not bear the agony of standing by and watching him be trapped in his autism while I could offer nothing more than a hug and some words I wasn't sure he understood.

Now, sitting beside nine-year-old Dov in his room, I looked around at the shelves of toys that hadn't really changed much since the earliest days. There were simple toddler puzzles, plastic stacking rings, and all the other toys he never played with. There were books we read to him not knowing if he understood, there were the remains of lots of good ideas that didn't work, attempts at teaching reading, attempts at teaching pretend play, attempts at teaching almost every early developmental stage a child could go through, or in Dov's case, could have missed. Then there were the blocks, the marbles, and the rocks—all the things Dov would obsess on and stim on incessantly if you allowed it. He would click the rocks together, pour the marbles in a stream before his eyes, put the blocks in his mouth.

We could not have imagined that he would be like this now. No, when Dov was two we could not have imagined that at the age of nine he would still be chewing on blocks and tapping stones, that he would actually be much worse than when he was two. We would not have believed that he would still not be able to speak, or to communicate in any way, or play with toys, or be left alone for a few moments without endangering himself.

I looked at Dov, sitting there next to me, staring straight ahead with a slight smile on his face, a smile which might be random or perhaps was because I was sitting there with him—I had no way of knowing. His eyes were dark like his dad's and he wore that faraway look as though his mind were on another planet. We hardly knew each other.

Now I reached over and hugged him, and held him in my arms as I had so many times before. He seemed to enjoy it as I rocked him gently back and forth, patting his back as I'd done when he was a baby. This was one thing we could do together, one out of millions of otherwise disconnected moments when we were sort of normal together, as mom and kid. At least we had this. I knew that some families did not. Some families had an autistic child who could not bear to be touched, and these parents were deprived even of these few moments of silent closeness.

My mind kept returning to Tito's e-mail. I had come into Dov's room planning to tell him about it. I wanted to tell Dov why things were so easy for us "normal" people that were so very hard for him, why he had to struggle to accomplish the smallest task, to understand things that the rest of us understand effortlessly or to do the simplest things, like walk into another room to find something he lost.

But I also didn't know whether Dov could understand a word I said. What if his brain was as intact as Tito's and he just couldn't tell us? It was at once an awful and fantastic idea. For if he was intelligent, then I could not bring myself to think about the years we had wasted and the emotional pain we'd caused him by treating him as if he knew so little. What if we'd drilled him with therapies that were far below his cognitive level for years only to discover he was actually intelligent?

"Dov," I started out slowly. The words rang superficially in my ears as if I were reciting a passage with nobody listening. This was the ultimate in "acting as if," a form of pop psychology that says if you "act as if," it will become so. But what did I have to lose? No one else was in the room with us, no one could hear us . . . and if God was anywhere nearby, he wouldn't laugh at us, I thought. He would find it a perfectly good thing to be talking to Dov as if he understood everything instead of almost nothing.

"There's something I want to talk to you about." I hesitated. "I've told you about Tito, the boy from India who can write—who can communicate." Was it my imagination, or was Dov, still never looking at me, smiling just a bit more? I studied his face for a moment, then squeezed him around the shoulders affectionately as I went on. "Well, he's been explaining to me how he experiences things, how he perceives the world around him. It's different, Dov. It's different from how the rest of us experience things."

Dov turned his head and stole a fleeting glance in the direction of my face. I caught his babyish cheeks in my hands and drew him closer to me. He avoided my eyes, staring blankly at a spot just to the side of my face. "You see, Dov, you may not realize it, but things are so much easier for the rest of us . . . because we can see and hear and feel things all at the same time." I sounded insane to myself, but I went on anyway. "Tito told me that he can't hear my voice if he looks at my eyes. He says he can't look at something and listen at the same time. He told me he can't feel his body."

I went on, "Dov, maybe some of these things are true for you, too. I don't know. Tito says he has to struggle to make sense out of things. Tito says everything is chaos for him, the world is overwhelming and hard to understand. He has to work really hard to make sense out of it, and by the time he does the situation is over for everyone else and they've left him behind. He says he relies on his hearing almost completely; he says he doesn't use his eyes very much at all. Dov, is that true for you? Dov? . . ." I trailed off. Even if it was true, I knew Dov could not tell me.

Suddenly Dov was looking right at me with an unmistakable look, a deepness in his eyes that, when they dwelled on mine for even a fleeting moment, I knew in my heart meant he understood me. A tear slipped down my cheek and I tried to hide it by hugging him tightly. We sat like that and rocked on his bed in silence for a long time.

5.

Loops Around
Our House

Throughout the months of waiting and hoping for Tito and Soma's eventual return, I corresponded with Tito several times a week. If no one else was interested in studying Tito, at least I could try to learn about autism from him myself. Being able to communicate with Tito was like opening the encyclopedia of autism—a previously forbidden volume where the definitions and the answers could now be had for the asking—and the phenomenon of autism itself was suddenly accessible. Although I greatly admired Tito's poetry, it was how his brain worked that I wanted to learn about—even more so than his lovely, ever-so-complex and very human heart and soul. And Tito explained.

I remember things by associating.

I tend to associate anything which I am experiencing now with a previously learnt experience. Like number three exists because number two exists. While number two exists because number one exists.

I am never very spontaneous with my visual experience as my auditory experience. I have to link the colour or shape to a previously experienced thing having identical colour and shape. And therefore it takes time.

Now dear Portia, the question comes as to how I recognise people? The answer is simple. 'I don't.'
Did you ever see me making any eye contact?
So Portia dear, it will be your voice, your choice of words and someone similar to your photograph, which I have seen many times, and which being constant, relating to changes are understood better.

Every face becomes a combination of eyes, nose, mouth and other parts. Yet the lengths and sizes of these parts differ from person to person. Now, can you imagine what a big confusion it will be if I started linking facial parts, with every detail, each one having a different expression, a worried look or a smiling look or a sad look or a puzzled look?

How many links I should require to recognise Portia smiling at me? Can you imagine the strain?

Now the question is do I know whether I am fast or slow in recognising situations? How can I say whether I am fast or slow when I have not experienced the way a normal human being processes images and sounds?

I have to thank my mother for that.
She has taught me Biology. The basic human body along with its systems.
She has taught me Physics. The laws which regulate our surroundings.
So I know 'what should be' and what I am experiencing.
I compare the two and believe that I need to process slowly to get the complete picture.

And Portia, difference is surely there.

Without any difference, how can I act different?
Again without acting different why on earth should I be called Autistic?

Tito

It was becoming very clear that Tito was not able to experience the world using all his senses in the seamlessly synchronized way that the rest of us do. It also seemed as if Tito relied almost entirely upon what he heard to make sense of the world—to such an extent that he was almost like a blind person. I was beginning to wonder if other nonverbal autistics might be experiencing the world the way Tito did and were presumed retarded when perhaps they were silently, helplessly listening their way through life with no means to express themselves.

The more I studied Tito's amazing replies, the more it seemed that his senses were split apart, that he literally could not see and hear at the same time.

At the end of each day, I found myself once again sitting with Dov on his bed. When he was not stimming or experiencing a bout of mania, Dov had the face of a beautiful angel. He was going to be very handsome someday. But now I took his small hands into mine, and summoned up the courage to talk to him as if he could understand me; telling him as best I could about everything that I was learning about Tito. It occurred to me that no one had told Dov how "normal" people experience the world. He might not know.

As the weeks turned into months I studied Tito's book and continued to correspond with him by e-mail, and I knew with ever-growing conviction that we could learn more about autism from Tito than from anyone else in the world, because he was living in the deepest, darkest trenches of it and yet could communicate with us. Convincing the scientists of this was another story. Each day I conjured up my nerve and made one more call, met with another researcher, wrote one more letter. Why couldn't I convince just one really great scientist that Tito was a gold mine of information waiting to explode every myth about autism and reveal a new understanding of it? For one thing, I was pretty sure most of them thought I was crazy.

Those who were familiar with autism asked me why Tito was any different from the autistics who a decade earlier had used the now-debunked communication method called facilitated communication.

The truth was, I hadn't even noticed the phenomenon called facilitated communication[7] when it came on the scene a few years before Dov was born. And by the time Dov was diagnosed with autism, facilitated communication had gone underground and had all but disappeared from the vernacular of autism. When I finally did hear about it, it was described as a hand-over-hand method of communication that had been used with autistics until it was debunked. Accusations of abuse communicated by some autistic in-dividuals using facilitated communication had led to tragic conse-quences for some families, causing the method itself to be put on trial. Attempts to validate the method had failed and no one used it any-more, I was told.

And yet I couldn't help but wonder: Was it *possible* that some of the communication could have been real?

"Oh, that's just a Ouija-board effect," Ed Cook, a widely respected autism researcher, stated with certainty and a touch of concern when I asked him what he thought about facilitated communication.

But that didn't stop us from eventually trying facilitated commu-nication. When Dov was about six and he had made very little progress using any kind of therapy we made a halfhearted attempt to try it. The method consisted of holding a child's hand and applying counterresistance, so they had something to push against, the ra-tionale being that this would help them control their movement enough to point at letters on a board and thereby communicate. Af-ter watching a demonstration, I tentatively held Dov's hand and let him push against mine, slowly, laboriously, he typed the letters D-Z-N-E.

"Disney!" the sweet, smiling lady exclaimed. "He wants to go to Disneyland!"

I wanted to believe, but so far we had no indication that Dov could spell, read, or even knew the alphabet. He still could not match letters or numbers reliably, even when given only two choices. Had he typed out the word independently, even if misspelled, I could have made the stretch from *DZNE* to Disney, I could have suspended my disbelief and abandoned my empirical thinking, but the real problem was that I could not honestly tell what was me and what was Dov. It was impossible to know who was doing the typing because our two bodies were so enmeshed in the movement of the pointing. And not surprisingly, without another person helping him, Dov could not type anything at all.

But Tito was different. For one thing he could produce handwriting. It was scrawled and barely legible, but ultimately you *could* read it. And what he wrote made sense. His were well-formed thoughts and ideas, well-constructed sentences, and he had an excellent vocabulary, if slightly odd grammar. And Tito often tried to speak the words aloud as he wrote them, though almost no one could understand him. But most of all it was the fact that his mother did not touch him while he wrote or typed that set Tito apart from what people thought of when they saw someone using facilitated communication. It was true that Soma had to verbally urge Tito on and rescue him by alerting him with her voice when he lapsed into transient paralysis, but she did not hold his hand, his shoulder, or touch him in any way other than to occasionally prod him back into the moment with a sudden jab to his arm or knee. In fact, not a single person who had ever witnessed Tito writing or typing could doubt that it was Tito who was communicating and not his mother.

Around this time, I was visited by my friend Elaine and her autistic son, Steve. Steve was about twenty years old and could physically talk but had a highly circumscribed verbal routine that seemed to prevent any actual communication from taking place. He would run from person to person, talking urgently about his favorite subject.

"Is your grandfather alive?" he would start out, regardless of the fact that he'd already asked me this question a dozen times in the past fifteen minutes. "No, he died." "Where is he buried?" he would ask next. "Chicago," I would reply again. And then Steve would launch into a detailed monologue about the train station in Chicago. He apparently knew a lot about every train station in the entire nation. But what was he doing? Was this a not-so-subtle strategy to get people onto his favorite subject, train stations? Or were these the only words that his mouth could utter when he tried to speak? His speech was flawless yet somehow he could not use it to communicate meaningfully. It was eerie. It was as if Steve were possessed and interacting with him felt like being in the company of an apparition, someone who was not really there.

Steve reminded me of Brian, another autistic teenage boy I'd met. Brian was a handsome high-school-age boy with the build of a football player who would have been a heartthrob if it weren't for his autism. During my visit, Brian raced from one end of his house to the other, stopping abruptly on each lap, inches from my face, shouting: "Portia! Have you seen *The Prince of Egypt*, Portia?" And then, not waiting for my reply, he would take off, sprinting through the house again. "He means the movie, *The Prince of Egypt*," his mother explained. Apparently Brian had seen the movie and also owned several books about it. At the time I met Brian, he had been asking everyone this question for over a year.

I had seen other children like Steve and Brian, in fact, many of the autistic people who could talk had their same problem: Although they could speak, it did them little good for the purpose of communication. I had witnessed the heartbreak of so many parents whose autistic child could speak by the age of three, suggesting a better outcome, and yet by age seven these same children could not communicate and often spoke only in repetitive, meaningless loops.

It had never occurred to me until now that speech itself could be an abnormal behavior, useless for purposes of communication. It seemed as if Steve's and Brian's words were not under their voluntary control. If this was true, their spoken words would not be considered language in the sense that we usually think of it.

How could someone like Tito have a highly developed, complex internal language and yet be unable to speak while someone like Steve who had all the required physical-motor ability to speak was unable to use his clearly enunciated words to communicate?

Even more perplexing was the fact that when Dov or Tito did try to speak, though their words were apraxic and barely intelligible even to those familiar with them, the words *were* communicative.

A larger idea was beginning to take shape in my mind, something that seemed important though I didn't know yet what to make of it. The autistic people like Steve and Brian were extremely visual. They seemed to rely on their eyes to make sense of the world, just as Tito had said he relied on his ears to understand things. I was beginning to suspect that there might be two major groups in autism, a visual type with better motor skills and the ability to speak, like Steve and Brian, and an auditory type like Tito, and perhaps Dov, with poor motor skills and no ability to physically speak.

There is an old folktale called "Stone Soup" in which a starving boy enters a small village that has fallen on hard times, claiming that he can make a delicious soup from a single stone. The villagers gather round to watch him attempt to perform his miracle. The soup, the boy tells them, is going to be most delicious they have ever tasted, but it would be fit for a rich man's table if only he could add a carrot or two. The villagers send for the extra ingredient at once. The soup is exquisite, the boy exclaims upon tasting it, but it would truly be fit to serve the king himself if only he could add a few potatoes. And thus the villagers continue to bring more ingredients and watch in amazement as the boy produces a magnificent soup from a single stone, until finally the entire village dines upon it, in celebration of the miracle of stone soup.

If only I could find the stone for my stone soup: One great scientist was all I needed to convince the CAN board and get other scientists to take Tito seriously. I knew that if I could just get Tito in front of one of these scientists in person, they would believe me. But so far the only scientist in the United States who had actually seen Tito firsthand was Mike Merzenich, the naysayer, the pessimist, the realist, the genius. Suddenly it hit me: Mike Merzenich might be my *only* hope.

And so it was that I finally got up the nerve to call Mike Merzenich again. As he picked up the phone that day, I pressed the receiver tightly to my ear and clutched a pen in my sweaty hand just to keep it occupied. Would he consider seeing Tito, studying him at his lab, if I could get them back to the United States for a few months? My heart was beating too fast, at once hoping that Mike Merzenich would come through and yet terrified that he would just tell me again that autism research was impossible and he could not get involved.

"*I would be honored,*" came his unhesitating reply, his voice resonating with intense interest and sincerity.

I loved Mike Merzenich.

Mike Merzenich's involvement proved to be the turning point for the CAN board of directors, who finally agreed to support Soma and Tito for four months, all expenses paid, so that Merzenich could work with Tito. Soon after Merzenich committed to studying Tito, a half dozen other scientists agreed to meet with Tito and study him as well.

E-mailing Soma and Tito with the good news was one of the most rewarding moments of my life.

Then came the more practical problems. Where would they live? A more unusual pair of tenants I could not imagine. I rented a small furnished apartment for them in Park LaBrea, a sprawling complex of buildings enclosed within a high wall right in the middle of Los Angeles. At least Tito could not run out directly into moving traffic there. Their apartment had a private entrance; there was a laundry on the first floor and outside was a patchwork of small green lawns crisscrossed by flower-lined sidewalks. There were stores nearby, an expansive city park and a public library, city buses stopped at the corner, and the other tenants kept to themselves. It seemed ideal.

No matter how much I tried to guess what they would want or need, I knew I could not. This was going to be a huge change for Soma and Tito. Tito was accustomed to roaming the streets of Bangalore at his mother's side as she described everything they passed. Tito barely used his eyes at all, relying almost entirely on his mother's continuous narrative in which she explained everything in their world. There were rickshaws and cars; the undisturbed, revered cow; old men at work in their shops; tailors and beggars; dogs that roamed the streets; and religious ceremonies taking place. There was a sun and sometimes clouds, the wind, a rainy season and a dusty season, day and night, a drought. All of these Tito learned about from his mother as she first described the environment and then explained the underlying principles and laws of the phenomena to him. Tito looked like a blind person as he clutched his mother's arm and allowed himself to be guided through the crowded streets. Back in their tiny apartment in India, Tito wrote about the things she described to him.

One day, after a summer dust storm, when everyone else had shuttered their doors and windows, Soma pulled Tito out onto their terrace to enjoy the wind. Later he wrote this passage:

Little dust grains could be seen all around me. Little dust grains
scattered in the air, floating with their own sublime peace, little
dust grains with the wheels of the trucks suddenly breaking their
peace and flying with a wakeful alertness, little dust grains in my
breaths and of course little dust grains on and around the road
making a greater togetherness to form a dusty everything. Dusty
road, dusty air, dusty bushes around the road, dusty fields and of
course a dusty self of mine with my dusty feet.

But Los Angeles was different from Bangalore. The cars moved
faster and I was worried for Tito's safety. I knew that he had occasionally escaped into the streets of Bangalore, where his frantic
mother would search for him.

As the day of their arrival grew closer, I stocked their apartment
with groceries and supplies. All I knew was that Soma loved Lipton tea
and Tito loved chocolate. If all else failed, an Indian restaurant was
within walking distance. I knew Soma had never shopped at an American megagrocery store like Ralph's, and that the experience could
be overwhelming. Soma had described shopping in Bangalore where
she purchased specific things from small, individual shops, directly
from the shopkeeper. Candy was from one shop, vegetables from another, socks from their own shop, and shirts from yet another. In India
she never let Tito near a candy shop, for fear he would fly into a violent
rage in public. How was she going to control him in Ralph's, where
everything you could imagine was not only on display but within
reach? Everything was different here. Soma was very brave, I thought.

Finally the day arrived when Soma and Tito once again stood
among the crowd in the Los Angeles Airport international terminal,
this time searching for my familiar face instead of a handwritten
sign. It was the Fourth of July, 2001. Nine months had passed since
their first visit.

And then suddenly, as happens in dreams that are borne out of
yearning and a longing for something impossible, I found myself sit-

ting across from Soma in a small furnished apartment, both of us smiling shyly at each other and neither really knowing what to say, while Tito sat and rocked on the couch nearby, wearing headphones, his eyes seemingly fixed upon some distant planet. They had arrived, at last.

It was summer in Los Angeles. It was hot, but not nearly as hot as it could get in India, Soma informed me. And Park LaBrea had air-conditioning, not to mention a dishwasher, a microwave, a coin-operated washer and dryer, and a hundred other devices Soma had never encountered before. I saw Soma and Tito almost every day at first, though between CAN and my family and especially Dov, I don't know how I did it.

That first weekend, everyone at our house was ready for Soma and Tito's visit. The table on the porch was set with cookies and tea and there was a stack of poetry volumes on hand, which Jon thought Tito might enjoy. I knew Tito loved sweets and I thought by visiting on the porch he could have some cookies and tea with us, look at the poetry books, communicate on his alphabet board for a while, and then roam around the yard when he got antsy.

I'd been talking to Dov about Tito for months and I'd explained as best I could to my other children, Miriam, who was eight, and Gabriel, who was five, that we were going to have a very unusual guest named Tito. I tried to explain that how Tito behaved was not necessarily how he wanted to act and that his mind might be thinking something different than what his body was doing. Miriam and Gabriel looked at me as if they couldn't believe I was falling for such a transparent excuse for bad behavior, and maybe they'd give this excuse a try in the future themselves.

No sooner than Soma and Tito appeared on my front steps, all best-laid plans were swept aside. Instead of joining us on the porch for tea as I'd envisioned, Tito ran straight through the front door and began ranging through the entire house in an alarming manner. Soma ran after him apologizing and halfheartedly repeating: "No, Tito! No!" as he tore up the front stairs and burst into every room, throwing open closets and dumping drawers, turning anything that could be opened upside down, emptying laundry baskets and toy chests, dumping out books and papers, knocking over furniture or anything else that obstructed his path toward the next object of his desire.

I could barely keep up with them as Tito raced back downstairs and into the library, overturning books and papers while Jon looked on in horror as some of his finest first editions went crashing to the floor. Tito raced to the kitchen where he threw open the cabinets, grabbed a mouthful of bread, and shot out the back door, leaving the refrigerator agape and food scattered across the floor.

Outside, Tito ran awkwardly, loping around the perimeter of the building as Soma and I chased behind him. I caught a glimpse of Gabriel and Miriam as we ran by the front porch, making the most of the situation, greedily stuffing more cookies into their mouths than they knew I would ever allow. I shook a finger in their direction as I galloped by.

Tito ran back inside the house through the front door and the foraging started all over again. There would be no sitting down, there would be no cookies and tea, there would be no reading of poetry books. It was hard to spend time with Tito. In fact it was exhausting.

"So, Tito," I blurted out, breathless when finally I caught up with him. "Can we talk for a minute?" Suddenly, Tito dropped to the floor and sat cross-legged, rocking and flapping his fingers furiously at the sides of his face. Soma held the alphabet board in front of him. "C'mon!" she commanded. Tito's hands dropped to his lap and his rocking ceased and he began to point at one letter, then the next, as she read out each word, alternately regarded the alphabet board and then looked away with a strange half smile, his eyes bulging out of his head. His long, tapered, double-jointed fingers tapped out the words with deliberateness. *"I want to talk about Shakespeare, but instead I will open and close a paper bag. I will laugh and sniff the brick wall."* Just as suddenly as he'd begun to type, he resumed his flapping and rocking, now adding a series of loud, guttural clicking sounds. I was unable to think of a reply.

Soma thought they should go. I couldn't argue. But first, there was something I was determined to do. Somehow in the end we got Tito into the library where Jon was reading Dov a book. I took Dov by the hand and pulled him over to where Tito was standing. As far as I could see, the two of them never even looked at one another. It appeared as if each didn't even know the other existed.

"Dov, this is Tito," I introduced them. "Tito, this is Dov. You are a hero to him and a role model," I continued with a sense of urgency. Dov grabbed the end of Tito's belt and began to flip it back and forth, stimming, even though I'd told him not to stim on people, that they hated it, that it hurt their feelings and made them feel like he was treating them like an object instead of a person. "Stop it!" I admonished him, pulling his hand away from Tito's belt. Dov let out a burst of manic laughter and his hands flew up in front of his face, his eyes crossing in some unknown surge of electricity.

Tito seemed oblivious. "C'mon!" came Soma's now familiar demand as she thrust the alphabet board in front of him again. "Tito, is there anything you'd like to say to Dov?" I asked. Tito now bent slightly at the waist and embarked on a furious session of rocking and flapping, as if he were having an intense religious experience. "Do you think Dov will be able to communicate like you do someday?" I persisted, wishing that Tito would give Dov some encouragement.

Hearing my plea, Soma ramped up her prompting: "Tito! C'mon!" she demanded so sharply that Tito suspended his flapping and began to point at letters on the board again. "C'mon!" she repeated in a forceful, even voice, urging him on to the next letter and then the next. Soma would read each word as he typed it out, until at last, in this way, a sentence emerged which Soma now spoke for him: *"I think he should do it."*

I knew what Tito meant. "You see," I said to Dov as I hugged him tightly, smiling ear to ear, "Tito thinks that you'll be able to communicate like him someday."

I was just as glad they didn't see that my eyes were filled with tears as Tito ran from the room, Soma close on his heels, out to the cab that was waiting for them.

6.

Sipping Tea

had been so looking forward to Tito's first visit to my home, and yet all he did was wreck my house and run around like a wild beast. I did not use these words when later that night I wrote to Tito and asked him what had happened. This was his reply:

Dear Portia,

I shall name this letter as 'Thinking of apples and doing bananas.'

Quite weird isn't it?
But it so happens. And it happens with me.
Specially, when I am trying to think of something emotional and when the emotion gets too large to express. While, at the same time, it becomes important to get it expressed.
So what if it comes out as a laughter-fit when the mind is filled with tears?
So what if the manifestation of the emotion comes out as running around or perhaps sniffing the closest possible object?

*The important thing is to let the body lose that burden of emotion that
makes it too small to hold it any further.*
So what if Portia wonders 'What is wrong with Tito?'
*'Instead of appreciating my rose which I have sent, he is running
wild, or touching things, or opening and closing the bag.'*
And Portia wonders whether she should get irritated or not.
And Portia wonders whether her rose is recognised at all by Tito.

*Yet Tito feels himself running around or perhaps giggling aloud fully
aware that it is not what he means to do. And he cannot do anything
about it because he cannot stop himself.*

*And Tito wonders whether Portia will ever send him any more roses
because she got the message, that her roses were not understood—
leave alone appreciated.*
No wonders she thinks that Tito is in his own world.
*And since 'Tito is in his own world, he needs to be brought back to
the real world.'*

*And what about the feeling of appreciation which was trying to come
out of his mind?*
It gets sucked drying up the senses and drying up the feelings.
'What use are the feelings, when you do not know how to feel them?'
And the mind thinks another 'apple'. Body does a 'banana'.

Tito

I could see that trying to interview Tito at my house was going to be
very difficult. I began to visit Soma and Tito at their apartment more
often. At least there, Soma and I could have tea and cookies and
talk. Lipton tea was considered a delicacy in India and Soma savored
it in abundance here, brewing a pot of black tea with a large portion

of sweetened condensed milk and even more sugar, she cooked it
slowly, until eventually it turned into a hot, caffeinated, liquid candy
drink.

Soma would raise her cup, sniffing in the heady perfume of Lipton's and then take her first sip—her eyes would narrow and then go
misty with pleasure. Then she would offer me biscuits and choco-
lates, indulging in a few herself. I always politely ate one, knowing
that they were the sworn enemy of the low-carb lifestyle I ascribed
to. But as life often does, in its unfair way, after years of such dietary
indulgence, Soma remained about half my weight.

If Soma was bored with my unrelenting questions, she never
showed it. Instead, she paced back and forth in the tiny apartment,
her jewel-colored sari flowing behind her as she gave forth magnificent lectures, recalling the glorious details of how she had figured
out how to teach her son and telling me about her own life growing
up in India.

When Soma was a girl, she went to a convent school. In her family, being educated was the most important thing in the world. And
of all the brothers and sisters and cousins, Soma was the most
fiercely competitive. She had to be the best.

At home, there was no place for toys or child's play, it was a serious world, and if you were smart you could survive. If you were
smart, you would be loved. At least the brothers and male cousins
were allowed to participate in sports, but even after the girls completed all their homework they were expected to practice the do-
mestic and cultural arts that would produce good future wives. They
were trained in traditional Indian dance, to cook and to embroider
and crochet, to paint and draw and to play classical Indian music on
the harmonium.

But Soma had even less time than the other girls; Soma had a special problem that caused her to work much harder than anyone else.
She could not comprehend what she read unless she wrote down the

words while saying them aloud. This was a laborious way of getting through her schoolwork. To remedy this, her mother would buy Soma's schoolbooks ahead of time for the upcoming school year, so that she could teach her daughter everything in advance. In this painstaking way, Soma not only passed all her exams but she excelled in school. She told me that she often delighted in telling her teacher all the answers to an upcoming exam before it was ever given. Perhaps it was her own struggle and valiant triumph over her own learning difficulties that made Soma so patient, so diligent, so uniquely gifted as a teacher. Whatever the reason, Soma was a brilliant teacher.

My desire to learn from Soma was insatiable. I wanted to know everything about how Soma had taught Tito to communicate. I spent hour upon hour interviewing her about this and over time I learned how Soma built Tito a mind when everyone else said it could not be done. I learned the specifics of what had occurred not only from Soma but also from Tito, as each one told me their stories, over many hours of talking and extensive e-mail correspondence.

Soma told me that as an infant, Tito was hard to handle, irritable, he cried incessantly and had trouble sleeping. There were times when Tito could not sleep at all except when he was in his mother's lap. During these episodes, which could last for months, Soma would sleep sitting up, propped up against the wall. It was exhausting and her back ached. She lived with her husband's extended family where her new mothering skills were under close scrutiny, making Tito's irritability all the more cause for anxiety.

When Soma told me the story of how Tito, at only four months old, would stiffen in her arms when she substituted the wrong word in a song, I wondered if Tito could remember any of this; I wondered just how far back he *could* remember. I asked Tito to try to recall his earliest memories. About a week later, an extraordinary fifty-six-page document entitled simply "Memories and Beyond . . ." arrived in my e-mail box, and, remarkably, Tito did recall his mother singing to him as an infant. This remarkable document began as follows:

MY MEMORY

Memory it is which makes a link,
Mark of which is darker than ink,
And Memory it is which makes complete,
My story in my moments of retreat.

My memories of life are twelve years old.
I am twelve, being born on July 30, 1988.
Did I know that I shall grow up to become an Autistic person,
and remain thus all my life?
I try to ask my memory again and again.
And my memory remains dumb about it.
So I search the family photographs where my four day old baby face
stares at me,
not giving me any chance to guess about the forecast.
My morning did not show me the day.

The memory of mine try to search the little shadow in the greater
darkness with screams coming out of me, and the sound of a
contrasting voice of mother singing some tune to calm me down.

Memories find me slowly calming down as I concentrated on the
tune and the words which went along with them. I knew 'by
heart' all those tunes and all those words which matched the tune
that mother sang.

I wanted the same notes and words to be sung again and again,
never to get bored by the repetition of them. The shadow substi-
tuted by mother's lap, while everything else got substituted by the
words of her song, ensuring me of my presence.

I existed with my ears wide open and wide alert

With all the sounds happening around
Sounds of songs and all the words

I asked Tito to try to recall his earliest experiences of his body, the sensation of having a physical existence. This too he wrote about in his "Memories and Beyond . . ." document.

I had no concept of my body. So I never paid attention to it. And I never enjoyed experiencing it. My hands were mere objects which I used to pick and throw. My hands which I flap now as a releasing tool of energy, was a mere extension of my shadow at that time. I remember that when I saw my shadow, I put the hands out to make my shadow complete.

My body was a mere reflection in front of the mirror. When I stood in front of a mirror, I remembered that it was me. For it looked like my photograph which I saw often because I pointed at the faces of the family album when mother asked me which face belonged to whom. So when I had to point at my own face, I knew that I had to point at the face which was similar to that of my reflection.

By the time Tito was two, he was staring at the calendar on the wall and not playing with toys or interacting with people. "He had very good eye contact with the calendar," Soma explained. No one could understand Tito's fascination with the calendar, which they viewed as an abnormal, even alarming behavior. But Soma, instead of dissuading Tito from obsessing on the calendar, decided to capitalize on the one thing she saw capturing her son's attention. In a moment of insight and inspiration, Soma tested Tito to see if, given a choice between a correct and incorrect answer, he could indicate which number came next in a short. For example, what number came between one and three? To her astonishment and delight, he could. Realizing that Tito could learn to recognize a sequence, she taught him to count, testing him by asking which number came next. In this way, Tito quickly learned the numbers up to one hundred. Once she saw that Tito could memorize a sequence of symbols, Soma progressed from numbers to simple arithmetic.

If Tito could learn a sequence of numbers, why not letters? Soma asked herself, in a flash of brilliant deduction.

As it turned out, Tito had no trouble learning the sequence of symbols we call the alphabet and he quickly progressed from the alphabet to simple phonemic combinations and then words. I was astounded when I realized that the methods Soma used to teach the sounds of the alphabet and their combinations closely resembled the standard phonetic reading approach used in typical elementary schools. This supported Soma's postulation that the autistic child's intellectual capabilities were intact no matter how dysfunctional their outward behavior might appear.

Soma's painstaking, repetitive approach of teaching *how* to indicate the answer by pointing was quite the opposite. She started out using hand-over-hand motor modeling to train Tito how to indicate his answer, at first motoring him through the motions, then slowly receding until she held only his wrist, then his elbow, and eventually just placing a single finger on his shoulder. In this way, Tito learned to point and later handwrite and much later type on a computer with no physical contact from his mother at all. This was what set Tito apart from other lower-functioning autistics who communicated while another person held their hand. This was what dispelled all doubt from even the most skeptical observer when they witnessed Tito communicating.

At first Soma's lessons were no longer than ten or fifteen minutes. She would read a short passage to Tito, asking questions every couple of sentences to ensure that he was actually listening. "Teach, then test," she dubbed this part of her method. Basically it seemed that Soma was able to alert and maintain Tito's attention for short periods while she fed him a stream of information in short bursts. This was true in the beginning, and, in spite of Tito's intellectual gains, it remained true even now.

"You have to outpace the stim. You have to become the stim," Soma advised me. I interpreted her advice to mean that if the autistic child's senses were rapidly drawn into the environment toward all the wrong stimuli, it took a lot of effort to compete for their attention.

To teach Tito how to construct narrative, Soma used Aesop's Fables. She would read one of these short stories and ask Tito questions every few sentences. Later she began to ask Tito to fill in a word and eventually a sentence. Finally she asked Tito to fill in the ending of a story with his own idea of what could happen. Over time, Tito learned to compose his own stories. A strange concept was beginning to form in my mind: Had learning to spell words, construct sentences, and build stories actually taught Tito how to think?

It is commonly thought that language emerges in the service of communication and that literacy may follow, though not necessarily. In Tito's case, it seemed that the reverse was true: Acquisition of literacy was the scaffolding that provided Tito's universe with the order and shared meaning needed to begin communication. Literacy had allowed Tito to join our world in a most unusual way. Soma had created a conduit between Tito's mind and the world outside, a thin, highly circumscribed thread of a connection that essentially bypassed his body and its behaviors, built tenuously upon a few simple motor sequences such as pointing, typing, and handwriting. He could read, he could write, he could communicate. The only thing he couldn't do was act like a regular person. And no one knew better than Soma herself that when it came to matters of behavior, she was out of her element.

Soma read aloud to Tito incessantly from very early on, from books of all kinds, classical literature and nonfiction alike. I thought of Dov and how he would circle around the room making noises, seeming to be oblivious when Jon read to the children before bed. Soma told me that Tito's behaviors had been just as disconnected. What in the world had made Soma think that Tito was listening when she read aloud to him during those first years before he could communicate? "He never left the room," was Soma's answer. Tito had simply not left the room when she read to him—and he could have. Soma called this listening behavior. I, on the other hand, had applied my ordinary criteria—the child who is sitting quietly must be listening. It was true, now that I thought about it, Dov never left the room either when we were reading aloud—and he could have.

At some point, Soma began to read poetry aloud, perhaps more to preserve her own sanity than anything else, and Tito listened.

Mother had a secret hobby. Whenever she was alone, she would recite poetry aloud.
She sometimes recited poetry even while she cooked or stitched.
She read out poetry aloud, perhaps to herself, perhaps to me. I am not sure.
She said, she was not sure too when I asked her who she read the poetry to.
All those words with their timbre, and placing got so much a part of my silent appreciation that I tried to make my own little word game with them.
And I got all those words get their proper place, in my own similar constructions.
I never knew or realised that I was constructing my own rhymes with those words.
I was not even aware that what mother recited, were called poems.
Mother never realised that I listened to her, in fact waiting for her to recite them again.
For me, those poems were mere extensions of her songs.

As Tito grew from a toddler into a little boy, he continued to show no interest in other children and there were no signs of speech emerging. Soma tried everything; she lured the neighborhood children with candy to spend time around Tito, but he seemed not to notice them and, when they became noisy, he ran away to some quiet place where he could go back to his favorite activity, rocking and staring at the rotating blades of the ceiling fan. Something was very wrong. By the time he was three years old, Soma and her husband were dragging Tito from doctor to doctor in search of answers. This, too, Tito vividly recalled in "Memories and Beyond . . .":

> I got diagnosed that I had Autism when the calendar showed 1992.
> I still remember the words of the clinical psychologist, explaining to my parents,
> why I was so, and what was needed to be done.
> Was I sad? Or was I happy? I cannot say.
> Happiness to me, during those days, was the immediateness of the environment.
> I was happy, because I was eating the chocolate.
> I was happy, because, I was looking at the fan.
> And I was happy, because I saw the fan moving.
> I was sad, because the shirt was new, and the body felt uncomfortable.
> I was sad, because my father was taking me through a new route and my body felt scattered.
> So, was I sad, when I heard that I had Autism? No. I do not remember that.
> I was sure for the first time, that I had something.
> I was sure of a few more answers.
> Answers to those questions, which formed around me.
> 'Why is he not talking?'
> 'Why is he flapping his hands?'

'And why is he not playing with other children?'
All those questions had one answer.
'Because he is Autistic.' Simple as that.
I felt quite comfortable with the answer.
However when my father looked disappointed and mother sang
less, I got worried.
'Was it wrong to be Autistic?'
The concept of what is right and what is wrong came from that.
With the crisis of the situation. And sure enough there was this
crisis.
Otherwise why should father look so sad? And why should he be
advised to take me to that doctor and then to that doctor and then
to another doctor?

I was worried now although I had all the answers to questions
about myself and my actions.
I began to be haunted by my own self which had Autism.
And then I began to be ashamed of my own self.
For some days I did not visit my image in front of the mirror.
I did not bother to even play with the words because I did not hear
mother reciting the poetry for the next few weeks.

Soma had been studying to get her advanced degree in education and relatives began to conjecture that this was the cause of Tito's abnormal behavior. Others believed he was just a late talker and still others felt he lacked parental discipline. During this desperate time, Soma tried everything from faith healing to medicine, whatever anyone suggested, whatever they could find. Still nothing worked and their son grew further and further away from them.

Each new expert who tested Tito once again pronounced him mentally retarded and autistic. And after each of those devastating visits, Soma would return home determined to teach Tito everything he needed to know to pass that particular test when they returned to that doctor's office. Soma reasoned that if Tito could pass the doctor's test, he would not be autistic and he would not be retarded. Soma had one burning desire: to fix Tito.

It was a warm Los Angeles summer day the next time they came over to our house. Tito was in an unusually calm mood and willing to sit out on the porch swing and listen to music with his earphones for a while. Jon was sitting out on the grass with Dov, trying, as he always did, to get him to catch a ball. They could have been any father and son, whiling away a summer afternoon sitting together on that idyllic-looking stretch of green grass, the brilliant orange clock flowers blazing behind them on the vine which covered the brick wall surrounding our yard, and the smell of jasmine spreading everywhere. It could have been heaven.

I saw Dov put his hands out. Jon animatedly urged him on as if enough encouragement and excitement would improve his abilities, as if it would work the way it does with normal children. Jon was just a dad and like any dad, he could not stop himself from trying to make his son catch a ball. Jon cheered and cajoled and jumped up and down as much as anyone could, while sitting cross-legged on the grass.

But Dov could not catch a ball, not now and not ever before. I watched from a distance and wished with all my heart that someday Dov would be able to catch that ball and even throw it back to his father. More than anything else, I was amazed that Dov still extended his hands into the air to try to please his father, even after years of failure. Why he persisted in the face of this perpetual failure was a mystery to me. For that matter, why did a child like Dov or Tito keep trying to talk, after so many years of not being able to articulate well enough to be understood? What drove them to keep trying in spite of a lifetime of complete and utter failure?

I only realized Soma had left my side when I saw her appear out on the lawn next to Jon and Dov. I could see her reaching out toward Dov. To my surprise, Dov reached toward her and allowed her to take his hands in hers. Just as quickly, he withdrew his hands and smiled, pressing his chin into his chest, squeezing his eyes shut and crossing his arms in front of his face, as he often did when he was overwhelmed. Soma turned to Jon and they started talking; I couldn't hear what they were saying. Now Soma was holding one of Tito's alphabet boards in front of Dov. The next thing I knew, Dov was climbing right into Soma's lap, where he sat with his back pressed into her, looking out toward the alphabet board in front of him. I held my breath.

I saw Soma tap on the alphabet board as she often did to get Tito's attention. But Dov's eyes never left the sky. Soma shook the board in front of Dov's eyes but still those eyes looked away, into the unknown distance, perhaps at a fluttering leaf or perhaps at the droplets of water that might be sliding down the garden hose and into the dry earth. One could not know.

She was saying something to Dov as she picked up his arm, suspending his limp hand above the board. "C'mon!" she commanded, as she did with Tito. "Yes, very good! That's it!" She encouraged Dov over and over again, but his hand just hung from her grasp, unable to point, while his eyes looked off into the distance as they always did.

"Okay!" she went on, in an upbeat and encouraging voice. "Yah, I know we are smart!" she continued briskly, as she prodded his shoulder and then took up his hand again. "We have a ball," she said, now holding the ball and placing Dov's hands on it, pressing them into the surface, as if trying to get him to make the connection between the object and the word. "A ball, b-a-l-l," she explained, now pushing his hand through the motions of tapping out the letters on the board. "Very good!" she concluded.

A vision of Helen Keller and her teacher Annie Sullivan flashed into my mind. Keller, completely blind and deaf since very early childhood, was essentially without language or social behavior until the momentous breakthrough when she first made the connection between perception and a representation of it. This happened one day when her teacher, Annie Sullivan, ran water over Helen's palm and spelled out the word *water* over and over again. After months of trying, Helen suddenly understood that the pattern her teacher was spelling out in her palm corresponded to her tactile experience of the water.

Within days Helen had learned hundreds of words. Her brain was ready to make the connections between perceptual experience and its representation, but someone had to help her make that very first correlation.

I found it incredible that in spite of the complete absence of the two most essential sensory modalities—vision and audition—Helen Keller's brain was ready and able to establish a complex and functional repertoire of mental representations that allowed her to experience shared meaning and in turn join the human race both intellectually and emotionally. I had an intuitive feeling that something like this was true in autism too. Autistic children seemed to be able to hear and see and yet working with a child like Dov was not very different from working with Helen Keller as she was described before her big breakthrough.

I watched as Soma tried again and again with Dov, moving his limp hand across the alphabet board: "B-a-l-l! Yah! Very good!" until at last she said that was enough for today. I felt my throat swell with unintended disappointment. What was I thinking? Soma had spent years intensively training Tito every single day, to get him to communicate the way he did. Of course Dov couldn't type the word *ball*. He barely knew the alphabet, even though he was now nine years old and had been taught it since he was three.

And yet the image of Soma sitting there in a sea of emerald grass that summer day, with Dov sitting so quietly in her lap for so long as she held the alphabet board before him became emblazoned in my mind and etched deep into my imagination. Try as I might, I couldn't make it go away. Nor did I really want to.

. . .

The next time I visited Soma and Tito's apartment my knocking was answered by the sound of a key turning and a padlock being removed from a hasp. I'd told Soma this was dangerous, because I knew she hid the key from Tito in another room. I tried to explain that if there was a fire, they might not be able to get out. Newspaper accounts of horrible factory fires that killed hundreds of trapped workers in places like Sri Lanka flashed through my mind. But Soma held fast to this arrangement because Tito had started leaving the apartment in the middle of the night and wandering around Park LaBrea. And if she tried to stop him, he became violent. It was becoming clear that Soma would not be able to handle Tito by herself much longer. She needed help.

Inside, Soma invited me to sit down and have some tea and cookies. The apartment was small and we could easily talk between the rooms. The kitchen opened into an L-shaped space that contained the living room and a small dining area. The single bedroom was the only room with a door where one could escape and it belonged to Tito. This was where he went slamming the door behind him when the situation in the main rooms overwhelmed him. It was where he went to listen to music or to watch the rotating fan blades to calm his nerves.

Today I watched Tito sitting on the couch in the small living room doing nothing in particular when suddenly he bolted up and ran into the kitchen and stood inches from his mother's face, making urgent sounds. "What's he doing?" I inquired, joining them. "He heard me unwrap the cookie package," Soma chuckled. Tito was transfixed by the package of cookies she held in her hand. "Tito, go sit down. I will bring it to you," Soma commanded, and Tito returned to the couch. Soma brought out the cookies and tea and immediately gave Tito several cookies that he began to shove into his mouth.

Soma wanted to show me something. She was trying to teach

Tito to "will himself" to do things, she explained. She hoped that the same approach that had succeeded in getting him to ride a trike, eat with a spoon, and write with a pencil could lead to Tito taking control of his behavior.

Soma stood up and moved into a position off to the side, a short distance from where Tito sat cross-legged on the couch. "Tito!" His head turned in her direction. "Will yourself to go to the kitchen!" I had seen him do that just moments earlier, I thought to myself.

Never removing his eyes from her, Tito clumsily pointed at his nose. "NO!" she shouted. Tito began rocking, staring at his mother. "What do we do first?" She implored. "We get UP!" she instructed, sweeping her arms upward. Tito, eyes still glued to her, rose from the couch to a standing position. "What do we do next?" she demanded, as he stood frozen, looking at her for the next clue. "We step forward!" she shouted, pantomiming a big walking step. And slowly, through dozens of such commands and demonstrations, one excruciating step at a time, Tito did walk to the kitchen. Though I would hardly say he had "willed" himself to do so. In fact, what I had just witnessed reminded me more of the Golem of Jewish folklore than anything else; the monster made of clay that would do man's bidding but could not think for himself.

It dawned on me that I'd seen the same sort of thing in Dov before. Just as Tito could bound like a gazelle into the kitchen, Dov could pick up the tiniest string off the carpet with perfect precision and yet he could not hold a pencil in his hand, much less write with it. Dov also made lots of nonword sounds, in fact he spontaneously produced every sound needed for spoken language—yet he could not use the sounds to speak. When I asked him to immediately reproduce a sound he had just made spontaneously, it came out unintelligible, in a hoarse, whispery voice. Dov could not voluntarily reproduce the very sound he had made spontaneously, only seconds earlier. This was not a problem of motor skills, it was a problem of what organized and drove behavior.

A fundamental question had begun to form in my mind since getting to know Tito: if Tito was not retarded, if he had language and could communicate, if he had emotions and even empathy—then *what was autism?*

What remained was a constellation of out-of-control behaviors, some repetitive, some impulsive, some obsessive. And the inability to generate voluntary behavior.

The good news, I supposed, was that if you could eliminate retardation, language deficits, and lack of emotion from the equation, then theoretically at least, autism ought to be a lot easier to figure out than we'd previously imagined.

Yet what I had just witnessed made me feel anything but hopeful.

Soma told me that without the proper credentials no one in India would let her try the techniques she'd developed for Tito on another autistic child. "Why not try it with Dov?" I suggested. I believed in Soma and what she had done for Tito, and even if there was almost no chance that it would work with Dov I was grateful that she was willing to try.

Soon Dov began to see Soma for thirty minutes a week at her apartment. I knew it was not reasonable to expect any results in such a small amount of time. In my heart, I wanted to believe that Dov might have a hidden intelligence like Tito, yet I knew Soma had devoted years of intensive, highly specific training to enabling Tito's mind. The chances of her methods working on another child starting out at a much older age seemed extremely unlikely. Dov was already nine and hadn't learned to speak, write, or even dress himself. He did things that were deeply disturbing, distressing, and unacceptable, things that no one with an intact mind would do, if only because of the sheer embarrassment of behaving that way. But then so did Tito.

On the day of Dov's first session with Soma, Dov, his therapeutic aide, Maria Lopez, and I trudged up the cement stairs to Soma's apartment loaded with gear. Dov's backpack was bursting with extra clothes, sensory toys, books, puzzles, educational materials, wipes, medications, special foods. I wasn't sure what Soma would need to work with Dov. As it turned out, a pencil and paper were all she ever needed.

Soma guided Dov to the couch and sat next to him. Amid a non-stop stream of encouraging chatter, Soma first tried holding Dov's arm, then his wrist, then finally his hand and prompted him to point at the alphabet board. But each time his hand fell limp into his lap while his eyes continued to stare up at a corner of the ceiling as they always did.

Maria continued to take Dov to see Soma once a week. I asked Maria to let me know if anything interesting started to develop. I didn't see the point in observing this sort of hand-over-hand technique, unless it progressed into something more independent—which it didn't look like it would anytime soon.

7.

A Disastrous
Dinner

Dan Geschwind and Bruce Miller were good friends of ours and now they were going to be the very first scientists to meet Tito and Soma. Dan and Bruce were prominent behavioral neurologists and geneticists at University of California, Los Angeles and San Francisco, and they were perhaps the most influential people in our lives when we started CAN. Over the years, they had become trusted friends, and having children of their own, they were painfully aware of Dov's struggle with autism and how it had affected our family.

What they didn't know was that simply having a dinner party was a monumental undertaking for us. Unless Dov was asleep, doing anything besides taking care of him was next to impossible. Although Dov was nine now, he still required the constant attention of a toddler. And as with any very young child, there was never a chance to sleep in, or go out to a restaurant, or a concert with the family, or to take a vacation away from the kids. There was no downtime. Dov didn't like to watch TV and there was almost nothing he could do by himself. The only difference was that unlike a toddler, with Dov there was no end in sight. Every social event became a painful conflict about whether or not to bring Dov. Would he be overwhelmed? Or would he feel left out? We did our best to guess at the answers to these questions, because we had no way of knowing.

Tonight the table was set with gold-rimmed plates, and a dozen white candles were blazing. It couldn't have been a more perfect setting for what I hoped would be a meeting of the minds—my scientist friends' and Tito's. I'd already told Dan and Bruce a lot about Tito and I knew they were skeptical that such a human being could exist.

I saw Soma and Tito's cab pull up and watched as Tito hit the pavement running and continued right through the front door, pushing me aside as I tried to introduce him to Dan and Bruce. There was no stopping Tito as he furiously rushed off on his mad circuit through the house.

It was a long and strange dinner. Tito sat at the head of the table shoving food into his mouth with both hands, as I waited for Soma to reveal Tito's amazing and unexpected mind. But she made no effort to show how Tito could communicate or to engage him in the conversation at the table. Without any kind of interaction, I was amazed that Tito sat with us as long as he did, although I knew he was listening to our conversation. Dan and Bruce talked about their latest genetic discoveries, bragged about their sons' soccer games, while our strange guest rocked and flapped himself into an agitated frenzy at the end of the table. Soma simply sat and quietly ate her dinner.

"He's tired," Soma finally said, apologetically, finishing the last bite of food from her plate and wiping her mouth with one of the French country patterned napkins I'd so optimistically set the table with that evening, hoping to inspire an informal and cheerful atmosphere. "Tired" was hardly an apt explanation for the extraordinary scene we had been witnessing down at Tito's end of the table, where food was flying in every direction, accompanied by his odd grimacing sounds, which were punctuated by Soma's intermittent, "Tito! No!"

If Soma didn't encourage Tito to communicate with people, how would Dan and Bruce ever know that he had any intelligence at all? Was she too shy? Was she afraid of seeming presumptuous? Was she intimidated by scientists? Or was there some cultural rule unbeknownst to us that she was afraid of breaching? Whatever the reason, it made me look like I was out of my mind after having described Tito as having a hidden intelligence.

I knew that Tito did have a mind, but that mind was not a guest at our table that night. I did not know what to do about that.

I e-mailed Tito that same night and asked him why he behaved like that at the table, grabbing food and acting like a wild beast, though I did not use those words.

Dear Portia
Ask me why I did something like grabbing food,
I will think rapidly about a reason most suited to
answer so that I may be satisfied too with it.

It seemed as if Tito wanted an explanation for his behavior as much as I did. Next he offered some logical, if generic, explanations for his actions.

There can be many answers.
I am a generally greedy person.
I wanted the food badly because of my oral fixation.
I acted with my instinct and not with my mind.
I was hungry.

Now which will I choose to tell you when the picture
of my grabbing food just does not replay.

Tito did not seem to have any visual recall of his own actions.

I will choose the most honest answer and that is,
I acted with my instinct and not with my mind.

Because, if I had acted with my mind, I could have
remembered it. I could have replayed it back.

Tito concluded that if his actions had been the result of his thought process instead of pure impulse he would have been able to remember them.

It was starting to look as if Tito often had very little mental record of his own behavior. Was it because his behavior was so split off from his thought process? Was his body on automatic pilot to the extent that his mind did not attend to or record what it did? Was such a thing even possible? How could one's mind be capable of so thoroughly ignoring one's body and its activities as to not even create a memory trace of it?

The next day, I visited Soma at her apartment and tried to talk with her about what had happened at the dinner. I wanted Soma to understand that being polite wasn't useful in these situations, that a dinner like the one we'd just endured ruined our credibility with researchers. We were on a mission to shake up the prevailing understanding of autism. If she would not help them to understand that there was another person inside her son, then scientists would not be interested in studying Tito and all the trips to labs would be for nothing.

I didn't want to overstep my bounds, but if we were going to visit scientists, she had to show them that Tito had a mind because Tito himself was incapable of initiating anything. I had never seen Tito ask for his alphabet board or pad of paper, or even reach for them when they were nearby. Instead, he would sit and listen, rocking and flapping feverishly until Soma thought to hand him a blank pad of paper or his alphabet board. Only then would he have the chance to blurt out his thoughts on paper. He was totally at the mercy of Soma to realize that he might have something to say and to help him do so.

When Soma left the room to make more tea, I tried to make contact with Tito on my own. It was eerie. I knew he was in there, behind those blank, staring eyes, beyond those crazy flapping hands. I had come to know the interesting, intelligent, and witty young man who lived inside the portrait of a madman that stood before me. I had gotten to know the person inside Tito at least a little and I was very fond of him. I cared about him, about his feelings, about his future.

"Tito, it's good to see you," I started out, hoping to establish a somewhat normal interaction, as I held the alphabet board in front of him, just as I'd seen Soma do. "Tito, how are you today?" I asked, tapping on the alphabet board. Nothing. It felt as if I were asking a tree.

I waved the alphabet board in front of his eyes and shook it helplessly, repeating my question over and over as if he were deaf. "Tito, just point at y for yes if you're fine, or n for no if you aren't," I continued, trying desperately to make the most rudimentary connection with the being who stood unresponsively before me. Tito bent slightly at the waist and commenced to rock at a rapid pace, flapping his long, tapered fingers wildly at the sides of his face. His eyes bulged as a gleeful grin spread across his face, culminating in an unsettling loud noise, like the quack of a duck.

"Tito!" I tried again to get his attention, reminding myself of Soma's definition of "listening behavior." He was not leaving the room; that was a good sign, I tried to convince myself.

Soma returned and saw what was happening. "Tito, how are you?" I repeated, as I handed the alphabet board over to her in resignation. "Tito!" Soma commanded sharply, capturing his attention at once. He stopped rocking and flapping just long enough to spell out "I am fine," and then resumed his routine.

Why couldn't Tito communicate with anyone but Soma? I wondered. When I read Tito's book *Beyond the Silence* and watched the BBC documentary, it was clear that other people had worked with

Tito when he was younger and that some had played a major role in his learning to communicate. But I also knew all to well that when a severely autistic child grows older, professionals lose interest. When it becomes clear that the child will never be a success story, parents are slowly left alone to supply all the social, emotional, and therapeutic needs of their child because there is no one else who will. After the early years of intervention, Soma too found herself alone wth Tito. How had Tito become so completely dependent on Soma? Was it the later years of interacting only with his mother? Was he so entrained with Soma that no one else could connect with him? That was how it felt when I tried.

Certainly during the years that Soma and Tito lived alone in Bangalore, they led a very isolated existence. I never understood how Soma had managed to move away from her husband and extended family with Tito. In India, wives do not just leave their husbands and extended family, taking their children to a town that is four days' bus journey away. Soma told me she explained to R.G. and her relatives that she was moving to Bangalore with Tito because of the therapists there, but in reality she wanted nothing more than to be able to work with her son.

And there were other reasons she left her home for Bangalore, Soma told me. She was expected to cook and clean and wait on her husband and his family members, while with each passing month it was getting harder to manage Tito and his strange behaviors. The role of traditional housewife simply did not leave enough hours in the day to help her son.

Things had gone from bad to worse when at first her relatives blamed Tito's disorder on Soma's career aspirations; later they grieved for Tito and his mother. According to Soma, the firstborn son was the one who would care for his mother when she grew old, and because of this both their futures were lost. There was nothing in the world Soma hated more than pity. Pity simply fueled Soma's ambition.

The final blow came one day when Soma's husband, R.G., arrived home obviously depressed by a magazine article he'd read, debunking facilitated communication. R.G. was now convinced that Tito's communication was not real. Soma now felt truly alone in her belief in Tito.

When I read Tito's recollection about what had happened, I understood.

One day, father came home from the club and dropped a magazine on the table.
He looked so depressed. 'Read it.' He told mother.
She read it and then she argued about my ability to communicate with him.
I knew at once that the magazine contained some article which had something to do with me.
But what could be written about me in it?
Obviously something hopeless about Autism.

I got the message.
My father did not believe in my communication any more.
I got the message.
Autism was something which made the people close to you doubt you.
I got the message.
I need not be proud about my communication.
Because I would not be believed.
Mother began to have a 'nothing to do about any literature on autism' after that.
'I don't need to learn about autism from any doctor when I can learn about it from my son.' She said in her most determined way.
She believed in me and in her own self.
She continued teaching me with increased speed and determination.
'Find a way or make a way.'

Not long after the magazine article incident, Soma and Tito moved to Bangalore, and, from that day forward, Tito and Soma saw R.G. only three or four times a year, when he came to visit.

Wasn't she lonely? Didn't she miss her husband? Didn't Tito miss his father? Wasn't it overwhelming to take care of Tito round the clock, by herself, with no help from family, with no friend to talk to?

She didn't have time to be lonely, she explained.

In truth, I don't think Soma could ever have felt more alone than she did before she moved away to Bangalore.

Free at last, Soma could now devote every waking hour to building Tito a mind. And this she set about doing at once, working day and night, experimenting and observing, then implementing her brilliant self-made programs. Her son might act like a wild beast, but Tito would have the mind of an Oxford scholar if she had anything to do with it.

Soma knew that she could command Tito's attention for about twenty minutes at a time. During these sessions, she bombarded Tito with short bursts of information followed by questions about what had just been covered. She told me that she never read more than a few sentences at a time before testing Tito, otherwise she could not know if he was still paying attention. Between these sessions, Soma would give Tito a ten-minute break during which she let Tito go wild, stimming and squeaking and generally being as autistic as he wanted. What he did when she was not teaching him was of no concern to Soma whatsoever and in this way, alternating mind and body, cognition and behavior, she managed to teach Tito several hours of academics a day, every day, for several years.

Soma discovered that when she held his attention this way, Tito could retain the information she taught him indefinitely. In fact, Tito could recall nearly every fact Soma had ever taught him. But when she was not commanding his attention, Tito could recall nothing. Much later I realized that this was even true of Tito's moment-to-moment experience of his own life.

To the astonishment and delight of his mother, when Tito was about six, he began to write short poems. Soma was not only proud of Tito, she was determined to prove to others that her son was intelligent. She took Tito and his poems around to anyone who would see her. But instead of being impressed, they saw Soma as a delusional mother dragging her autistic son around with a satchel full of poems she claimed were his despite the fact that the handwriting was obviously hers.

Unwilling to give up, Soma took Tito from doctor to doctor in hopes of proving his intelligence to them. But the doctors wouldn't believe her either, even when they saw Tito pointing. Pointing did not matter, they informed her, if Tito could not write by himself.

Soma's quest to prove Tito's writing was his own ultimately led her to the daunting task of teaching Tito to handwrite.[8] This was done over a period of about a year. Soma began by teaching Tito to hold a pencil and then painstakingly, slowly, step by step, Tito learned to first make one short line and then another, until at last he was able to form letters and words himself. It was a long, painstaking process, but the reward was tremendous—at last people believed Tito's words were his own. Tito remembered it this way:

> I had to finally write my words and language.
> Mother had placed my communication board next to a page.
> She asked me to write the spelling of 'cat'.
> I pointed at the letter c and I copied it.
> Next I pointed at the letter a and I copied it.
> Then I pointed at the letter t and I copied it.
> That was the beginning and that was my passport
> to make people believe that my words are no one's but my own.
> I wrote my compositions and my answers by copying from my
> board.

But I wrote them.
After that what?
After that mother was believed.
And after that I was believed.
Not only by father and uncles at home, but by doctors and psy-
chologists
who love to prove that you are wrong and they are right.

Like any child, Tito had good days and bad days. When he grew too restless to be contained in their tiny apartment, they escaped into the streets of Bangalore. Soma was not particular about the setting for her classroom and everywhere they went was another opportunity to teach Tito. She taught him as they walked the crowded city streets, narrating the scenes they passed, breaking them down into their parts, their categories and specific facts. She taught him about plant life when they passed the vegetable stands in the clamor of the open market. She taught him about the social classes when they passed the beggars on the side of the road. She taught Tito about zoology as they sat beneath the mango trees in the park where monkeys clamored above, sometimes throwing fruit at them. The whole wide world was their school.

For the next several years, Soma worked with Tito in this way, almost entirely alone.

When I asked Soma what she and Tito talked about when she wasn't teaching him, she said: "We never talk anything personal." At first I thought this was just another expression of Soma's formal, almost Victorian way of relating to people. But in fact, Soma had not talked about anything personal with Tito since he was five years old.

I was shocked by this admission. And I felt sad for Tito. If Soma was the only person Tito could communicate with and she never talked about anything personal, Tito must be even more lonely and isolated than I had imagined.

Whether driven by logic or custom, nothing Soma did was arbitrary. I knew there must be a reason for her radical decision. There was a specific incident, she said, which had led to her decision never to talk about anything personal with Tito again.

One day some years back, when no one believed in Tito's intelligence and the whole world seemed against them, R.G. took Tito out for lunch and when they returned, Soma asked Tito what he had eaten. Later she learned from R.G. that Tito had given her the wrong answer—a food he had eaten in the past but not with his father that day.

This alarmed Soma deeply. People already doubted her son and thought she was crazy. If Tito couldn't answer a simple question like what he'd had for lunch correctly, there could be no hope of convincing anyone of the authenticity of his communication. There was only one way Soma could be sure Tito would answer questions correctly, and that was if she stuck to what she was sure he knew. From that moment on, Soma vowed that she would stick to facts and facts alone when she communicated with Tito. Why Tito could answer correctly when asked to name the prime minister of Japan or describe Newton's first law, and yet was often unable to report what he'd eaten for breakfast remained a mystery until much later. No wonder Tito became a poet. Poetry was not just a metaphor for Tito's feelings, poetry was the only form in which Tito's feelings were allowed to exist.

According to Tito, the greatest event in his life occurred at the age of eleven when he was discovered by the National Autistic Society of the U.K. and a book of his poems was published. Since that time Tito constantly dreamed of getting published again. It was the single most powerful way in which Tito could be acknowledged as an intelligent person by the greatest number of people. Helping Tito get his writing published again was probably the most meaningful thing I could do for him personally.

I didn't have the heart to tell Tito that I had already contacted all of the small presses that published autism-related books and I could not even get a response from them about his writing.

After their first few visits to our house, Tito developed an unbreakable compulsion to complete a circuit through the house and around the property, leaving a swath of destruction in his wake, and no one, not even Soma, could stop him. He had to complete the circuit eight times and he could not stop himself, Tito explained.

It was depressing to admit that perhaps it wasn't going to be so easy for a person like Tito to go to college after all, no matter how superior his intellect might be. I had naively thought that Tito could attend college with some simple accommodations like an aide who could help him get to class and then sit beside him to help keep his mind focused on the lecture. But these early visits to my house had demonstrated the deadly power of Tito's obsessive-compulsive behaviors and his uncontrollable impulsivity which could lead to aggression in an instant—even toward Soma, who loved him and had devoted her life to him. I was beginning to grasp Tito's tremendously daunting limitations and I felt sad.

But I would not let this stop me from having Tito over again. They needed to get out and go places. They needed to be with people. They'd had enough years of being alone.

This time I was prepared to chase Tito around the house and yard with my pad and paper in hand to try to have a conversation with him whenever and wherever I might have the chance. This time I thought I knew what to expect.

As usual, Tito burst through the front door before I could even greet them. And as usual, Soma ran after him as he dashed through the house and raced toward the fridge, the first stop on the terrible circuit he could not break free of. He flung open the refrigerator door and wildly rifled through its contents. A cake I'd made especially for Dov landed frosting-side down on the floor. "You'll never get a publisher with this kind of behavior!" I commented in a low voice, at which Tito's eyes bugged out at me in furious acknowledgment.

Tito took off out the back door and headed toward the neighbor's house. I caught up with him and was trying to slow him down when he stopped and turned toward me. Suddenly, I saw a seething, murderous look in his eyes. He grabbed the collar of my shirt tightly, choking me. He was breathing heavily and his eyes were filled with a red, uncontrollable rage that I had never seen before. At thirteen years old, Tito was already my height and he was strong. Now it seemed as if Tito were possessed by a demon.

I stood my ground stoically as he twisted the collar of my shirt until I could barely breathe. It would not last long, I told myself, vowing not to show my fear. Soma had described these episodes to me. Now Soma was trying to pull Tito off me. "No! Tito, no!" she pleaded as she tried to pry open his grip on my collar. But she was no match for Tito.

Suddenly Tito let go of me. I backed away from him and tugged at the twisted cloth around my neck. I took a deep breath and rubbed my neck, trying to act calm. But then I realized that Tito was turning on his mother in a renewed fit of rage. Baring his teeth, he twisted her hair and pulled her down toward the ground. She had a desperate look in her eyes but said nothing. I didn't know what to do. Then just as suddenly as he had let go of me, he released Soma and headed back to the house.

We found Tito in the kitchen stuffing a fistful of cake into his mouth before he rushed out the back door, presumably to continue on his circuit.

We ran after him as he made a beeline for the next-door neighbor's house, bounded up their steps and began pounding on their door. Then Tito spun on his heels and tore out across their front lawn. Never looking once, Tito raced across the street. Thankfully, there were no cars driving by at the time.

Finally he stopped and we caught up with him. He stood completely still, his eyes cast into the distance again as if returned to their former blindness. Soma breathlessly admonished him while apologizing to me. "I am so sorry," she repeated over and over, in a dark and troubled voice. "It's okay," I said, not knowing what else to say.

Tito began to cry and in a broken, barely understandable voice, between sobs, he said, "I am so ashamed." I was starting to understand some of his words when he tried to speak, since his attempts at speech sounded very much like Dov's. Although they could rarely be understood, Dov and Tito had never stopped trying to speak.

Later that night, I couldn't stop thinking about the disturbing scene of what had happened. What was Tito's mind thinking when he acted like that? It was clear from earlier interviews that Tito was aware of his terrible behaviors, at least after the fact, even if he could not replay them in his mind. And now I'd witnessed him reacting with remorse and tears after his own violent outburst.

The next day at their apartment, I asked Tito about what had happened and what was his mind doing while he acted as he had? "Nothing," he replied, "I can think the same way as you can when you coil your hair and talk on the phone." I considered this for a moment. We all have unconscious or barely conscious behaviors that we engage in, things like twirling hair, biting nails, or tapping a foot. Was Tito's entire behavioral repertoire like that? The thought frightened me.

Tito went on to explain a further subdivision of his unconscious behaviors. He called these *constant happenings* and *instant happenings*. Constant happenings were the unconscious behaviors he engaged in most of the time to manage his sensory experience. These were the repetitive behaviors we called stimming, the rocking and flapping he used to help regulate his erratic nervous system. And then there were the instant happenings; these were the sudden, impulsive behaviors which also took place at the edge of awareness. These instant happenings could be as simple as grabbing the food off someone's plate or as explosive as strangling his mother. Tito explained that he was powerless to stop these instant happenings. And somewhere entirely apart from these two calamitous states, lived the sensitive mind of a young poet.

When I left their apartment that day I felt as if I'd glimpsed into the mind of an alien being. It was far easier to think about Tito, to correspond with him by e-mail, or to read his book than to spend time with him. The truth was, it was very hard to relate to someone like Tito in person. What should I be relating to? Should I ignore his behavior entirely and relate only to the words he typed out? I didn't know what to do. I didn't know how to act. I didn't know how to be around someone like Tito.

And yet I had to try to be Tito's friend, even if I didn't know how.

8.

Chaos of the Mind

It was the end of July and we were about to embark on our annual summer vacation at Capistrano Beach, where we rented a house. We'd long since forgone our yearly pilgrimages to the Jersey Shore with Jon's parents. The thought of traveling with Dov—the plane flights, the special foods, the baby-sitters, the aide, the therapies—was exhausting and expensive, not to mention the emotional toll it exacted on our already shattered nerves. So when we discovered a vacation paradise right in our own backyard, on a stretch of sandy beach less that two hours' drive away, we never looked back. Each year since then we rented a house there and tried to have as close to a normal family vacation as we could pull off.

It was hard to believe that Soma and Tito had only been in Los Angeles for less than a month. They now felt like family members, like some long-lost eccentric cousins, and I hated to leave them behind in Los Angeles, even for just two weeks.

Finally I convinced Soma to come down on the train with Tito. It was going to be Tito's fourteenth birthday and we could celebrate it at the beach.

This would be the first time Soma and Tito traveled alone in the U.S. and Soma was nervous. She was still getting used to American currency and American food. Soma would have to figure out the train schedule, how to get to the station, how to use the electronic ticket kiosk, where to get on the train, and when to get off. And beneath it all lurked the unspoken fear: Could she handle Tito alone? What if he had an anxiety attack or flew into a rage while they were on the train?

At last, the day arrived when Jon and I picked up Soma and Tito from the old brick platform of the train station in the sleepy little town of San Juan Capistrano, famous for its old California mission and not much more. It was a relief to learn that their trip had been uneventful, even pleasant.

At the beach house, Soma was greeted by my sisters, Sarah and Lenore, who were eager to meet her after hearing about Tito and how Soma had taught him to communicate. My sisters loved their nephew Dov, even if they didn't always know how to be with him, and in the back of their minds, they also harbored the unspoken hope that if Tito could communicate, maybe someday Dov would too.

The house was an old ramshackle place in the Spanish mission style with six tiny bedrooms arranged around an open courtyard. It was built in the '20s and was owned by the Sisters of Social Service, a much-loved order of leftist nuns. It was a spartan place with a cross hung on the wall of every room and dark red cement floors that seemed to welcome the constant trail of sand tracked in by bare feet. The front of the house opened onto the sand of a golden beach that stretched for miles in either direction and down toward the rocky shoreline. In spite of the fact that the house was inhabited by nuns the rest of the year, nothing in the place seemed too sacred, from the threadbare couches to the banged-up white-painted table in the courtyard, where we loved to sit with a fire roaring in the outdoor hearth and enjoy long, late-night dinners together.

As Miriam and Gabriel pulled Jon down toward the water for yet another swim, Sarah and Lenore fussed over Soma, bringing her tea and sweets as I'd coached them to do and engaging her in long bouts of gossip and chitchat. I stood and watched from the kitchen door. I had never seen Soma look so happy as she did now, a cup of tea in her hand and two girls to chat with, one on each side. They doted on her, knowing she had performed a miracle with Tito, and for that reason she personified all the hope there was for their nephew Dov.

After a while, Dov and Maria came into the kitchen. Dov sat on one of the tall chairs at the short stretch of kitchen counter, where he often spent time while food was being prepared. As Maria cooked Dov's food, in this case plain noodles with butter and salt, one of the three or four things he would eat at the time, I brought Soma over to Dov. "Dov, look who's here," I said gently. Dov smiled a smile that lasted only an instant, then turned into a manic laugh and then a grimace as he crossed his eyes and then his wrists in front of his face, as his blank expression went racing right past the fleeting smile and became an excruciating overexcitement that wracked his whole body. It was as if there were no brakes on his nervous system.

"Do you want to try the alphabet board with him?" I asked Soma.

"Sure, why not?" she replied as my sisters gathered closer in hopeful attentiveness. "I know, we are nervous," Soma told Dov in a reassuring voice as she brought the alphabet board right up to his face, tapping his nose lightly with it to get his attention. "Let's spell 'cat,'" she said, pulling it back again. "Yah, I know we know it. We are a smart boy!" she reassured in a friendly voice. Still he did not look. "C'mon!" Soma continued, urging him on. For a split second he seemed to glance fleetingly at the letter board, at which Soma picked up his wrist and tried to get him to tap out the letters. It looked like she was juggling his hand in midair, trying to keeping it alight just long enough for it to discover itself—hoping that, like a bird pushed out of the nest, his hand might just naturally take flight as it fell. But instead, his hand dropped like a deadweight the moment she let go of it. Now he was laughing again and making high-pitched noises and squeals; still, nothing was happening. "We'll try later," Soma concluded. No one said anything more about it as we moved a slight distance away from Dov to another area of the kitchen and continued talking as before.

Maria brought Dov his food and urged him to eat it. Dov was too thin, much too thin. Autistic children were known to be extremely picky eaters. Many would not eat anything except a few specific foods. For years, it was thought that this was a psychological trait, a kind of mental rigidity. But the strange thing was that most of these children preferred similar foods. White foods, parents called them: french fries, bread, noodles. Foods that were highly predictable and didn't take much examination to determine what to expect upon putting them in your mouth. I thought about what Tito had told me about how he experienced the environment. If it was so difficult to compute ordinary experience, everything needed to be routinized and as predictable as possible for the autistic person to function.

Sarah was teasing Soma, who said she would never, never put on a bathing suit, much less get into a hot tub. As Soma and my sisters chatted, I watched Dov. It felt so strange. Even though the beach house was filled with sea air and optimism, the scene before me played out as always; there he sat, clinging to a string of beads he would not let go of, making the same strange sounds we'd never gotten used to, sliming drops of water on the countertop, eating with a primitive grasp as he funneled the food into his mouth.

In spite of being in the presence of Soma and Tito, nothing was changed with Dov. It was an odd feeling; I knew I was in the presence of the problem and at the same time in close proximity to the answers. Yet the gulf that stood between them was the size of the universe, the unfathomable distance that exists between the realms of possibility and probability.

Out in the courtyard, the early evening light was slowly fading through the fuchsia bougainvillea that wrapped the wooden posts holding up the tile roof. Tito sat cross-legged in an old, unraveling wicker chair, wearing headphones. His eyes, looking blind as they often did, stared upward, toward an early moon that had crept into the last afternoon sky. A smile crossed his face intermittently, but it seemed unconnected to anything.

When I visited their apartment, I often found Tito just sitting there on the couch with the same blank expression on his face. Didn't he get terribly bored, just sitting there, unable to read a book on his own, unable to turn on the radio or TV, unable to do anything at all? Listening to books on tape or even music was a good way for Tito to pass the time, I speculated, if he couldn't initiate any activities himself or be engaged in the social situation very easily. I wondered why Soma didn't provide him with more material to listen to.

I'd purchased many CDs for Tito since they arrived, a first collection of my very favorite poet Maya Angelou's poetry, poems by A. E. Housman, Robert Frost, and Robert Louis Stevenson. I bought audio versions of short story collections and novels and CDs of reggae music, his current favorite. I also bought Tito books, poetry, art, biographies, novels, even popular neuroscience books like Antonio Damasio's *The Feeling of What Happens*, which Soma read to him in its entirety. Besides candy, these were the only things I could think of to give Tito, who didn't care a bit about clothes, toys, games, or gadgets of any kind.

Soon my sisters were setting the dinner table and lighting candles in colored glass votives around the courtyard. Soma appeared at my side and together we watched Tito rock to and fro wearing his headphones. I asked her why she didn't have more books on tape for Tito.

"After the first few minutes, I don't know what his mind is doing," she explained.

It was beginning to dawn on me that without Soma's constant attentional prompts, one could not know what Tito's mind was doing at all. And inside those headphones, Soma had no control over Tito's attention.

Was Soma saying that he was just stimming, not even listening, as he rocked and flapped and made those clucking noises? Yes, she admitted, without her prompts to alert his attention, Tito could not keep his mind focused on the material that was being broadcast into his ears through the headset.

It was just like when he could not continue to write if Soma didn't prompt him to keep going. Or when I'd seen him staring up at the ceiling, writing one letter on top of another in an illegible jumble until his mother prompted him to resume writing from left to right on the page—as if his eyes were not connected to his own hand. Or the only way Tito could read—he needed Soma to hold open the book for him and command "Read! Read!," tapping each word and making sure his eyes glanced at the page again and again, moving from left to right.

Suddenly I was scared. Such a profound inability to attend to stimuli in the environment was a frightening thought. It made Tito seem even more helpless than he appeared; it made his intelligent mind seem even more isolated and out of sync with the world than I could have imagined.

Tito did best in the mornings. So each day he and his mother were up at dawn. Sunrise on the ocean was full of promise and Soma and Tito and I would sit on the giant trampoline out on the sand, which was Dov's favorite spot in the world, and watch the last morning star fade as the pinkish sky turned slowly into the blazing blue of another California summer day.

But on this particular day Tito was already having a hard time at breakfast. He became agitated, pushed his chair away from the table, and rushed out into the courtyard, where he suddenly stood frozen, flipping a leaf at great speed in front of his eyes, until Soma led him back to the table. Maybe Tito sensed my own nervousness, for this was the day our good friend Tony Edwards was coming over to meet him.

Our friends Tony and Jeanine owned the beach house next door to ours and I really wanted them to meet Tito. Tony Edwards was Dr. Green in the television series *E.R.* and his wife, Jeanine, had her own hugely successful cosmetics line. Being in the entertainment industry was one of the main reasons Jon and I thought we could pull it off when we started the Cure Autism Now foundation. And we shamelessly called in every favor we could for CAN from our celebrity friends.

One night, shortly after we had started CAN, we went out to dinner with Tony and Jeanine; back then, we knew them only casually. Sitting across from them in the small dark restaurant booth, we were prepared to make our appeal—would they help us? But before Jon or I could get a word out, Tony started in: "Everyone wants Dr. Green to be their spokesman," he began. "It's like I'm the new Marcus Welby. Remember when they had him advertising drugs on TV, like he was a real doctor?" He chuckled. It turned out that everyone wanted Anthony Edwards to promote their products, from vitamins to medications, and they were willing to pay big bucks to get him to do it.

Tony and Jeanine knew that Tony's stardom was valuable, but had no price, and they wanted to use it to do good. Jon and I hardly said a word as Tony and Jeanine went on to explain that they wanted to do something grassroots, something where they could make a real difference, something personal and real. They knew Dov and they wanted to help him; they wanted to help us. What could they do for CAN? they asked. Could they use Tony's celebrity to give a voice to children who literally had no voice of their own?

We were nearly in tears; it was a dream come true. Tony Edwards, the fabulous Dr. Green, was going to be a spokesperson for autism, a spokesperson for CAN. We were so thankful we were quite literally speechless. And from that night on, Tony did exactly what he promised. Dr. Green became the spokesperson for CAN and for autism, and he became the first celebrity to step forward in what was then still considered an obscure cause.

Now I was eager for Tony and Jeanine to meet Tito in person. They'd heard me talking about Tito a lot. I'd hoped that Tony would be able to come over that morning, when Tito was at his best, but he didn't have a chance to stop by until later in the afternoon. And now, despite the early hour, Tito was already falling apart. What was wrong? I decided to try to find out, and with Soma's help I asked Tito if something had been disturbing him at breakfast.

"It took me some time to understand that I was eating a bread because this was the first time I was eating a round bread."

Now I understood why Tito had gotten off to such a bad start at breakfast. It was the "round bread." Tito had never seen an English muffin before. Therefore an English muffin could not be identified in his "knowledge base" as a piece of bread, and he could not recognize it at first. This caused him great distress because he was hungry and couldn't determine if the foreign object could be eaten.

When Tony arrived that afternoon I introduced him to Soma and Tito and invited him to sit down with us at the table in the courtyard where we'd set up Tito's laptop. I was hoping that perhaps the larger open space would help Tito stay focused and not panic and run away, as he often did.

Tito blinked into the sunlight, seemingly oblivious to Tony. Soma smiled shyly at Tony and nodded hello, then suddenly turned and shouted, "Tito! Where are your manners? Say hello to the gentleman!" Tito made a sound that was meant to be "hello." Satisfied, Soma nodded and smiled again and Tito began to flap feverishly. Tito's eyes stared with great intensity at the space between his fribulating fingers as if something might materialize there at any moment.

I was wracking my brain, how could I break the ice? And what an ice it was to break.

I'd explained to Tito that Tony was a television star and that he had helped CAN and the autism cause greatly. Tony was one of the kindest and most sensitive people I had ever met, so it didn't surprise me when he simply said, "Hello, Tito," and sat there waiting quietly, wondering what was next.

In the back of my mind I knew I had unrealistic expectations. What could Tito say that would be so revealing, so insightful, to make a big impression on Tony? I wanted Tony to see how amazing Tito was and that autistic people, in spite of their outward behavior, could be intelligent and have feelings. And yet how could I show him this in these few, self-conscious moments we had together?

Tito knew what an actor was—I would try to start an interaction with that.

"Tito, maybe you have some questions for Tony about being an actor?" I ventured, absurdly. "C'mon!" Soma commanded Tito, before my last word was out, visibly startling Tony. At this, Tito abruptly ceased his flapping and began typing on the laptop. *"I think that is quite a talent,"* he typed and then resumed rocking, more violently than ever.

Tony smiled, appreciative of Tito's answer. Things weren't going as I'd hoped, but at least Tony had now seen some evidence that Tito could understand what people were saying to him and that he could communicate.

Again, there was a long, painful pause. I had no idea what to do next and Soma offered no help. "This is Tito's worst time for conversation because he writes and communicates best in the mornings," I explained to Tony. Tony nodded understandingly. Suddenly Tito stopped rocking and resumed his typing, this time without Soma's voice to start him.

We all watched as Tito struggled to type out another sentence, wondering what he was going to say. *"I am physically sick from the time, because this is not my time to write. I am helpless. Time and action is so important for me that I relate my actions with respect to time. That is why I cannot be polite, because of this relative thing."*

Tony again nodded understandingly, "That's okay," he said as he stood up to say good-bye. His kids and ours were waiting for Jon and Tony to take them to the boogie-boarding beach one more time before sunset, he explained. So we bid farewell to the illustrious Dr. Green.

Relieved that our visit with Tony was over, I asked Tito as I always did before concluding our time together, if there was anything else he wanted to say. To my surprise, he leaned forward and began to type, once again without Soma's prompting. *"I do well and concentrate in the morning."* He seemed to be apologizing for the paucity of his communication with Tony. Perhaps Tito understood how important Tony was to us and how much I had wanted Tony to witness Tito's bright mind. "Yes, I know, things become difficult as the day wears on," I reassured Tito.

I knew he wanted to quit for the day and I understood. "Okay, we're done."

I expected Tito to jump up and rush off at this point, but instead he continued to hover over the keyboard. Then something happened that had never occurred before or since: Tito invited me to ask him about something in particular that he wished to tell me about.

Slowly, deliberately, he typed out: *"I would love you to ask me why."*

I had never seen Tito initiate a conversation like this before. Excited, I answered, "Okay. Why do you do so much better in the morning?"

"Because of the association of the time and action," he answered. Now it was my turn to ask a question. "Are you very aware of actual time?" Without hesitation, Tito continued to type: *"Yes, it's the body clock."*

"The body clock? What is the body clock?" I asked, astounded at this mysterious-sounding concept.

"Like, why do you sleep at night?" he answered my question and then continued typing, *"I am thinking better in the morning. For me it is my creating time. Evening is for experiencing."*

"Does the body clock tell you when to do things, like write, eat, sleep—any of those, or other things?" I asked him.

"Yes, dear Portia, and I keep to it because I am more sure of that—rather than chaos. It keeps me a whole."

Then Tito jumped up and rushed away, leaving me to ponder what he had said. I thought about primitive man and that perhaps what Tito was talking about was our internal clock, something modern man is scarcely aware of and rarely relies upon. Yet what else could Tito rely upon to know what was going to happen next? Or what he should do next?

He had so little control over his life, which was made up of his constant and instant happenings. He could not *will himself* to stand up and walk into the kitchen to look at the clock on the wall. He couldn't even will his eyes to look at his watch on his own wrist and read it. Perhaps the body clock gave Tito a sense of order, and a sense of time, but without the external devices modern man has come to rely upon.

Tito went to bed by seven o'clock each evening. Dinner with the group was too much to expect of him at that late hour, when he had barely a shred of self-control left. After dinner, I asked Soma to tell me more about Tito and his sense of time.

He did not experience time the way most people did, she explained. He was anxious all the time because he could not anticipate what was next. When she told him anything having to do with future events, his anxiety redoubled because he could not tolerate the thought of getting from the present moment to a designated time in the future. He had absolutely no ability to wait for anything and it seemed that in this respect, in spite of his otherwise well-developed intellect, Tito was developmentally more like a toddler. If he wanted something, he had to have it right now. She told me that when Tito got the idea that they were going out for ice cream, he would immediately get up and stand by the door until they went. It was this inability to wait that often turned to obsession and led to some of Tito's most intense, even violent outbursts.

Tito could not anticipate, he could not wait, he could not pace himself, he did not know how to live in the measured flow of time, defined by predictable events and expectations, the way most people can. This caused him untold anxiety and at times pure, raw, uncontrollable fear and rage.

Consequently, Soma often avoided telling Tito what was going to happen next. This established an unfortunate cycle in which the less Tito knew what was going to happen, the more his anxiety and sense of uncertainty grew. Yet any future event of which he was informed, be it in one hour or in a year, seemed to arrive with the full urgency of the here and now. This drove Tito crazy. If Soma told him that his father was coming for a visit, Tito would become obsessed with waiting for him, and knowing moment to moment exactly how many more weeks, days, hours, and minutes remained until his arrival. This obsession would occur to the extent that it interfered with every other aspect of Tito's life. And the anxiety would grow over the weeks and days until it finally exploded in a violent outburst.

Thinking about Tito's sense of time and the body clock he described, I recalled one of the poems I'd read in *Beyond the Silence*, in which he refers to "the continuous flow of happenings." Without any way to live in a present built upon a past, or to predict a future, without a means to demarcate the beginning and end of the events that make up daily life and finally all of life itself, Tito truly did live his life in "a world full of improbabilities, racing toward uncertainty."

Men and women are puzzled by everything I do
Doctors use different terminologies to describe me
I just wonder
The thoughts are bigger than I can express
Every move that I make shows how trapped I feel
Under the continuous flow of happenings

The effect of a cause becomes the cause of another effect
And I wonder
I think about the times when I change the environment around me
With the help of my imagination
I can go places that do not exist
And they are like beautiful dreams.
But it is a world full of improbabilities
Racing toward uncertainty.

It was Tito's fourteenth birthday and the last day of their short visit to the beach. Birthdays were different in India, Soma explained to me. They were no big deal. There was no celebration, no presents or birthday cakes. But we had other plans for Tito's birthday. Tony and Jeanine and all their kids came over at the appointed hour. Jeanine had picked up a giant ice cream cake for Tito, complete with fourteen blazing candles and white icing and yellow roses made of sugar.

"Happy Birthday, dear Tito!" we sang out enthusiastically. Tito bent his head down and rocked and with much encouragement from Soma, he was able to blow out some of the candles, while the other kids finished off the job for him. Everyone clapped and the cake was cut and the ice cream was served and the presents were given.

It was late afternoon and the sun shone brightly in its summery orange way and cameras snapped, capturing the brilliant rainbow colors of the children's tie-dyed T-shirts and the red and yellow and purple of the potted flowers in the courtyard and the bursts of ribbons and balloons. And then it was over. Soma and Tito left that evening on the train. A few days later I received this letter from Tito about his fourteenth birthday:

Sometimes I wonder what could have happened if I were to be
a normal individual rather than an autistic person.
The day would have been the same one. A Saturday.

The month would be the same month of July.
And I would be turning fourteen after a few days.
There would be the same experience of a warm summer noon
as I am experiencing now.
And may be I would be playing with other boys my age
or writing some love letters to a newly found face in secret.

Many things could have happened and many things could not have
happened.

For example I would be an ordinary normal boy not even having the
term autism in my vocabulary. I would be aware of the term disabil-
ity and may be knowing about two types of disability.

I would know about the physical disability and about the mental
disability. And I would perhaps be vaguely curious about them.
I would hear someone's distant cousin has some mental disability or
someone's uncle had problem walking and so he needed a wheelchair.
The word disability would come up as an idle topic to chat. I would
try and imagine a middle-aged man struggling on his wheel chair or
imagine a distant cousin of somebody being 'baby talked' to although
he is twelve years of age.

And then I would have forgotten about them because I would be too
engaged with all the fun happening around me.

It would be none of my business to think about that because I would
be pretty far from every thing that was imperfect in this world. I
would rather stay away from it.

And one day I would meet some strange individual on a super market
who would be of my age perhaps and would act in a different way

like someone from a distant planet, by chance coming down to earth, not knowing the ways of this planet.

I would see him flap his hands, as if he had nothing to do with any thing else, other than his own hands. I would stand near him to have a second look but then realize that I should not hurt his mother who is trying with her great effort to grab his hands so that the boy stopped flapping because like me many more eyes are now on him.

I would realize that I was getting late and hurry myself away from the place.

I would have belonged to this planet.

Many other things could have happened now while I sit and write all these could haves.

And again what could not have happened is this. I would not have the rich experience of this strange life of mine. I would be staying in a distant remote corner of India and growing up with the experience of any one who grows up with a secured belief in a secured family environment. There would be dreams of becoming a doctor or an engineer so that I could join the world in the rat race of success.

What about my dream of becoming a writer? Perhaps it would be there waiting with a dormant kind of probability. Perhaps I would not even recognize that dream because it would have been buried under the load of home works and the responsibility of passing the tests.

Or what about my book Beyond the Silence? It would not even have any existence because there would not be any kind of silence.

-Tito

9.

Four Minus One

The precious glimmering days at the beach were now behind us, and the hard work we'd placed all our bets on was about to begin. It was with a combination of dread and excitement, knowing I was about to jump into a powerful river that might carry me away in its strong current and wash me up on unknown shores, that I tried to imagine what might occur in the days and weeks ahead.

I placed all my hopes in these scientists. I was doing all that I could by myself, conducting extensive interviews and relying on my observations to try to unravel the mystery that was Tito and the greater mystery of autism. But I was limited in what I could do. I could not, for instance, peer directly into Tito's brain, as I hoped they would. Nor could I even imagine those highly complicated tests they called psychophysics tests, which only experts in neuroscience and psychology could administer, analyze, and understand. And whatever they lacked, I trusted they would brilliantly invent on the fly. Wasn't four months long enough to figure out autism?

. . .

"I don't remember you being this driven, this obsessed," Jon said one night over a glass of wine shortly before Soma, Tito, and I were about to embark on our schedule of scientific testing. I thought about his observation for a moment. *Was* I always like this? "Yes, I always was," I answered finally.

"What was your obsession before?" he challenged me.

I couldn't help but smile. "You were," I said quietly. And he was. I was determined, driven, mad about him—from the moment I first saw him, I knew I was going to marry him. He was mine and I was his. And I knew that this was not the first time we had met—no, we were ancient souls, ancient partners in something bigger than this life as we knew it. What I didn't know was how unique a journey we were about to embark upon together. A destiny we innocently and aptly named Dov, the Hebrew word for "bear."

Jon looked tired these days. His wife had departed on some inexplicable journey to a distant universe called science. It was no fun to be left alone with Dov and the other kids and a baby-sitter for weeks at a time. He was working out of the house, constantly in meetings with writers. By now he barely bothered to explain to his guests when Tito ran by, tearing through the house on one of his obsessive loops, with Soma chasing close on his heels. Jon fluctuated between being patient and understanding and being furious. But he believed in whatever I was doing, if only because he hoped that my strange journey might in some way eventually help Dov.

In what had become my main gateway to brilliant scientists and their ideas, I had discovered Fred Schiffer and the concept of the "dual brain" in one of Sandra Blakeslee's *New York Times* Science Times articles. A science reporter for more than two decades, Sandy was my secret hero. She had a rare knack for translating the complicated language of science into words that everyone could understand. And it was through Fred Schiffer's work that I became inspired to delve more deeply into the subject of hemispheric laterality: the distinctly separate personalities of the brain's two hemispheres. A psychiatrist at Harvard, Schiffer had a unique and convincing way of explaining the existence of the two minds he claimed we all carry around inside our heads. And on the many occasions that I tried to refer to these two minds as states of mind or as a metaphor, Fred stood fast and unmovable in his conviction that he meant it quite literally: We actually have two brains.

I had begun to wonder if the split between Tito's mind and his outward behavior might have its origins in some abnormality of hemispheric laterality. A catalog of the separate and contrasting traits that differentiate the left hemisphere from the right could have been a list of the conflicting attributes that described Tito's mind and his behavior. It was generally held that the left brain was where language, logic, and reasoning resided. The left brain was also thought to have the capacity to store long-term memory and mentally project into the future. Conversely, the right brain was thought to be the seat of emotion, visual thinking, nonverbal intelligence, intuition, and creativity. The right hemisphere was reported to have a very limited memory capacity of only a few minutes and likewise could not project into the future more than a few minutes. You might say that the two hemispheres were like the two sides of Tito, the left was involved in thinking and higher-level mental activities while the right brain lived in the here and now.

A small handful of studies suggested that there *were* abnormalities in hemispheric laterality in autistics[9] and I couldn't help but wonder if the remarkable split between mind and body, between voluntary and spontaneous behavior, between thinking and acting, that I observed in Tito could be the result of abnormal development of connections between the left and right hemispheres that was thought to occur in autistics. It seemed more than just coincidence that the extremely distinct and opposing characteristics attributed to each of the two hemispheres could easily have been used to segregate Tito's own dual personality traits.

Most of what is known about the two hemispheres has been learned by studying patients whose hemispheres are not functioning together normally. The most informative of these have been the patients whose hemispheres were surgically separated to prevent the spread of catastrophic epilepsy. Referred to as split-brain patients, they end up with their two hemispheres functioning independently from each other, allowing scientists to study the separate function of each hemisphere. Another group known as hemi-neglect patients have lost some or all function of one hemisphere, either the left or the right. The study of hemi-neglect patients has also shed much light on the separate functions of each hemisphere.

The more I read the literature about split-brain patients, the more I saw many common symptoms and behaviors that were shared between Tito and these patients. As it turned out, Eran Zaidel, one of the best-known experts in the study of hemispheric laterality, was a professor at UCLA, only a few miles away. Before Soma and Tito returned to the States, I'd spent hours in the UCLA faculty lounge talking with Zaidel about Tito. "Why, that's remarkable," he'd said when I described Tito. "What you're telling me sounds exactly like our split-brain patients."

Our first visit with a scientist would be local. We would start out easy, with no travel involved. Soma and I chatted nervously as we drove across town to Zaidel's lab. In the backseat, Tito, his ears hidden under a large set of headphones, rocked in his customary way, staring intently a few inches in front of his face, thinking thoughts we could not guess at. I was grateful and even took it to be a good omen that on this particularly hot, smoggy summer day, Tito did not even once try to jump out of the moving van as we sped along the freeway toward UCLA.

Eran Zaidel had assigned a postdoc student to work with us. David Kaiser threw open the unmarked door to Zaidel's lab as we unwittingly passed by. He was a large person with a head so huge it looked like it might roll off his shoulders. How he detected us there, just outside his door, remains a mystery. Zooming up and down the hall that ran through Zaidel's lab was a small boy, perhaps three years old, with a wide, pale face, big blue eyes, and quite a large head also, but covered in blond curls. The little boy chattered nonstop and unintelligibly to no one in particular and he never stopped moving. This was David Kaiser's son. He had autism, his father remarked, as if this were in no way surprising.

We followed David Kaiser down another gray hall to a small, brightly lit room. This was where Tito would be tested. He instructed Tito to sit down and place his chin in a contraption just in front of the computer monitor and not to move. "Say 'Left' if you see something on the left and 'Right' if you see it on the right," he instructed Tito. I reminded him that Tito could not speak and David Kaiser quickly jotted the words on two index cards and taped them above the monitor.

I'd described Tito in great detail to Eran Zaidel and I'd corresponded with David Kaiser by e-mail, knowing that the tests would probably have to be altered to accommodate Tito's limitations. And yet I realized it must be very difficult to believe that someone possessing Tito's mental abilities could not handle anything but the briefest and least complicated kinds of tasks.

The instructions were simple. Tito was to sit perfectly still while holding his chin in the contraption, and when he saw something appear on the monitor he was to answer by tapping one of the two cards, labeled *Left* and *Right*, which were now taped above the monitor. What David did not realize was that getting Tito to look at the monitor was an accomplishment in itself. Sometimes Tito did look. And sometimes he kept his chin in the contraption. Sometimes he tapped the left card and sometimes he tapped the right card. And sometimes Tito lashed out with multiple random taps while other times he did not respond at all. Tito could not hold still. He could not keep his chin in the contraption that was meant to position his gaze, never mind the fact that he could not gaze. But most of all, Tito could not bear to stay in a tiny room for more than a few minutes at a time.

By the end of the day David got the idea: Tito could not be tested. At least not in the usual way.

After completely wearing ourselves out, we left the lab feeling discouraged and defeated. Not a bit of usable data had been collected that afternoon. But I did not tell this to Soma and Tito—they could not know how utterly useless our struggles had been that day. I did not want them to know that this first, miserable attempt to study Tito made everything that lay ahead of us seem impossible. We had seven more labs to visit in less than a month and some would involve extensive traveling.

We had to keep going. Things would get better. The scientists would listen to us. Somebody would listen. If they did not listen, if they did not adapt the tests so that Tito could actually do them, none of the things Tito was telling us about autism could ever be tested or validated.

But we weren't done with hemispheric laterality yet. The next day we were scheduled to meet David Kaiser for lunch at the California Pizza Kitchen restaurant and then drive to a private EEG clinic nearby.

And in what I would eventually realize was simply Soma's style, she never warned, never advised, never informed, but instead politely accommodated, even as we coasted full speed ahead into the next disaster. At the restaurant, there was a forty-minute wait. It was an indoor-outdoor restaurant on the second level of a downscale mall. Standing near the hostess station, David Kaiser and I watched apprehensively as Tito rode up and down the escalator with Soma. I was only beginning to realize what an intense, exhausting, full-time job it was to keep Tito within an acceptable range of behavior while he was in public.

To commemorate the experience, I took Soma and Tito's picture on the landing by the escalator, in front of a giant clay vessel filled with artificial reeds, a knockoff of ancient Egypt. How or why ancient Egypt related to this scrappy little mall was beyond my imagination. Soma stood as tall and proud as anyone under five feet ever could, smiling demurely in her flowing aubergine-colored sari with gold-embroidered edges as she wound a small arm around her large son. Tito's head was turned away from his mother, as he stared upward, transcending the inconsequential architecture, staring up through clouds, out into the cool expanse of the universe. An unexpected shaft of sunlight suddenly illuminated Tito's profile, his fish-shaped eyes, his aquiline nose, and stoic smile, and he was transformed into the majestic head of a pharaoh. I snapped my photo.

At last our name was called and we were seated. Inside, the place was very, very loud. I'd never noticed just how noisy it was before, or how the lights glinted at odd angles off the shiny black tables, the walls, and the floor. I'd never noticed the galaxy of ceiling fans with their large, slowly rotating blades, overhead. But I did now. And so did Tito.

Soma did not know what to order. She'd never heard of anything on the menu. Playing it safe, I ordered them both the kid's meal of chicken nuggets and fries. Eventually Soma would expand her repertoire to include fish and chips, and one day, after I'd gotten to know her much better, I discovered that she loved crème brûlée.

Soma tried hard to keep Tito in the wiry black chair that tipped and scraped and threatened to shoot out from under him, as she repeatedly pushed him back down onto it. Why he so desperately wanted to jump up or where he wanted to go, we had no idea. Soma apologized repeatedly as his food went flying and admonished Tito each time he made a grab for our food. I made a few attempts at small talk, but each moment was so disrupted, so fragmented that I soon concluded conversation was impossible. What the hell were we doing in the California Pizza Kitchen anyway? I wondered to myself. No answers came, only the oath "Never again," which I kept repeating silently until we escaped.

Back in the van, we shot out of the subterranean parking lot, into what was left of the day. What I hadn't learned yet, but was receiving my first lesson in, was that taking Tito out—taking him out anywhere at all—was tantamount to using Tito up.

When we arrived at the EEG clinic, David Kaiser set about the challenging task of hooking Tito up with the wire leads from which the EEG would be recorded. While Soma and I coaxed, cajoled, and pleaded at full tilt, David sanded Tito's scalp with a bit of coarse sandpaper, a sensation Tito did not appreciate, and then applied glue to Tito's head where he would stick on a small patch that attached a wire lead to Tito's scalp. After several failed tries, David managed to attach one lead to Tito's scalp. There were only a couple dozen more to go, he reassured us.

There are battles and there are negotiations, and the next hour was an intense combination of both, a complex dance bordering at times on violence and at other times on blatant bribery, a dance that thoroughly exhausted us all. Against all odds, every lead was finally attached to Tito's scalp and Tito's head was swaddled in a tight cap to hold them in place. David Kaiser motioned Tito over to a small couch, hooked him up to the EEG monitor, and turned it on. Glowing wavy green lines shot out across the dark screen like a regiment of synchronized snakes as he adjusted the controls until he got a clear signal. The waves told a story, a story only experts could decode and analyze. Now we could trace Tito's brain activity in real time. We could learn which of his two hemispheres was more active under different conditions, which regions of his brain were activated when he was stimming, and which were activated when he was typing. We could see what was happening in his brain when he did something impulsively and compare it to when he willed himself to do a voluntary action.

Our fatigue forgotten, we stood there, breathless with anticipation, our eyes riveted to the monitor. But nothing seemed to be happening. David Kaiser walked over and adjusted some controls, then tapped on the machine, as if he were trying to knock a bad TV picture back into focus. But there was a different kind of technical difficulty, one we could not solve: Tito had fallen fast asleep. And all the cajoling and antics we could muster would not rouse him. He slept like a baby on that couch for quite some time. My questions about the role of hemispheric laterality in autism and particularly in Tito would have to wait until another time.

I was exhausted after those two harrowing days, even though I knew this was only the beginning. But when Soma invited me to come inside the apartment as I was dropping them off that night, I couldn't say no. I felt I owed her the world for everything she and Tito had agreed to go through for the sake of helping others. Inside, Tito immediately went to his room, slamming the door behind him. Soma smiled and beckoned me to sit down. I was feeling more at ease with Soma now, so much so that I now regularly dared to ask her if I could put my feet up. She always nodded yes. In fact, I was becoming so at home with Soma that I knew I could even stretch out on the couch and close my eyes for a few restorative moments whenever I felt overcome by mental exhaustion.

That Soma was a musician was something I had only discovered a few weeks earlier when she shyly revealed her talents on the electronic keyboard to me. Only when I was supine and power-napping would Soma softly begin to play the keyboard and sing traditional Indian songs. Soma's voice was lovely and although I could not understand the words, the melodies expressed a universal harmonic beauty. Lulled into a state of deep relaxation, I could not have moved if the place were on fire. It was only then that Soma would begin to read Tito's poetry aloud. This was like a wonderful dream, half conscious, half floating in some other realm, as fantastic pictures rose and fell in rhythm to the words Soma read. Her voice, filled with love and adoration, bestowed an added tenderness to her son's poems as I saw their images floating beneath my eyelids in full splendor.

Here are the opening lines of a poem Tito wrote called "Gypsy Song." It is one of the hundreds of poems he had written and one of the dozens I was privileged to hear read aloud by Soma.

GYPSY SONG

A narrow road on an orange day
Sleeps in silence with a vacant peace
A gypsy song floats through wind
With idle tune, with idle ease.

A yellow field of dried grass
With dust on its breast and on its heart
Orange day floats a song—
It calls the song a 'gypsy song'.

A mellowed wind behind a hill,
A sudden rush with sudden thrill,
The gypsy road wakes in still,
Between the grass and the hill.

A lonely float on a lonely cloud
A gentle glide on its shadow dark

A patch of shadow on the orange day
Gliding in and moving away.

A gliding shadow on the road
Under a flying eagle's wings
A familiar song floats the air
The old gypsy somewhere sings…

After some time had passed in this way and Soma finished reading, I would sit up deeply refreshed as if from a hundred-year sleep. My brain cells and my determination both renewed, I was ready to get back down to business. Soma and I had important subjects to talk about before our next trip. Hemispheric laterality would have to be shelved for the time being, but I promised we would get back to it. Right now we had to push forward and begin investigating the single-modality sensory processing that Tito had repeatedly described to me.

But when I glanced over at Soma I could not believe the dreamy look that had stolen across her face. And only then did I become aware of the country western music that was playing. Whenever she saw me getting serious, Soma would try to throw me off track, take me off guard, derail me. And she was good at it. She had slipped a tape into the boom box and now she sat perched on the edge of the gold-marbled coffee table only a few feet away from me. We were listening to her favorite song, "No Charge," by Melba Montgomery.

For the nine months I carried you,
Growin' inside me: no charge;
For the nights I've sat up with you,
Doctored you, prayed for you: no charge;
For the time and the tears,
And the cost through the years, there's no charge;

When you add it all up,
The full cost of my love is no charge.

I tried to avoid Soma's intensely staring eyes, but she was sitting too close and I couldn't. Her face was flat and wide, with a tiny chin balanced by two huge eyes. Her skin shimmered with a fine sheen of oil, exotic oil, like cardamom or saffron or elephant musk. Her black and naturally curly hair was one of her best features, she told me. You could do anything to it—cut it, curl it, or just run a brush through it and it would immediately assume a wonderful style all on its own. Now Soma was staring at me even harder, with a strange faraway, misty look. What did she want from me? I didn't know what to do.

"Who is your best friend?" she asked suddenly, out of the blue.

I thought for a moment, "I have three best friends," I answered, trying to be accurate.

"Who?" she wanted to know.

"Kara, Teresa, and Sharyn," I said.

Now her eyes became slitted, like grenades of emotion, ready to explode. "I hope someday you will say I am your best friend," she said, her voice quivering with a restrained, Victorian kind of yearning.

I didn't know what to say. I didn't know what to do. You didn't just say you wanted to be someone's best friend like that. That was what children did, not grownups. Those kinds of friendships evolved over years, not weeks. I felt profoundly embarrassed and inadequate. Most of all I did not want to hurt Soma's feelings, when she'd made herself so vulnerable. I tried to smile, but it felt fake, like I was wearing a pair of wax lips. *"Don't put me on the spot like this!"* were the words my mind wanted to shout at her, but instead, I told Soma a story, hoping it would explain my basic nature and temperament.

Two Norwegians went on a fishing trip. They walked in silence for three days until they came to a lake. There they cut a hole in the ice and proceeded to fish. One of the men pulled out a bottle of aquavit

and poured two drinks. Raising his glass, he toasted: "Skoal!" where-
upon the second man said, "Are we here to talk, or are we here to fish?"

Soma beamed at me. "Yah!" she said coquettishly, smiling ear to
ear, as if I'd written "best friends forever" in her yearbook, and then
she got up and went to make us some tea.

Eric Courchesne was, without question, one of the best researchers
in the field of autism. He was an innovative thinker and a prolific researcher. He published at an incredible rate, and his studies covered
nearly every important area of research in the field of autism. Attention shifting in high-functioning autistics was the focus of his current research but I knew that Tito would not be a suitable candidate
for this type of testing because his sensory abnormalities were so profound. Eric had agreed to see Tito, though I suspected he thought I'd
gone off the deep end when I described Tito to him.

Eric Courchesne's expansive lab was situated on an idyllic
bougainvillea-covered hillside overlooking the ocean in La Jolla, a
couple hours south of Los Angeles. When we arrived we were
greeted by Natacha Akshoomoff, one of Courchesne's collaborators.
Natacha was quiet and reserved, with long brown hair that swung in
a shiny sheet whenever she moved. Despite her reputation as a very
productive and highly focused researcher, Natacha had an unexpectedly comforting air about her, like a good nurse—an excellent
quality for a neuropsychologist. We were still in the hallway, where
after exchanging friendly greetings I was trying to emphasize the fact
that Tito was a very intelligent person, when he broke away from us
and shot through an open door into Natacha's office. "Tito!" Soma
admonished as we ran after him. But Tito had that crazed, obsessed
look that I now recognized and dreaded, as if he'd spotted some object worth giving up his life for. Then I saw it. Soma and I made a
mad dash to intercept him, but it was too late. On top of Natacha's
file cabinet there was a very tall stack of research journals, and Tito

loved to sniff magazines. Apparently, the most enticing ones were at the very bottom of the stack. Natacha's eyes widened as Tito yanked journals from the bottom of the teetering stack, opening and sniffing the interior of each one and then casting them to the floor and on to the next delicacy. A great crash occurred as the tower of magazines collapsed and the journals went flying in every direction.

The look on Natacha's face succinctly illustrated her unspoken words: "*Intelligent? You've got to be kidding.*" Indeed, once again, Tito's mind was nowhere to be seen. "Don't worry, I'll get those later," Natacha said kindly, as we tried to clean up the mess. "Let's just get started."

Although Natacha was a calm, patient, and respectful person, I was still afraid that Tito again might be tested in such a way that he could not answer the questions and that Soma would say nothing. It was very difficult, even for a person as well-meaning and open-minded as Natacha, to believe that words, whether spoken or written, were easier for Tito to understand than pictures. Or that by using pictures to test Tito, she might greatly diminish Tito's ability to demonstrate his knowledge. It was generally accepted that autistics were visual thinkers with profound deficits in language processing, and in all fairness, Natacha had probably never met anyone like Tito before.

Unfortunately, most of the easier tests they started out with involved using pictures, and Tito did very poorly on these. Natacha continued with the battery of standardized tests used to characterize intelligence and social/emotional functioning that were given to all autistic subjects to establish a baseline. I watched them vigilantly on the video monitor outside the testing room as Soma prompted Tito to answer questions and corralled him back into the room each time he ran away. After two hours had passed in this way, it was time for lunch.

We ordered sandwiches to be brought in and eaten in the lounge. I knew by now not to take Tito out to a restaurant if we didn't have to.

At last it was time to see Eric Courchesne himself. Courchesne was a handsome man with rugged good looks; he was also a compassionate man, but I knew he had a harsh insistence on not whitewashing the truth. He once told me that he hated giving false hope to parents and their children with autism because his own parents had promised him he would recover completely from a bout of childhood polio, but he never did.

I always thought that when the answers about autism started to emerge, we would realize that Eric Courchesne had already discovered all the separate parts that make up the bigger picture. The problem was that nobody had ever put it all together.

As we finished our sandwiches Eric told us about his studies on attention shifting in high-functioning autistics and announced that he planned to test Tito's attention-shifting ability that afternoon. Before we arrived, I had carefully described Tito's reports of single-modality sensory processing to Eric. How could Eric test Tito's attention shifting when Tito's attention was operating primarily in only one sensory modality at a time? It seemed that it would be essential to characterize this more basic sensory processing abnormality before testing the shifting of higher-level integrated attention. I was getting upset. Was this just going to be another waste of everyone's time?

As so often happens in science, a person can become too enamored by their own brilliant idea and miss what is right in front of them. And so at great expense to Tito's limited capacity for self-control, much time and effort was again devoted to placing EEG electrodes all over Tito's scalp and securing them with glue under a cap. I was surprised that Tito sat through the procedure because there were many more electrodes than even David Kaiser had used. Instructions for the test were read to Tito, and although I knew he understood them, I was sure he would not be able to carry them out.

Tito was escorted into a tiny room and asked to sit in something that resembled a dentist's chair, surrounded by mechanical apparatus that would present the testing stimuli and record his responses. There would be two kinds of visual stimuli, a blue square or a yellow triangle; there would also be a beeping sound. Tito was to respond when he perceived various combinations of these images and the sound in time. It was a test that consisted of the very thing Tito told us he could not do.

I was getting angry. I knew he could not do it. For one thing, Tito could not reliably push a button, much less quickly, or on cue. In fact, Tito could not do anything quickly or on cue. For another, I knew it was only a matter of time before the EEG cap, the small room, or the restrictive chair would cause him to panic. And, if Tito used only audition most of the time, as he'd told us, and did not use audition and vision simultaneously, how could he perceive the images and sounds occurring at the same time in this test? It was missing the whole point. Tito had given us lots of valuable information about how he perceived the environment, and needed to be documented and investigated. Now I realized they were not going to be testing what Tito had reported at all. I was beginning to suspect, though I hoped it was not true, that scientists might just be using Tito to try to prove their own ideas, not to investigate what Tito was telling us about what it is really like to be autistic.

The miserable, frustrating session finally ended when Tito tore off the EEG cap. Shocked, the technician who'd spent over an hour putting it on Tito told me that in all their years of testing, they'd never had a patient do that before. Which made me realize that Eric Courchesne's lab had only worked with high-functioning autistics. After the technician removed the last few straggling electrodes and some of the bigger wads of glue from Tito's mussed-up hair, Soma took Tito for a desperately needed walk up and down the long hallway outside.

Tito was upset. The experiment was a failure; no data had been collected. Eric sat down with us. "I'm afraid he just didn't understand the instructions," he said, shaking his head.

As I felt the outer edges of my ears become hot as they filled with blood, it occurred to me that this must be where the term *hot head* comes from.

"Do you really think Tito didn't understand the instructions?" I asked incredulously. Had they listened to nothing I'd told them about Tito?

Just then Soma and Tito returned. I handed Soma a pad of paper and asked them to sit down. "Tito," I said, "did you understand the instructions?" Tito made a sound that I knew meant "yes." "Then tell us what they were," I said, through teeth I could not unclench. Trembling with anger, I handed the pencil to Tito. Eric and Natacha and the technician looked on, embarrassed by what must have seemed like my irrational insistence.

The moment the pencil came into his grasp, Tito began to write furiously. His handwriting was a scrawl, barely legible. Soma read each word aloud as Tito wrote it, but her accent, combined with the unnatural pacing, made it hard to grasp what Tito was writing. Finally Tito stopped and began rocking; he was finished. Soma took the pad from Tito and began reading the words Tito had written back to us. Word for word, Tito had written out the instructions that had been read to him. Eric moved in closer to examine the scrawled words. They were difficult to read, but you *could* read them.

There was a long silence, intensified by the hum of the fluorescent lights above. Eric's face looked white. It was the technician who finally broke the silence by asking Tito why he had ripped off the EEG cap.

Tito scratched out this reply: *"I was distracted with my body and started to realize that I needed preoccupation. I can't tell, I suppose I was feeling so responsible this test is so important."*

We proceeded to another lab area where Tito was scheduled for some auditory testing. Other technicians and psychologists came and went and Eric disappeared. When the testing was finished, Eric returned accompanied by a distinguished-looking gray-haired man, his mentor, the famous Dr. Steven Hillyard. Dr. Hillyard took a seat at the table and introductions were made. Meanwhile, though no one was commenting, Tito was up to something extreme in his seat. In all fairness, Hillyard had little preparation for what he was about to encounter.

Someone had given Tito giant jawbreakers and they were deep in his pants pocket where, in something of a frenzy, he was trying to root them out, making noises and digging around, squirming so violently that he shook the whole table. Dr. Hillyard peered hard at Tito over his glasses, obviously trying to think of a question to ask Tito. We all waited respectfully. Finally he held up three fingers. "Tito," he said, speaking slowly and deliberately as if Tito were deaf, "Tito, how many fingers am I holding up?" Tito began writing and Soma read out his words as before. "*Four minus one.*'" Everyone laughed at this witty answer: Tito had answered in this peculiar way because he was trying to show this man he was smarter than that question. But Tito was getting agitated. Now he dug in his pocket even more furiously, nearly overturning the table. "He's got some candy in his pocket and he's very distracted by it," I tried to explain. Once again, Tito's mind had left the room.

Dr. Hillyard scratched his head, thinking some more. "Tito," he started again, now talking very loudly. "You like your candy?" Tito started writing again, this time more furiously than ever. An insane smile flickered across his lips and he rocked like mad. Soma read the words aloud: "*Operant conditioning.*'"

We reconvened for the last time that day in a conference room with a long teak table. Eric and two psychologists sat across from Soma, Tito, and me. Eric was at a loss, trying to think of what to ask Tito now that he realized the gold mine of information that sat before him. But he was unprepared and now could only think of the old standard, wrong questions, which they always asked autistics.

"Tell me about your friends at school," Eric started out.

"*Nobody. I have classmates,*" Tito replied.

"Do you like them?"

"No."

There was a pause, and then Tito continued writing. *"What are you aiming at?"*

"Some people say that people with autism don't have friends and have difficulty relating to people. What do you think?" Eric continued.

"You should be realistic," Tito wrote. *"Why should you want something when you cannot have it? You can ask me more. I have come to a point when nothing matters."*

I knew what Tito meant. Why should he want friends if he could not have any? And I knew he was trying to act tough, to show Eric that nothing could hurt his feelings anymore. Not even cruel questions like these. I asked Tito if he felt depressed.

"No I am just looking forward. I have beyonds to touch. And dreams to reach."

"What are your 'dreams to reach'?" one of the psychologists chimed in.

"Goals to make a publisher. To succeed."

I felt a twinge of remorse in my heart, as Tito reminded me in no uncertain terms, exactly what was important to him: He needed to find a publisher. He wanted to be recognized for his mind by as many human beings as possible. Eric gave it one more shot.

"What makes you happy?" Eric asked.

"Attention, acknowledgement," Tito replied.

Eventually, unable to think of any more questions, Eric left.

The psychologists sat across from Tito, mesmerized. They rested their chins on folded hands and stared at him coquettishly while he impressed them by writing silly, flirtatious poems about them on the fly. Then it degenerated into poems by request. "Write one about the moon and the stars in the sky for me, Tito!" one giggled. This went on for a while and then they began to show Tito pictures and ask him to write poems about the pictures. Entranced, one showed Tito a postcard of Matisse's *Nasturtiums and Dance,* to which he wrote:

Dancing grace with disgrace
Why have you forgotten your party dress?

The enchanting dream in blue
Maybe a thought I have of you

They couldn't get enough. Tito was a dandy in heaven. I thought I was losing my mind.

10.

I See
or I Hear

*The best and most beautiful things in the world cannot be
seen or even touched. They must be felt with the heart.*

—Helen Keller

W hy hadn't I thought of it before? We were gearing up for our trip to the East Coast when it hit me. My father-in-law, Jerry Shestack, when he was not busy being a fierce trial lawyer, collected poetry books and befriended the poets who wrote them. Maybe Jerry could somehow help Tito get published. I sent some of Tito's poems to him at once. Jerry had heard me talk about Tito, but now I sent him the BBC documentary because I knew that seeing Tito's behavior made the beauty and depth of his poems all the more startling.

Jerry was moved and so impressed with Tito's poems that he asked if he could send them to his friend, the renowned American poet Steve Berg.

Berg knew nothing about autism, except that his good friend Jerry had a grandson named Dov who was autistic and that it broke Jerry's heart. Jerry was a friend who had always been there for Berg, through his early years as a struggling poet, through his bouts of self-doubt and his creative triumphs, and even when his old car broke down. Berg was grateful to be able to do something for Jerry, especially when it came to matters of the heart. When Berg watched the BBC documentary about Tito, he saw an extraordinary boy who behaved as if he were retarded, yet could think and write, and Berg felt even sadder for his friend Jerry.

As it happened, Steve Berg not only read the poems Jerry sent him but he too was impressed with Tito's poetry. I quickly sent more of Tito's poems to Berg and then I introduced Tito to Berg by e-mail. Soon they were corresponding. The next thing I knew Steve Berg and Jerry Shestack were talking about a poetry reading for Tito at Jon's parents' home in Philadelphia and Berg had offered to edit a collection of Tito's poems for the occasion. This was quite an honor, Jerry told me, explaining that Steve Berg was the founder and co-editor of the *American Poetry Review*.

I often wondered what made Tito want to be a writer. What inspired and motivated him? What drove him toward his goal of getting published again? It was obvious that the process of writing required extraordinary effort from Tito, both mentally and physically.

Tito answered this question too in the document "Memories and Beyond . . ." that he wrote for me. It seemed that the same motivation that drives us all was behind Tito's irrepressible desire to be a writer: the deep and abiding longing to be included.

So there is a great desire within me to get included in the world of happenings.

But how to get included?

Maybe through my writings and poems.

Maybe as you read this page.

Maybe and maybe.

Every maybe make its own dream.

And do dreams have any boundary?

And sure all those dreams lead me to one bigger dream.

A dream to make a place in this world not as a mere representative of the Autistic people, but also as a writer.

I have no objection to my label tag of Autism attached to me.
Because I have no escape from it.
However I would also love a tag of a writer which I suppose is nothing wrong to dream about.

I knew from our discussions and e-mail correspondence that several steps were involved in Tito's creative process. First, there was his experience of the thing that inspired him. This was usually an auditory "impression" but sometimes it was a visual impression.

What exactly were these "impressions," I wanted to know. I corresponded with Tito by e-mail about how he "saw" his stories.

"My dear Portia, words are put together when I am on the swing, when I am sitting in a bus and watching that old blind beggar by the road side or watching a photograph of Portia smiling at me."

But how did Tito look at something and write about it if he processed the (auditory) words and (visual) images separately, as he said he did? And what became of these auditory and visual components when Tito imagined things in his mind? What were the mental representations that resulted?

"I use sounds and I concentrate on the sounds more than my sights. And so I need to recite and re recite the words over and over again. Suppose I am writing about something as unpredictable as a market place I borrow the sounds heard and then build up my picture around them. It is difficult to explain but I imagine pictures around the sounds."

How did Tito access these representations, I wondered? In short, how did he think and how did he remember things?

"I think in terms of words.

"Talk about the Prime Minister and all the information I know about the Prime Minister, his office tenure, his duties and power come to my mind. What comes last to my mind is his face.

"I shall yet have no picture in my mind. However if the TV shows some clipping, I would remember the event as that clipping. Or if the news paper shows a still image, I shall have the image of the event that way.

"The world is full of different events. Each event is unique. There is no opportunity to practice seeing one particular event. Because, it would never be repeated in the same way."

I asked Tito about the next step in the process—how did he actually compose his stories and poems? According to Tito, he assembled entire poems, short stories, and chapters of his book in his mind, before ever writing them down. He told me that he had composed one of his earlier books, *All Through the Rainbow Path*, entirely in his mind before writing it.

"About the book 'All through the Rainbow Path'
Will you believe or not

If I tell you that
The book was composed much before
Much before than I even did start
All I needed was the right time
And all I needed was to start."

When it came to communication of any kind, including pointing, typing, handwriting, or even Tito's attempts to produce speech,
initiating the physical act of doing so was perhaps the greatest obstacle of all for Tito. I observed Tito picking up his alphabet board un-
prompted on only a few occasions and only once I heard him say,
"*I need my paper.*" I asked Tito about this, and he explained in an
e-mail.

"Starting needs initiation from my part. Observing Dov you must be
aware how difficult this is.
So starting is quite a task for me.
All I need is a page
And all I need is to start.
And the words are there in her smile
And words are there in my heart
Words are there in wait
All I need is to start."

Once Tito had his pen and paper or his laptop and began to write
or type, he still required his mother's verbal prompts to keep him going. I was never sure how or, at times, even whether Soma knew
when Tito intended to stop writing.

For all these reasons, it was hard to imagine exactly how Tito and
Steve Berg were going to work together to edit Tito's poems. It occurred to me that I did not even know whether Tito had ever edited
his own work or if he actually could. And if he did, how did he do it?

I knew Tito could read, although this too required Soma's verbal prompting to keep Tito's eyes moving along the lines of text on the page. Why didn't he read his own poems when he was editing them? Tito explained that he preferred being read to, because concentrating on the act of reading was so laborious that it made him *"miss out"* on the meaning of the text.

"Because I am concentrating on the letters and fixing my eyes on the position and wondering how to articulate them, the essence of the passage gets missed out," Tito explained.

"Do you mean you're trying to translate the letters into sounds?" I asked.

"Yes." Tito replied.

"How do you manage to read your own poetry?" I inquired.

"I don't."

His answer perplexed me. "Then how do you edit or make corrections to your poetry?"

"I ask mother to read and tell her to stop at a word she gives me the page and I change it."

Tito's reply reminded me of something else that I had observed. When Tito attempted to speak, he needed his mother to echo every word. It had even occurred to me that perhaps Tito could not hear his own voice.

"Tito, can you hear your own voice when you are talking?" I inquired.

"I am not deaf," he replied.

"Yes, I know that you can hear other people's voices and sounds in the environment," I assured him. "But what happens when you talk? What do you hear?"

"I need my mother to say the words, then I can hear them," he confirmed.

Imagine: Your mind thinks, creates ideas and thoughts. You forge a tiny pathway to the outer world to express them, but you need someone else to initiate the use of this pathway. And when the person does initiate for you, they must constantly prompt you along and keep you in your chair long enough to write out what is in your mind. Even then, having succeeded in getting it out, you can't access your own words by reading them yourself or by speaking them.

I thought of Thoreau's *Walden*. In it he writes that even if he were a prisoner in an attic, he would be a free man as long as he was able to think. But in spite of Tito's ability to think, I could not classify Tito as a free person. Yet whether free or imprisoned, Tito could dream, and if I could help make those dreams come true, by finding him a publisher, I would.

It was the second week of August when we set out to visit the lab of Dr. Guinevere Eden at Georgetown University in Washington, D.C. Our plans had changed to include an excursion to Philadelphia. It was definite: a poetry reading was going to be held for Tito at the Shestacks' magnificent apartment overlooking the expansive oval green of the parkway and the Philadelphia Art Museum. Best of all, Tito was going to meet Steve Berg in person. Finally there was something for Tito to look forward to.

Tito was happier than I'd ever seen him. In truth, I can think of few times in my own life that I have been happier than I was for Tito then.

The flight to Washington, D.C., was uneventful, and when we finally arrived at our hotel, we went straight to bed. It wasn't quite 6:00 A.M. when I knocked at Soma and Tito's door the next morning. As I expected, they'd been up for some time. Soma opened the door, brimming with energy, and invited me in, announcing that they'd already had breakfast. The sitting room of their suite, dimly lit by a couple of lamps to fend off the predawn gloom, had the kind of rarified and mysterious atmosphere that you feel when you happen upon someone sitting at the kitchen table in the middle of the night.

Tito was sitting on the couch, fully dressed and ready to go, as was Soma. Her hair was neatly coifed and she was wearing a saffron-colored sari and gold bracelets.

Soma poured a cup of tea for me, then one for herself, stirring in a half dozen spoonfuls of sugar as she always did and smiling as sweetly.

The room was growing brighter as the sun rose outside. I sat down next to Tito on the couch. "What are you thinking about this morning?" I asked him. *"The German man,"* he answered to my surprise.

I noticed the book I'd given Tito recently lying facedown on the couch next to him. On the cover there was a botanical print, a delicate engraving of a pupa, a caterpillar, and a beautiful butterfly. The title was: *Messages from an Autistic Mind: I Don't Want to Be Inside Me Anymore.* It was written by a young man with autism from Germany, Birger Sellin, who in many ways sounded a lot like Tito. Since getting to know Tito, I had been wondering how many others there might be in the world like him—if there were any at all.[10] So when I discovered Birger Sellin's book, I was excited. Originally published in German in 1993, and then in English in 1995, it was now out of print and had been difficult to locate. The author was even more difficult to track down and my endless searches on the Web yielded nothing. Birger Sellin's book was fascinating and bore many similarities to Tito's accounts of his life. The fact that two nonverbal autistics described their perceptual problems with such similar details, and that the way they learned to communicate through pointing was also so similar, suggested that perhaps the existence of an intact mind in nonverbal autistic people like Tito was not so uncommon, but rather that having a mechanism to express that intelligence was the one-in-a-million phenomenon. I had given Birger Sellin's book to Soma and she'd been reading it to Tito.

According to the experts, autistics are supposed to lack empathy, they don't understand what others are feeling or care about their feelings. I didn't believe this was true of Tito, because he had already demonstrated sensitivity to the feelings and thoughts of others on many occasions in the short time I had known him, and yet I was surprised that he was thinking, perhaps worrying, about Birger Sellin. "What are you thinking about Birger?" I asked Tito.

"Shining eyes and a perfect mind. What are they doing about him?"

"Are you worried about him?" I asked.

"I think so," Tito replied. *"The poems are like someone who is very hurt."*

"Maybe we can get in contact with him," I said, not knowing what else to say to assuage Tito's worry, even though I already knew that I could not find Birger Sellin.

Tito rolled his eyes up into his head, then sniffed his shirt vigorously and continued to write. *"There is nothing to feel hurt because if you have the will to succeed no power can stop you. Do you know my ambition?"*

"What is it?" I asked.

"Nothing less than the Booker Award. Try to keep it to yourself."

I smiled. Tito was embarrassed at the loftiness of his own aspirations. "That's not a bad ambition," I said reassuringly. "Why not aspire to the best, to do the most?"

"I want people to respect autistic," Tito explained.

"Hopefully that will get better," I said.

"I feel responsible," Tito wrote and then he abruptly shoved the pad of paper aside, jumped up, and went into a bedroom.

Some experts define autism as a deficit of "theory of mind,"[11] referring to their apparent inability to understand and relate to what is going on in another person's mind. One such expert and a pioneer of this conceptualization of autism is Simon Baron-Cohen, who coined the term *mind blindness*. And yet I knew this could not be true of Tito, for who could possibly say it was, after reading Tito's "Poem 8" from his book *The Mind Tree*?

POEM 8

In a place called Somewhere there lived happiness
Somewhere was a place of Paradise
But one day from Nowhere
Came Sorrow from the place called Nowhere
Happiness asked Sorrow to leave
The place called Somewhere
Sorrow went back to Nowhere
And then occupied the hearts of people
Who are kind and compassionate
As they never refused anybody a place to stay
So if you feel the pain
Which a person who has lost his mind bears
If your heart aches when you see a tear in someone's eyes
If you are ready to accept such a person and help him
You can be sure
You have sheltered Sorrow in your heart.

"Everything comes big in autism," Soma said of Tito's feelings. She had said this before and I was slowly beginning to understand what she meant. Tito could understand what emotion was—the concept of it, in himself and others—but when it came to experiencing it directly in himself, there were no shades of gray, no degrees of intensity; he was like a two-year-old—he experienced his own emotions in an all-or-nothing way.

For Tito, the experience of emotion seems to have lagged far behind his cognitive development, remaining raw and immediate, urgent and overwhelming and completely unmodulated. No one as far as I knew had ever described this before—that autistics could have empathy and theory of mind (the ability to know what another person is thinking or feeling) and understand their own emotions and the emotions of others cognitively, but not be able to filter, modulate, or tolerate the direct experience of emotion itself. This idea made sense when one considered Tito's other perceptual abnormalities and the lack of modulation and integration across his sensory systems. Why would the experience of emotion escape this same lack of normal filtering and integration?

The Booker Award was one of the most highly esteemed literary awards in the world. I thought it was fantastic that Tito dared to dream of winning it someday. I hoped that one day Tito would have a chance at winning a literary prize. I hoped and wished for a lot of things for Tito.

I glanced at the clock. It was almost time to go. Soma was still contentedly sipping her tea and she was drawing something on a napkin. "Hey, yah! Look at this!" she said, holding up the portrait she'd sketched of me. "I'm really good, aren't I?" She laughed. "I'm the best! Tell me, I'm the best, aren't I?"

"You're the best!" I said, as I always did. "But . . . it's a little two-dimensional. A little left brain," I added, immediately regretting it.

"Noooooo!" she protested. "I'm good! Admit it! I'm the best!"

"Okay, you're the best," I conceded.

"Can your other friends draw like I do?" she wanted to know. "Can Sharyn or Teresa or Kara draw like I do?" she demanded.

I had to think about that question for a minute and yet I knew I should not. "I'm not sure," I answered truthfully.

"Nahhhh! No one is as good as me! Admit it! I'm the best!"

"Okay, you're the best," I laughed.

Soma *was* the best. She was amazing. Soma never complained. She never alluded to her loneliness, she never said she was tired or overwhelmed, at least not while we were together in person. It was only in her phone messages and e-mails that she was able to express her anxieties, to reveal her fears and admit to a profound loneliness at times. She was constantly worried about Tito and how she would be able to manage him. The truth was, she would not be able to control him much longer by herself.

Soma brought Tito out from the bedroom and made him use the bathroom before the long cab ride ahead. She combed his hair and reminded him "to be a gentleman today." The fact that Tito was so tall and so big made Soma's tenderness toward him strike a chord in my heart all the more. Suddenly I missed Dov very, very much. What was he doing right now? Who was he with? How would he ever get better enough to have a good life? He just had to, that's all I knew. Or at least that's all my aching heart could tell me.

Dr. Guinevere Eden was a neuroscientist specializing in disorders of reading like dyslexia (impaired ability to read) and hyperlexia (the inexplicable ability to read without having been taught, often without comprehension, which is found in some very young autistic children). It is widely thought that many forms of dyslexia are related to an imbalance between auditory and visual processing capacity.[12] Dr. Eden's expertise in this area seemed like a perfect background to frame the investigation of Tito, I thought. Surely someone with such advanced knowledge of the cognitive and perceptual processing involved in literacy would be able to investigate the single-modality processing Tito was describing with great skill and innovation.

I'd already sent several e-mails and had a long phone conversation with Dr. Eden about Tito in advance of our visit, so I felt I would merely be adding a few details to what she already knew about him as I stepped into her office. Dr. Eden was tall and thin with long straight hair and a lovely voice made all the more so by her English accent. Her white blouse and the navy wool skirt she wore evoked the genteel look of British aristocracy. When she offered me a cup of tea, I accepted politely. Then, slipping into a proper doctor's white coat, she gestured for me to sit in the chair across from her desk and sat down herself, preparing to take some notes.

In spite of the elegant, civilized exterior, I knew very well there lay a fierce and highly competent scientist just below the surface. As I talked, she began to write, looking up with interest occasionally as I reiterated my growing suspicion that there might be two major subgroups in autism, the higher-functioning visual type, who were the ones usually being tested, and the lower-functioning auditory type like Tito, who because of their lack of speech, extreme behaviors, and motor-skill deficits were rarely tested.

I had forwarded Tito's detailed descriptions of not being able to see and hear simultaneously to her already and I hoped she could test some of the perceptual abnormalities he was describing. I thought it could be particularly revealing to learn more about how Tito reads, I told her.

"How exactly *does* Tito read?" Dr. Eden wanted to know.

If I knew the answer to this question, I would be back in L.A. sipping a cappuccino at this moment, I thought to myself. Tito preferred to be read to, I started out. And certainly if he were read to, we knew that Tito could absorb and comprehend the material quite well. Yet in spite of the cognitively and academically advanced material Soma read to Tito, she would only read a few sentences at a stretch to him, followed by questions. Soma referred to this as her "teach, then test" method. By asking questions at frequent intervals, she could be sure he was listening and paying attention.

"Could Tito read to himself?" she asked.

The answer was yes, in a way. He would glance at the page when prompted by his mother and afterward could answer questions about the content. That meant he could read silently to himself, but not unassisted. Not surprisingly, another obstacle was that Tito could not initiate reading on his own, just as he was unable to pick up his alphabet board or pen and paper, or go to his laptop to initiate communication. But perhaps the most insurmountable barrier to Tito's reading independently was that he could not physically handle a book by himself in such a way that it could actually be read. Not only could he not scan the words with his eyes without the guidance and prompting of his mother but he could not even turn the pages in an ordinary way and would quickly revert to stimming on the pages, flipping them back and forth in front or avidly sniffing them.

"Could Tito read aloud?" Dr. Eden inquired.

Again the answer was yes—sort of. Soma tried to teach Tito to talk by having him read aloud with her; she called this method chorus reading.[13] Later Tito graduated to reading aloud without his mother's voice accompanying him, but still Soma had to initiate for him, hold the book for him, turn each page, and prompt each word that he read aloud and his spoken words were mostly incomprehensible.

Tito reported that it was much harder for him to comprehend what was written by any method other than listening. He explained that this was because the struggle to read aloud or silently demanded so much effort that it was extremely distracting and diminished the attention he could focus on understanding the text.

"How can a mind that is literate and a body that is capable of physical movement not work together well enough to be able to read unassisted?" I wondered aloud.

Dr. Eden looked up from her notes, tapping the eraser of her pencil on her chin, not answering my question as a series of undecipherable thoughts seemed to pass behind her eyes. "Bring them in," she said suddenly in the direction of the door. Her assistant, a pleasant young student, popped her head in. "Right away," she replied, disappearing again.

Soma had been walking Tito up and down the carpeted halls, trying to keep him calm and in a cooperative state while they waited. Tito was growing more anxious with each passing moment as he always did whenever he was waiting for anything. They sat politely before Dr. Eden, who explained the testing. It would be a battery of cognitive tests related to reading ability. Soma smiled politely and cocked her head to one side repeatedly, in a motion I had learned was the Indian equivalent to our nodding yes, and not an early sign of Parkinson's.

Dr. Eden wanted to ask Tito a few questions. She started by asking him to describe how he read, to which Tito replied: *"I think doctor that I either see or I hear."* Then she asked whether he ever read by himself. *"I have a problem of beginning anything and so prompting is necessary,"* Tito wrote. She wanted to know if he could read aloud. *"I can't understand my speech,"* Tito answered.

"Do you have any questions for us?" Dr. Eden concluded. *"The machine part I want to rehearse. I have claustrophobia,"* Tito answered, referring to the neuroimaging that was planned for the next day.

Dr. Eden nodded. "Anything else?" she asked. *"I am bad with drawing I like to converse,"* he said. I knew that Tito was trying to tell her to please not test him using his vision but rather to rely on verbal instructions. He was worried that they would give him tests that required normal visual ability and that he would fail. Tito could not tolerate failure and especially if he was simply unable to demonstrate his intelligence because of the kind of testing he was given.

I was surprised and somewhat alarmed when Dr. Eden asked Tito if he would need to have his mother in the testing room with him. *"I will do better if she is there,"* Tito confirmed.

My heart went out to Tito for his trust, his patience, and honesty, and above all, his willingness to be put through all these tests for no other reason than to help others.

Dr. Eden stood up, preparing to leave, when I noticed Tito was still writing. "Wait," I said, reading his last few words aloud. *"I suppose you are English. I love England."*

Dr. Eden smiled for the first time.

Soon Soma and Tito had disappeared behind the door of a small testing room with one of the psychologists. The rest of the afternoon passed uneventfully with the exception of one strange incident. During one of their breaks, Soma came to me quite perturbed.

They'd been giving Tito a test used for dyslexics, wherein letters are presented both visually and auditorily at the same time, and the subject is asked to distinguish between similar-looking letters, for example *b* and *d*. It seems that there had been a malfunction of the equipment and the visual image of the letter had lost sync with the auditory component, so that the voice was saying a different letter than what was seen on the screen. It took a few minutes before anyone realized what was happening but in the meantime, Tito was only answering with the auditory information. He seemed completely oblivious to the fact that the auditory and visual tracks were no longer synchronized. Soma was excited because this was just the kind of demonstration that Tito was not hearing and seeing at the same time that she thought the scientists were after. But Soma said all they seemed interested in was fixing the equipment and continuing the original test. I didn't know what to say to Soma. I had a sinking feeling that they weren't really studying Tito but instead were seeing if Tito fit into their own research paradigm.

The next day, the researchers tried to do a structural MRI on Tito, but as he had predicted, Tito could not tolerate lying still in the scanner despite the practice sessions he'd had and the unrelenting cajoling and chatter Soma and I tried to distract him with. The prolonged attempts at neuroimaging proved very traumatic for Tito, who felt terrible but could not control his acute claustrophobia. That evening we returned to our hotel once again feeling defeated, frustrated, and worn out.

I thought nothing could make me feel worse about this experience until I received the testing summary a few months later. Tito's scores were terrible in almost every area, even those in which we knew he excelled, such as verbal intelligence. When I read the descriptions of some of the tests, I felt even worse—everything in them required normal sensory integration, normal motor coordination, and even the ability to speak.

"Students are provided with different-colored blocks that are used to represent sounds."

"Students are to name as rapidly as possible items presented visually on charts. Students are scored for errors and time (in seconds) to complete each chart."

"It is clear that Tito can perform certain reading-related tasks at his age and grade level. However, he struggles to perform well on tasks that require him to utilize his hands, vocalize responses, or maintain visual fixation for even short periods of time."

My heart was filled with anguish as I imagined Tito struggling blindly to complete those impossibly visual tests, which also required motor skills he did not possess, knowing all the while that he was failing and that it would not be possible to demonstrate his intelligence.

But the final blow came in the very last sentence of the report. "We want to thank you and Tito for participating in our study."

Now I understood. There had been no investigation of Tito. There had been no tests designed specifically to investigate the unique set of characteristics Tito possessed and that he had so painstakingly described. I now realized that Tito had merely been included in an ongoing study designed for high-functioning autistics or patients with dyslexia to see if he might fit in with existing theories about autism and literacy.

I felt I had betrayed Tito and Soma's confidence and violated their trust in me and in scientific research. Tito had experienced the same unbearable, enraging inability to show what he knew, to show that he was smart and could think. I had promised them that what we were doing was for the betterment of people with autism, yet the scientific investigation Tito had undergone to date was shaping up to be just more of the same old thing with absolutely nothing new coming from it.

.   .   .

I leaned back and closed my eyes to enjoy a few minutes of peace as our train lurched toward Philadelphia. But Soma would have nothing of the kind. I knew even with my eyes closed that Soma was staring at me. Her eyes sparkled with delight when she saw mine open and she quickly seized upon the opportunity to impress me by demonstrating that two plus two does not always equal four and other mathematical tricks that could be executed with a pen and paper, and which had delighted her since childhood. Next she tried to beat me at tic-tac-toe, employing a blatant trick, which I soon detected and turned against her, causing her to lose all interest in the game.

I gazed out the window at the gray towns that blended together in a blur of chain-link fences and brick. When I turned back, there was that dreamy look that had stolen across Soma's face again. Trying to avoid those dewy-lashed orbs of intensity, I studied the wire luggage rack above the seats across the aisle. Soma moved closer. There was something she had to tell me, she said, in a voice so intense that I could feel my eardrums become taut. Never taking those huge quivering eyes off me, she pursed her lips so tightly they disappeared. Breaking with emotion, her voice finally crashed the barrier of her lips: "Inorganic chemistry is the most beautiful thing on earth," she confided. If only I could get to know about it. Then she drew the periodic table on a napkin as if to illustrate the fact. Soma loved inorganic chemistry so much that I truly wished in that moment I *could* understand it.

The truth was that Soma and I had almost nothing in common and it was hard to talk. I had a degree in art; she had a degree in inorganic chemistry. Soma knew only one thing about art, which was that it had to be realistic for her to like it. And I knew only one thing about inorganic chemistry, which was that it had nothing to do with the word *organic* as I understood it.

If Tito's connection to the world was only as big as the tip of his finger tapping on an alphabet board, so was the tenuous connection between Soma and me, for even in that intersection of our lives called autism, we shared only a tiny sliver of sameness. Our personalities couldn't have been more different. Soma was outwardly very modest, she believed in the status quo, and maintained a "don't rock the boat" attitude in life. She believed in the traditional role of woman as wife, housewife, mother. She preferred very traditional music, art, and writing. Yet, Soma was also a very social person who sought drama and emotional sustenance in her friendships with other women. I was a feminist, a boat-rocker, a nonconformist, and a liberal who favored the avant-garde. I was not a modest or traditional person, and socially I was an introvert.

There are two reasons why one sustains a relationship with another person who is so very different from oneself and who can make one so very uncomfortable at times. The first is that she is a relative and you have no choice. The second is that she is bestowed with some kind of genius and worth putting up with. I felt both ways about Soma. For what she had done with Tito, for the years of devotion and the sheer determination by which she'd succeeded in bringing his mind into our world—for this I loved her in such a way that I felt I had no choice in the matter—and in this way she felt like a blood relative to me. And there could be no doubt there was genius in what Soma had done for Tito.

It was late in the day when we walked out of the Philadelphia train station. A wall of heat enveloped us as the automatic doors closed abruptly behind us, separating us from the air-conditioning we'd become accustomed to. It was almost dark by the time we got to the hotel.

Tito and Soma were staying directly across the street from my in-laws' apartment building, at a modest hotel distinguished by the giant coin atop it bearing the likeness of Ben Franklin. We were worn out, especially Tito. He needed to sleep, but he was nervous about the poetry reading the next day. After checking them in, I ordered their usual dinner of chicken nuggets and fries. Once these had been consumed and the tray removed from the room, I turned my attention to Tito to discuss the events of the next day. I was hoping this would calm his escalating anxiety. Tito was sitting on one of the beds rocking when he suddenly jumped up and stood by the door, making loud, urgent sounds and pulling at the lock. He shot an intense look at his mother, as if to say, "Let me out!" I knew he was nervous about the poetry reading the next day and I also knew he was claustrophobic. I handed Tito a pad of paper and asked him what was happening to him. He immediately sat down and began to write.

"*I am pretty anxious now but I think that time will stabilise it. The new situations take time for my body to get neutralised.*"

"How does your body feel right now?" I asked him.

"*Now that my thoughts are occupying my mind I feel more stabilised,*" Tito replied.

"In the past you've explained that when you're anxious you need to feel your body so you flap your hands. Are you saying that thinking also calms your anxiety?" I wondered aloud.

"*I am writing which is something I am pretty sure of so even if the situation is different I can do something familiar which stops the scattered sensation,*" Tito explained.

"Does that mean that when you're anxious and need to feel your body, writing can help the same way that flapping your hands does?" I asked.

"*I am not sure because the surroundings may bar my thoughts.*"

"What do you mean by 'bar my thoughts'? What in the surroundings bars your thoughts?" I asked, not understanding.

"*Noise may interrupt. For example people can,*" Tito informed me.

Not wanting to let this go, I pushed on. "If the surroundings bar your thoughts, can you still write?"

Irritated, Tito replied: "*No can you?*"

"No."

I got his point.

And I got the idea: flapping his hands was an instant physical sensation that calmed Tito's scattered senses and his anxiety. Writing was calming too, but it was not an instant fix. Writing depended on a more complex and precarious sequence of events, it depended on having thoughts that could easily be disrupted by the environment, and writing itself depended on someone handing him a tablet of paper and a pencil and prompting him. All these things were entirely out of his control. Hand flapping and rocking were the most accessible, rapid, and reliable means Tito had to regain a sense of his body when he was anxious, which in turn calmed him down. I thought about all the hours of therapy Dov had undergone in an attempt to make him stop stimming. I had always wondered why Dov was so driven by those strange repetitive, stereotyped movements.

Once when I asked Tito whether he thought all the testing he was undergoing would apply to other autistics, he said that autistics were like birds in that there could be many classifications. "*Yet all flap wings,*" Tito added, in a wry play on words, meaning that although there were many classifications of birds and of autistics too, each shared a set of common behaviors—all birds flapped their wings and flew and all autistics flapped their hands and stimmed.

Yes, stimming was a universal symptom of autism, shared in varying degree by all levels of autism, from high to low functioning. About that, Tito was certainly correct.

Suddenly Tito was very tired and needed to sleep. I said good night and walked across the moonlit street to my in-laws' apartment building. I was tired too.

As I recall it now, the day was yellow. Everything about it was yellow: the hotel room walls were yellow, a patch of sunlight fell on the pale yellow covers of the twin beds, Soma and I drank tea from yellow Melmac cups. Unexpectedly, our friend Sharon Wolmuth came by the hotel room to meet Tito, carrying an armful of giant yellow sunflowers that were a gift for him. Tito embraced the sunflowers like an unwieldy sack of flour. Then he turned them upside down, dangling their heavily seeded heads precariously above the floor in a disturbing manner. "So Tito . . . what do you like?" Sharon asked him, not knowing what else to say. Soma shoved a paper pad in front of Tito. *"Music,"* he replied, writing with a yellow school pencil.

Unsure of how it happened, the next thing I knew, Tito was taking a spin in Sharon Wolmuth's convertible with the top down, blasting music as they circled round the Benjamin Franklin Parkway with Tito's hair flying out behind him and a wild-eyed look on his face.

The Shestacks' apartment was huge, with expansive sun-washed rooms filled with modern art and Jerry Shestack's immense book collection. Marciarose was waiting for us at the front door. Jon's mother was a former anchorwoman and one of the most beautiful women I'd ever known. This was the first time Marciarose was meeting Tito and when she saw him, she smiled into his faraway eyes and took his two hands in hers, and greeted him as she would any guest of honor.

Tito arrived carrying the sunflowers Sharon Wolmuth had given him, and he wouldn't let go of them for some time, which quite delighted Sharon. "You are handsome," Sharon told Tito. *"I feel shy,"* he replied. Sharon jotted down her e-mail address for Tito and asked him to write to her. *"I think you have gotten into my heart,"* Tito responded.

Steve Berg was the first official guest to arrive. Berg not only sounded, acted, and wrote like a poet but he looked like one too. He entered the room with an expression on his face that said there was something very serious on his mind, as doubtless there always was. He wore a long dark wool coat and dark-framed glasses that gave him a Dylanesque look, equal parts writer and musician. He was intense. I introduced Tito and Soma to Steve Berg and pushed Tito closer toward Berg to get a picture of the two of them together. Then I asked Tito if he wanted to say anything to Steve Berg, who stared sternly over the top of his glasses, waiting to see what Tito had to say.

Soma gave Tito his tablet and steadied it as he wrote.

"I was glad that a picture was taken," Tito wrote, as Soma read the words aloud.

"Me, too," Berg replied.

"I think I am loving it," Tito continued.

"Good," Berg said, no longer resisting his own smile.

"I need a publisher," Tito stated.

"Be patient. I was nineteen when I first got published," Berg told Tito.

"Dear Steve Berg it will be my pleasure to work under your guidance but should I wait till I turn nineteen?"

"Not *under* my guidance, *with* my guidance!" Berg corrected him. "We have already started!"

"I meant get published," Tito continued, unwilling to depart from his point.

"Certainly, someday," Berg said, trying to be encouraging.

"When?" Tito asked.

"As soon as possible," Berg replied.

"Thanks," Tito said, concluding their exchange.

By then, the guests were filtering in and the place was filling up. I recognized many faces and knew their names. They had been at our wedding, and later, when they heard about Dov, many had made generous donations to CAN. This was a distinguished group of highly successful people: lawyers, doctors, judges, politicians, TV personalities, artists, writers, and poets—longtime friends of Jerry and Marciarose. People who would have done anything to help the Shestacks, which now included attending an autistic poetry reading.

I noticed Tito's sunflowers had found a new home atop the baby grand piano in a large crystal vase, and I prayed that he would not suddenly feel the uncontrollable urge to run over and reclaim them during the reading. The fifty or so folding chairs, which crowded the living room and spilled out into the library, were now occupied and people were standing around the periphery of the room. An air of expectancy hung over the room. It was nearly time to begin. A booklet of Tito's poems, edited and organized by Berg, was handed out. Marciarose and Jerry and Steve Berg would read the poems.

Just then I saw Jerry approach Tito with a different pamphlet in his hand. I recognized it as one of the many Jerry had written himself. Jerry wrote political and historical essays and had them bound in small volumes for the reading pleasure of friends and colleagues, and Tito would be no exception. Jerry showed Tito the pamphlet, which was entitled *Lincoln*. "Tito, do you know what this booklet is about?" Jerry ventured.

Soma dutifully handed Tito his paper and pen. "*Lincoln*," Tito wrote.

"That's right," Jerry said, smiling, obviously impressed. "Would you like to have this booklet, Tito? You could learn more about Lincoln."

Tito's anxiety was visibly growing as the start of the poetry reading rapidly approached. "*Thank you. I will like that. I am trying to concentrate,*" Tito answered Jerry. Satisfied, Jerry nodded and handed Tito the pamphlet, then turned to go to his seat, upon which Tito immediately began sniffing the pages of *Lincoln*. It seemed to me that whatever calming essence rose from those pages to meet Tito's insatiable nostrils must have traveled straight and potently to the area of his brain that made him sit in his seat, for that is what Tito miraculously did for the next hour.

I stood up to greet the sea of expectant faces. I had prepared a short introduction, with a little background on how I'd met Soma and Tito, how we hoped Tito could lead us to a better understanding of autism, and what an amazing poet Tito was. Then I introduced Soma and Tito and asked Tito to say a few words. All eyes were on Tito as Soma forced him to stand up; Soma put a pencil in his hand and steadied a clipboard in front of him. He began to write, and Soma read his words aloud to the hushed crowd: *"I think that Portia has said it all."* For a moment there was complete silence, then Steve Berg stood up and announced: "The first poem I will read is called 'Mutilated Spirit.'" I looked over and saw that Soma was beaming with pride. Sitting at her side, Tito was furiously rocking, and sniffing, and I saw a faint smile playing across his lips.

The room was spellbound as Berg began to read one of Tito's most hauntingly beautiful poems. The poem was forty-four stanzas long in its original form but Berg had edited it down to a dozen. Here is the first:

Mutilated Spirit
Dark from the claws of death
Has grown to love
Its own lost breath
A longing look at mankind
Which has dared to survive
Not knowing their own mutilated spirits
Mutilated spirit sits on the grave of sighs
Weaving its thoughts,
answering
The whats and whys.
Mutilated spirit with tender pain
Watches the earth
Watches all that remains
And Mutilated spirit with breathless pain
Blinks a blind look
Towards heavens.

Poem after poem was read that afternoon and the room stood still as if suspended in a crystalline series of frozen moments, etched in memory the way an unforgettable dream sometimes is.

After the last poem had been read, the room was silent. No one knew what to say; no one knew what to do.

Slowly, unsurely, I raised my hands and I started to clap. Applause swelled to fill the apartment. I couldn't stop smiling.

11.

Something's Burning

B   ack in L.A., there was no time to bask in the glory of Tito's po-
    etry reading, no time to see the kids or Jon, and barely time to
pack another suitcase. We were scheduled to see Dr. Vilayanus S.
Ramachandran, a professor of neuroscience at the University of California in San Diego.

Ramachandran was yet another brilliant mind that I had culled
from my usual source, an article by Sandra Blakeslee in *The New
York Times* Science Times. In fact, Blakeslee had even written a book
with Ramachandran entitled *Phantoms of the Brain* (1998). Rama, as
he was called, was known for the elegant "thought experiments"
that he used to solve some of the most mysterious neurological conditions known to modern science. He was also one of the world's
foremost researchers in the study of synesthesia, a condition in
which a person experiences bizarre overlapping of the senses, such
as seeing numbers as having distinct colors, or experiencing sounds
as having flavors.[14]

It was Rama's expertise in sensory processing that initially drew
me to his work. A link between sensory abnormalities and autism

was first suggested by researcher Carl H. Delacato in the early 1960s. Delacato, who worked with sensory-impaired individuals, was intrigued when he noticed autistic people displaying many of the same stereotypical repetitive behaviors exhibited by blind and deaf people, including hand flapping and body rocking. Delacato hypothesized that hidden sensory abnormalities must be driving these movements, even though the autistic people apparently could see and hear.

Parents of autistic children know their kids have sensory problems. You can't really miss this fact. The children spin themselves in circles and never get dizzy, they walk on tiptoes, they flap their hands and rock their bodies and sometimes they bang their heads. Many cover their ears because sounds distress them terribly, and most look away from eyes and faces, and instead may gaze at shiny or spinning objects.

When I first discovered Ramachandran's work in the late 1990s, I wondered whether he could shed light on the sensory problems in autism. I will never forget the first time I met Ramachandran. His office was crowded with bizarre objects, antique medical devices and dusty tomes that resembled spell books. All that was missing were the cobwebs. I found Rama sitting behind his desk deep in thought. When he saw me he gestured toward the only other seat in the room, a three-legged stool with tassels that draped to the floor. If only he'd been smoking a hookah pipe, somehow the scene would have been complete.

I couldn't help but notice a large stone egg covered in obscure symbols displayed on a pedestal nearby. "An ancient clock," Rama remarked when he saw me staring at it, as if everyone owned such a timepiece. Somehow after a number of hours of me spewing forth a river of facts and speculations about autism and Rama alternately appearing completely distracted, then getting excited, we managed to cover a lot of territory about autism, neuroscience, and Rama's extraordinary research. I knew I had succeeded in my mission when I suddenly realized that Rama was talking in his odd, brilliant way about autism. He was hooked. All I needed to do was bring him an autistic kid and he'd get going on autism right away.

A few weeks later, I arrived with an autistic kid and his mom in tow; we were ready to solve the mystery of autism that very day, if possible. Donald was a chubby, red-cheeked twelve-year-old who had Asperger's syndrome, sometimes considered a milder form of autism.[15] He was able to speak, had adequate motor skills, and could follow directions. Donald and his mom lived in San Diego and I'd met them through CAN.

When we arrived at Rama's lab, a tall, handsome man with reddish blond hair, wearing a tweed jacket and looking as if he just stepped out of an English hunting print, strolled across the lawn to greet us. Apparently Rama had assigned his protégé, Bill Hirstein, to deal with us and with autism. At first my heart sank with resentment and disappointment. Why was Ramachandran pawning us off on one of his students instead of applying his own genius to autism? Yet I couldn't help but like Bill Hirstein, with his soft reassuring voice and kind, patient manner. Not only did we receive more attention from Bill than we ever could from his mentor but as I grew to know him better, the depth and originality of Hirstein's thinking revealed a mind that was extraordinary and rare.

Bill had a background in computer programming, a degree in philosophy, and under the tutelage of Rama was getting his Ph.D. in neuroscience. This was a fantastic combination, since on a practical level, Bill could quickly devise or adapt psychophysics experiments on the computer, and what could be a better combination than philosopher and neuroscientist to contemplate an existence like Tito's?

One of the brain's most hardwired kinds of sensory integration is the integration of visual and tactile perception, Bill explained, as we followed him down the narrow set of cement stairs to Ramachandran's lab. They were planning to do Rama's famous "rubber hand" experiment, he said cheerfully. Donald's mom shot me a nervous look, but I was thrilled that they were going to do this experiment. I had read about it and knew it was perfect for finding out if the visual and tactile systems were working together in autism.

The lab was a large disheveled room with wood paneling and torn papers flapping off bulletin boards and a dozen old computers with tangled wires lined up on folding tables. A couple of shabby-looking couches rested near the sagging bookcases stuffed with aging textbooks. Bill walked over to one of the computers and turned it on. A graph filled the screen and a waveform appeared. Bill moved over to a dusty blackboard and gestured for us to be seated on one of the couches. "Let me explain what we are going to do today," he began. Bill glanced over at Donald, who had already co-opted one of the lab's computers for his own use. "Donald, would you like to hear how the experiment works?" Bill asked him. But Donald did not respond. He had already found a computer game and was playing it obsessively. Donald's mom smiled apologetically.

Bill began to pace back and forth in front of us. We leaned forward in our seats. "Everyone has heard of the lie detector test," Bill stated, "but few people outside the world of neuroscience know what it really is." We nodded in eager agreement. "The device actually measures moisture emitted from a highly specialized set of sweat glands called eccrine sweat glands," he continued, stepping over to the blackboard to do a quick sketch of an eccrine sweat gland. "These highly specialized sweat glands are located only on the palms of the hands and feet," he continued. "But the most important thing to know is that these glands can give us a direct readout of autonomic nervous system activity, which regulates the body's state of physiological arousal." He smiled, raising his eyebrows in an expression that said, *Pretty cool, huh?*

"The autonomic nervous system readout is called the galvanic skin response or GSR,"[16] he explained, writing the terms on the board as he spoke. "This readout is obtained by attaching electrodes to two fingers and measuring the level of electrical current that travels between them across the surface of the skin through the layer of moisture which is emitted by the eccrine sweat glands." We stared at the board. Bill adjusted his glasses and drew in a deep breath, then forged on. "This readout appears as a graph." He pointed to the computer nearby that displayed a slow-moving wave traveling across the screen. We all stared at it.

"But what *is* it?" I asked, at the risk of sounding like I didn't get it, which I didn't.

"Simply put, GSR is a psychophysiological index of changes in autonomic sympathetic arousal that are integrated with emotional and cognitive states."

"Right," I said. The truth was I'd been studying molecular biology for the past five years and I was just beginning to learn this brain-behavior stuff.

Bill explained that most people generated three to five of these GSR peaks per minute on average but that there was a very wide range of GSR activity that was considered normal and only the most radical differences could be considered meaningful. Just then a high-pitched sound broke our concentration. Donald was hopping up and down in front of his computer, waving his arms and shrieking. I had a hunch the difference might be detectable.

"Okay," Bill said, moving over to a nearby table. "It's time to do the rubber hand experiment."[17] Donald's mom looked alarmed again. Wasn't Bill going to explain *that*? Next he produced a disturbing-looking rubber arm from a dusty cabinet. It hardly looked scientific. "Found this at a Halloween shop!" Bill chuckled as he threw the thing across the table. It landed with an unpleasant thud and I saw Donald's mom wince. "Why don't you try the rubber hand experiment on me first?" I suggested.

I sat down at the table and, following Bill's instructions, I kept my left hand hidden in my lap and placed my right hand on top of the table. Then Bill put up a small screen, which blocked my view of my right hand. He positioned the rubber hand in front of me, orienting it similarly to my right hand, which was now behind the screen. Then Bill began lightly stroking the rubber hand while simultaneously stroking my right hand, behind the screen. In less than a minute I "felt" the rubber hand as if it were my own. I knew perfectly well the rubber hand was not mine and yet my brain's integration of touch and vision was so robust that it felt exactly as if the rubber hand was my own hand. It made me feel momentarily seasick.

At last we tried the rubber hand experiment with Donald. As it turned out, he experienced the illusion exactly as I did—his brain was fooled into "feeling" sensation in the rubber hand just like it was supposed to. Donald's brain *could* integrate vision and touch normally. The rubber hand experiment seemed like such a great idea to prove that vision and touch were not integrated in autism. Too bad it didn't work.

But there was more. Rama had added an additional test to the rubber hand experiment, Bill told us, as he fastened a couple of electrodes for testing GSR to Donald's fingers. Finally, the GSR!

Bill repeated the rubber hand experiment the same way again. And then, startling the bejesus out of us, he suddenly pulled back the fingers on the rubber hand so violently that if they were your own, you would scream out in pain. Most people did scream or jump up and their GSR spiked like crazy when they experienced this. But not Donald. In fact, Donald had no response at all. His sense of touch and vision *were* integrated, but there was a disconnect between his perceptual experience of his fingers being bent backward and his arousal.

This perplexing observation led Bill Hirstein, Rama, and me to collaborate on a study of GSR activity in children with autism.[18] As it turned out, each of the forty subjects had an abnormal GSR activity. The degree of abnormality in their GSR activity seemed to correlate positively with the severity of their autism. The more impaired, non-verbal children had a GSR readout that looked like a fast-paced roller coaster with higher highs, lower lows, and more cycles per minute.

The activity seemed disconnected from anything going on in the environment. Higher-functioning children, on the other hand, seemed to be able to drive their GSR activity to astonishing heights and maintain this level when they engaged in visual stimming. Since our original study, a number of other reports have been published that also describe abnormal autonomic arousal in autistic subjects.[19]

I wondered at what point in early development these arousal abnormalities began in these children. Until recently there was no data on autonomic arousal even in normal infants, but in the past few years a number of studies have characterized GSR in early infancy,[20] suggesting that it may be possible to monitor arousal activity in infants and perhaps even detect early departures from the norm. Could early detection and treatment of abnormal arousal prevent an infant from going off the developmental track, maybe even avoiding autism altogether? And how does abnormal autonomic arousal contribute to autism? Is it a cause or an effect? These are the questions that ran through my mind and still do.

It had been three years since the initial GSR experiment with Donald, and now Tito, Soma, and I were driving to San Diego to see Ramachandran and Bill Hirstein. Traffic was moving at a crawl and Soma was sitting in the back to prevent Tito from leaping out onto the freeway. As we approached San Diego, the sky turned blue and the industrial wasteland gave way to rolling green hills with an occasional glimpse of the sparkling ocean. We settled in a pleasant little hotel on a hillside, surrounded by palm trees and brilliant hibiscus flowers, just as the sky began to turn pink. Tito fell asleep immediately, which meant that Soma and I had time for a quiet cup of tea. I sat down in one of the armchairs and took off my shoes and put my feet up. Soma disappeared into the kitchenette to make some tea and returned beaming, carrying a tray with two cups and a steaming pot of black tea saturated with cream and sugar.

I knew Soma wanted to talk. About husbands and children, mothers-in-law and cooking, about astrology and her school days and playing pranks and winning contests. I drew in a deep breath. "So," I began, not knowing what in the world I would say next. "Yah . . ." Soma replied in her most mellifluous voice, nodding, as if we were in the midst of a conversation. I tried to think of something to say, but I could not. I wished I could give Soma some kind of gift to express how much I admired her. But I knew Soma was too practical for gifts; in fact, the little tokens of friendship which most people adore were meaningless clutter to Soma and only annoyed her.

I knew there was no gift I could give Soma except the gift of time, the gift of being a casual, intimate friend—that person whom she so dearly wanted and needed—the very kind of person I was not and never could be. But my biggest failure was that I was inept at Soma's favorite pastime—gossip.

I was grateful beyond words when Soma came over to where I was sitting and began rubbing my shoulders. I hadn't realized how tense I was. My shoulders felt as if they were made of stone. Soma's hands were small and delicate, she wore a tiny gold ring set with a single garnet given to her by her husband, R.G., and though her hands were not strong, they possessed that powerful quality of human touch that exists independent of physical strength. I slumped forward and let myself relax for the first time in what seemed like weeks. By the time Soma began to read one of Tito's poems aloud, my eyes were closed and I found myself drifting off.

THE BLUE SUMMER

It was the bluest summer.
The stray clouds at times
In the sky did wander.
Otherwise

The blue of sky
Was around the house
Around the length of garden
Around the Eucalyptus trees
With feathery leaves
Touching the higher domains.

I awoke with a start and saw that Soma had fallen asleep in her chair with Tito's poetry journal open across her chest. Quietly, I draped a blanket over her and tiptoed to the door. She looked like a child sleeping, so small and vulnerable, so alone in a foreign land, her face lost in a dream.

The next morning, Bill Hirstein met us at the hotel and escorted us to Rama's lab. It had been three years since I last saw Bill, but he had the familiarity of an old friend, as if no time had passed at all.

Rama's lab was below ground level just as Zaidel's had been. What was it about these eccentric neuroscientists that they ended up in basements? Except for the reassuring presence of the young grad students who drifted in and out, something about these labs reminded me of a castle dungeon where mad scientists performed their experiments.

Bill carefully carried out the same rubber hand experiment again, simultaneously stimulating the rubber hand and Tito's real hand, which was hidden from view.

"Tito, can you feel that?" Bill asked him as he continued to stroke the real and the fake hand at the same time.

Tito did not reply, and after a moment Bill repeated the question. "Can you feel that?"

"*I think it is not my hand,*" Tito replied.

"Can you feel anything?" Bill continued.

"*I think no,*" Tito answered simply.

A little later that day, Bill tried the rubber hand experiment again and he asked Tito if he felt anything.

"*I cannot feel that way because it is rubber,*" Tito explained. I suspected Tito thought Bill was nuts.

Bill abandoned the second part of the experiment because there was no point in suddenly yanking back the rubber fingers, if the tactile-visual illusion had failed to occur in the first place. ·

Here we were, three years after having given up on the idea that autistics might not be able to integrate their senses of touch and vision normally. And now Tito had showed us that he couldn't.

This time, the result was exactly what I'd predicted the first time around: Tito did not experience the illusion that the rubber hand had feeling.

Bill went on to test Tito's galvanic skin response (GSR) and determined, as we already suspected from Tito's own reports, that reading, writing, and doing math—in fact any cognitive activity—had a remarkable and obvious regulating effect on Tito's arousal level, his GSR.

The next day, Rama wandered in and out of the lab area in what seemed like a random fashion, sometimes asking Tito questions, sometimes showing him pictures in a book, sometimes speaking in metaphor or telling a joke to see how Tito would interpret it.

"Tito, I want to tell you a joke," Rama started out. "This chap goes to the museum and he sees this big dinosaur skeleton—a fossil. He asks the curator, 'How old are these dinosaur bones?' The curator replies, 'They're sixty million and three years old.' 'How do you know?' the chap asks. 'Well, I started working here three years ago,' says the curator."

Rama paused, checking Tito's face for any reaction to the joke, but Tito just stared ahead, seeming oblivious. "Was that funny?" Rama finally inquired.

"*Yes,*" Tito replied.

"Why?" Rama continued.

"*He added three years,*" Tito explained.

"Right," Rama agreed.

Rama's jaw jutted out and his eyebrows rose, as if to say, *Hmmm, very interesting.* Then he abruptly turned and left the room again.

I felt like time was running out and we were getting nowhere. I wanted them to test Tito's assertion that he could not see and hear at the same time. Why couldn't anybody do this? How hard could it be? Suddenly I had run out of whatever patience I had in reserve. And I made a decision—I was going to test Tito's perception myself.

Was there a pack of index cards around the place I could use? With a black Sharpie, I wrote a plus or a minus sign on each of twenty index cards and shuffled them. Then I asked Bill Hirstein to stand behind Tito and to say the opposite of what he saw on the card that I would show Tito. Tito's instructions were to write down what he saw on the card. The first card was a plus sign, and so Bill said "minus" when I showed it. Nineteen out of twenty times, Tito went with the word he heard Bill say behind him and not with the visual information that was on the card. Just to be sure, when we were finished, I held up one of the cards, which he had inaccurately identified, and said: "Tito, look at this card again—what do you see on this card?" Tito answered again with the word Bill had said, and not the picture that was right in front of his eyes. It was eerie, as if Tito were actually blind to the visual information once he'd registered the auditory information, even when the visual information lingered and was pointed out to him again without the sound. Bill, the two undergraduates, and I witnessed this test as Tito performed it again and again. At the end of each trial we gave Tito multiple chances to view the image in front of him; but try as we might to bring his visual attention to what was on the card, the auditory impression seemed to have permanently overridden the visual information. Later this test would come to be called the cross-modal Stroop test.

I felt a sense of relief that the experiment I'd been waiting and hoping for had finally been done. Yet it was extremely discouraging that I had to do it myself, because I knew that coming from me it meant absolutely nothing. What was the point of proving something to Bill and a handful of graduate students if the discovery didn't get out to the rest of the world?

The black silhouettes of palm trees stood out against the deepening pink of the sky as we said our good-byes in the hotel parking lot. I was grateful for the work Bill had done with Tito and even more so for the way he had given himself over so completely to trying to understand the puzzle that was Tito. Now, for the first time, I felt there was a scientist who was as intent upon understanding Tito as I was; someone who could see the incredible value of what Tito had to tell us about autism.

I shook Bill Hirstein's hand and then hugged him quickly, my cheek pressed against the woolly tweed jacket he wore even in summer. I felt lonely. I wondered how Jon was doing—it felt like I hadn't seen him for a long time. Suddenly I felt sad, as though I had lost something—but what? I climbed into the van where Soma and Tito were already belted up and waiting. We headed back to L.A. in the dark, stopping only once, for gas and Twinkies.

I missed Jon so much I could hardly wait to see him when I got home. I was still so in love with him. He was still the most handsome man in the world to me. I could see his face, those dark eyes, those kissable lips, and then there were those strong arms. . . . I couldn't wait to see him. I was determined to get a fresh start. I wouldn't let us argue and fight when I got home, no matter what. If he started, I simply would not respond. I would be happy and positive and in love enough for both of us, and then surely Jon would feel better too, and remember how we used to be and we would be happy together, no matter what. I wanted to be in love with him, to have back what we used to be like together, to have romance and sex and love.

Back in L.A., I dropped off Soma and Tito at Park LaBrea and thoughts devolved into a lovely daydream about Jon as I stared at the night sky before heading home. It was then that I saw it—a single, brilliant shooting star. And in that instant I felt it again: the feeling I'd had when I arrived so many years ago—that this was a city of dreams waiting to come true, a place where anything could happen and nothing was impossible. How our dreams had changed. And yet, *I needed that feeling more than ever now.*

It must have been midnight when I walked into the house and immediately smelled something burning. "Jon?" I yelled up the front stairs. "What!" shouted an angry voice from above. "Something's burning!" I said, throwing down my bags and hurrying toward the kitchen. The electric kettle was on fire. The room was filled with smoke and small blue flames danced from the sizzling mess of melted plastic and scorched wire that once boiled water for our tea. "Damn it!" I cursed, yanking the plug from the wall. The evil thing hissed at me as I doused it with water until it fell silent. "These things are supposed to shut themselves off!" I ranted.

"Get a refund," Jon snapped from the kitchen door, where he now stood, wearing only boxers. "Feel free," I snapped back, having completely forgotten my vow to be "in love enough for both of us." Jon was carrying a huge load of sheets and towels and balancing a mop over one shoulder.

I knew immediately that Dov was involved.

"He's still up," Jon growled through his teeth, gesturing upstairs with his eyes.

"Get some new underwear," I blurted out, staring at the pair he had on, which hung like curtains on a rod, there were so many holes along the elastic waistband, which ironically bore the name GAP every few inches.

"Feel free," he retorted with a snarl as he tossed the tangle of bedding through the laundry-room door and slammed it shut with such loathing you'd think he'd trapped a rabid rat in there.

My eyes scanned the countertops until I found an open bottle of wine. "Welcome home," I said, as if being sardonic would somehow improve the tenor of our exchange.

"Ditto," came his predictable reply. I poured myself a glass of wine, thought for about a second, and then poured another one for Jon, who snatched it from me and gulped it down in one great chug, slamming his glass down on the marble tabletop with a startling crash that to my surprise did not shatter the glass.

I poured another glass of wine for both of us and sat down at the table. "So what happened?" I said, not wanting to ask, yet knowing I had to.

"Which do you want to hear first . . . the bad news or the disastrous news?" he said, grunting as he struggled to open a window to let the residual smoke escape, or so I assumed until I saw him light up a cigarette.

"Don't smoke in the house."

"Everyone's asleep." He exhaled the words in a stream of smoke.

"Cancer isn't asleep," I replied with growing fury.

He extended a hand out in front of his chest, like a traffic cop telling me to stop. His chest still looked sexy, even though I hated him right now. "Okay, okay," he conceded, inhaling his own words as he stole one last deep drag off the thing and snuffed it out on a dirty plate next to the sink. He'd gotten enough of a nicotine fix to cope with whatever came next.

"It was a nightmare," he said, shaking his head in disbelief at whatever he was about to tell me.

I closed my eyes for a minute. The hotel room back in San Diego looked like paradise right now.

"Do you want to know what happened or not?" He was leaning toward me now on his mop, clearly needing to tell someone.

"Okay," I sighed.

Just then, a long shrill shriek echoed down the stairs and pierced our hearts. It was the kind of scream that would have sent most parents running to see what happened. Neither of us moved. "He's all yours," Jon said, vehemently propping the mop up against the wall. Then he turned and left the room as if he were going somewhere, though I knew he wouldn't get very far in those boxers.

At the foot of the stairs, I heard another volley of high-pitched shrieks that meant Dov was experiencing a manic episode. I dreaded that laugh. I hated that laugh. I lost my temper sometimes when he didn't sleep for days, and when he laughed hysterically at everything. I knew he couldn't help it, but I got so tired after a while. I'd probably be better off not seeing him when he was like this.

"Hello, Dov," I said, standing in his doorway. It looked like Jon had remade the bed that Dov was standing on, naked and giggling with a string of shiny beads in his hand. Jon didn't believe in pajamas, or, for that matter, teeth brushing, hand washing, or going to bed on time. He didn't see the point, which made him an instant hero in the eyes of our kids. I wasn't sure why he didn't think a bare mattress was acceptable, but I didn't question it and was just thankful there was a sheet on Dov's bed.

"I missed you," I said, pulling Dov down to sit next to me on the edge of the bed. I wanted so much to take his hand into mine, to kiss his cheek, to hug him and hold him. Instead I just stared at the tangle of uncombed hair at the back of his head. I wished he would look at me, but I knew he couldn't. Not when he was like this. Just sitting beside me without shrieking, for this precious moment, was the greatest gift Dov could give me. I knew it took every ounce of his energy and concentration to do it. "I love you," I said quietly, getting up as slowly as I could.

"How about some pajamas?" I asked, rummaging through his dresser drawers. I tried to help him put them on but whenever I touched him he doubled over, laughing hysterically. He could not stop. "Was everything okay while I was away?" I asked, trying to ignore his behavior and my despair. "C'mon, let's get these on." I was on the verge of tears. Dov couldn't stop laughing; he laughed until he was screaming.

Then suddenly, just as inexplicably, he began sobbing uncontrollably, a deep, mournful, despairing kind of crying. Huge tears rolled down his cheeks. I stared at him in utter grief, unable to know what was going on in his mind or heart. Finally, I just hugged him tightly, locking my arms around him and rocking us both, brushing away my own tears on my sleeve.

I didn't really believe in praying. But that didn't stop me from doing it. In fact, I prayed all the time. And not just for Dov but for all the children in the world who suffered from autism. They all deserved a miracle.

But I wanted a modern miracle. The old-fashioned miracle where one person at a time was saved just wasn't acceptable anymore. No, modern miracles were much bigger than that: They had to be reproducible; they required clinical trials and publication in peer-reviewed journals. Modern miracles were for the masses, not just one individual. That's why we started CAN. What good was a miracle, after all, if it saved only one little boy? No, I never prayed just for Dov—until now.

I felt defeated, destroyed, inadequate, broken down. I would accept any kind of miracle right now, even the senseless, one-in-a-million, unreproducible kind that cured only one person. I was too devastated to be altruistic any longer. I just wanted God to fix Dov—to save him, to cure him, to help him get better—because this was no way to live.

"Jon!" I called out, hoping he would come upstairs and finish putting Dov to bed. A few minutes went by and I called out for him again, but still no one came. Maybe he didn't hear me, or maybe he just couldn't take it anymore himself.

Just as suddenly as Dov had started crying, he stopped. Taking advantage of the lull in the storm, I gave up on the pajamas and tucked him into bed as he was. I leaned down to kiss him good night, but the moment had already passed and the mania returned with full force. Once again, he could barely suppress his laughs and screams as he struggled to remain under the covers. "Good night," I said, lightly brushing the hair from his eyes, but this was more than he could bear and elicited another volley of uncontrollable laughter. I could see that he was trying very hard to be quiet, to be still, but the helpless laughter kept breaking through and he could not hold his body still. It must have been utterly exhausting, I thought as I stared down at his face. There were dark circles around his huge brown eyes, and his curling lashes, still wet with tears, looked painted on against his pale skin; he probably hadn't slept much while I was away. I kissed his forehead as lightly as I could and told him that I loved him very much and then I turned out the light, hoping that he would fall asleep for at least a few hours before we all had to get up again.

And, if Dov was glad that I was home, there was no way to know.

During this time, daily life was a drag. Every morning, Dov awoke at about 6:00 A.M.; by 7:00 A.M. Maria Lopez, his therapeutic aide, arrived to help him get ready for school. There were so many loads of laundry to do that we wore out a washing machine every two years. Even though Dov was now eight years old, the bedclothes were always soaked and we wore out a washing machine every two years. We popped Dov into a bubble bath with some beads or blocks to stim on and headed to the kitchen to make him five or six foods, hoping he would eat one of them for breakfast. After his bath, Maria handed him a towel and instructed him to dry himself; with some help, he could roughly do the front half of his body. Then Maria would lead him to the dresser, where she laid out two or three shirts and would ask him to pick the one he wanted. We realized that Dov had few choices in his life and so we tried to provide them wherever possible. Maria repeated this with his pants, his underwear, socks, and shoes. Maria would then lead him to sit at the edge of his bed, where she patiently instructed him step by step and assisted him hand over hand in putting on each garment and taught him to put on his socks and shoes and secure the Velcro closures. Dov had been working on these skills for as long as I could remember. Dov hated having his hair combed or his teeth brushed, and he always resisted. But Maria never grew impatient. Instead she cajoled him and humored him, she sang Mexican songs, called him "Mi corazon," and tickled and teased him until he couldn't help but smile, and all the while she was stealthily helping him, and at the same time trying to teach him to become more independent at these skills.

An enormous red binder sat on the kitchen table those days. It was filled with hundreds of tiny laminated photos: pictures of the foods Dov ate—and many he did not—a water bottle, the bathroom, the special swing in his room, his beads, the shaving cream he loved to feel in his hands, Play-Doh, blocks, marbles, his favorite rock, a bowl of dried beans to plunge his hands into, the ball pit, the bathtub, the swimming pool, the speech therapist, the occupational therapist, the music therapist, the behavioral therapists, the reading tutor, his teachers at school, his weekend baby-sitters, family members. Dov's whole world was contained between the covers of this red binder. There was also a smaller version of the red binder from which he could pick out what he wanted for lunch before going to school. The little binder traveled with him to school, thereby avoiding the fits of rage he used to have when he chose something that couldn't be supplied on demand at school.

In the classroom, Dov had yet another small binder for "break activities" as well as a picture schedule on the wall. Dov's small class of six- and seven-year-olds was the only autism classroom in the school. His teacher, Karen Spratt, was a cheerful, upbeat, perpetually optimistic person whom everyone loved, especially the children. She valiantly tried to teach her students the alphabet, numbers, and other kindergarten and first-grade subject matter. She assigned each of her students a buddy from the regular classroom next door and gave the children their snacks together, then had them brush their teeth together and comb their hair and look in the mirror side by side. For many of her students, this would be the only time in their lives they would have anything resembling a friend.

The small classroom had a chain hanging from the ceiling where a platform swing or a net swing could be suspended and used to help the children who were having sensory meltdowns throughout the day. Sometimes, a particularly distressed child would simply be rolled up in a rubber mat and squeezed until he calmed down; the children seemed to crave this deep pressure and they loved it. After school, Maria drove Dov to his other therapies, and finally they would arrive home, both exhausted.

The weekends meant even more driving—an hour to speech therapy, another hour to therapeutic horseback riding, and more time driving to therapeutic swimming lessons. On weekends, babysitters came in shifts and one of Dov's most beloved therapists, Erika Karafin, was attempting to come over to teach him a sight-reading program. She constructed a board with Velcro sentence strips that had one missing word. Dov had to choose between two answers and place the word card in the sentence. In this way, Dov learned to identify twenty sight words over a two-year period. We were thrilled, because it was the first progress we'd seen him make in years. Yet it was only under these extremely controlled conditions that Dov could demonstrate his ability to recognize these words and the chance that this could develop into any form of communication seemed remote.

We were not only running out of steam, we were also going broke. Jon and I had devoted our most productive earning years to

CAN and it was beginning to take a serious economic toll on our lives, even affecting our ability to support our family and especially all that Dov needed.

I was afraid we were becoming threadbare, worn around the edges and middle-aged, and still Dov was not getting better. Meanwhile, we couldn't stop pushing autism research ahead. But we knew that soon at least one of us would need to focus again on earning a living. The problem was that neither of us cared more about anything else in the world than finding treatment and a cure for autism.

I turned out all the lights and checked the doors, though what more evil could get past these locks and into our lives, I could not imagine. I tucked Miriam in and ran my hand over her smooth forehead. Her room was light blue with white flowers painted on the walls and a massive doll collection that watched over her from atop the fireplace mantel. She was nearly seven years old and it was as if we had missed her childhood while we were struggling to save her brother Dov. Her long dark hair was neatly braided and she looked content, snuggled up with twenty or so Beanie Babies that I'd brought home for her from airports everywhere. Thank God she and Gabriel loved Beanie Babies. They were not hard to please. I looked in on Gabriel, who was asleep with Herbert, a stuffed pig of monumental proportions that took up half his bed. "Why Herbert?" I asked him when he named the creature. "Because Herbert is a very piggish name," he explained, as if I should have known.

In my wallet, I carried a picture of Gabriel and Miriam and Dov, which was taken at the beach house during our summer vacation. Autism had segmented our lives into a hundred separate compartments and our summer vacation was about the only thing we did together as a family. At home, I spent time with Dov trying to get him to play and communicate. Jon read to Dov at bedtime. Gabriel wrestled with Dov. And when Miriam saw her brother laughing manically, for no reason at all, she told him jokes. Miriam and Gabe went to our Temple school and Dov went to a special school. When Miriam told me she wanted to grow up to be a doctor for autistic kids, I said I hoped there wouldn't be so many autistic kids by then. "But I like having an autistic person in the family!" She protested. Miriam thought every family had at least one autistic kid, because most of the families we hung out with actually did.

I thought I saw candlelight flickering through the crack of our bedroom door and for a moment my hopes soared, but then I remembered the burning kettle. Quietly, I entered our room. Jon was lying on the bed. He had fallen asleep on top of the covers, surrounded by the books and newspapers he always meant to read.

The house was extraordinarily quiet now as I closed our bedroom door and went over to blow out the lone candle that flickered on Jon's side of the bed. I decided to let the flame burn and optimistically searched behind the socks in my top drawer, hoping to find one of those skimpy nightgowns that I recalled stashing there a lifetime ago. Not that I was in the mood exactly, but the fact that I could even remember there was such a mood was one small, old-fashioned miracle I would definitely accept.

12.

Echoes
of Doubt

The limits of my language are the limits of my reality.

—Ludwig Wittgenstein

San Francisco was my next stop with Tito and Soma and I found myself once again counting on Mike Merzenich to come through. Because, so far, we were batting zero. We were scheduled to see several more scientists over the next two months. Soma and Tito's stay was now half over and the four months they had been granted by the CAN board, which had seemed like so much time, now seemed like nothing. I was starting to have serious doubts about whether anything would come of all our efforts.

It was still light out when our taxi pulled up in front of the Stanyon Park Hotel, an old Victorian house across from Golden Gate Park in San Francisco. Soma and Tito spotted a McDonald's down the street and headed there for dinner.

I dragged my huge suitcase and Soma's tiny duffel into the decrepitly charming Victorian lobby. Tea was served from four till six every afternoon in the green lacquered sitting room by a Chinese gentleman, the wisp of a woman at the front desk informed me in a fragile voice. Sometimes it felt as if nearly everyone you encountered in San Francisco was just out of some rehab program.

I went straight to my room, gleeful at the prospect of getting a good night's sleep—tomorrow was going to be a big day. I unpacked and got into bed with a stack of papers on infant auditory and visual development. It took a lot of concentration to read this kind of research and I figured it would put me right to sleep. But it didn't. I wondered if Soma and Tito had gotten back from McDonald's all right and hoped they'd found their room without any problem. I shouldn't have to worry so much about them. Soma was much more independent than when they'd first arrived. She knew American money, she was able to take a cab or a bus on her own, she knew how to make a long-distance call and how to use a can opener and a microwave oven. I called the front desk. The concierge assured me that the Indian lady and her son had come back more than two hours ago and had gone to their room.

I woke up to the shrill sound of the rotary telephone ringing near my head. It was Sandy Blakeslee from *The New York Times*. She was in town and she wanted to do an interview with Tito. Could she come over in an hour? "No problem," I said sitting up, smiling. I'd been hoping for several years that Sandy Blakeslee would write a piece about autism for *The New York Times* and lately I had been telling her about Tito and what an extraordinary window into autism he was. But I hadn't expected her to show up here, today.

I immediately called Soma in her room. Sandy Blakeslee from *The New York Times* would be arriving in one hour to interview Tito, I announced breathlessly.

I joined Soma and Tito in their room, where I found them sitting properly on the two velvet chairs at the round table in the window, framed by the heavy green drapery. A few minutes later Sandy Blakeslee was knocking at the door. She blew into the small room with a gust of enthusiasm and curiosity. Sandy didn't look anything like the serious science journalist I'd pictured; instead, she looked like a college student, wearing a T-shirt, with a backpack slung over one shoulder. I stood up and reached out to shake her hand. "I am so glad you are here!" I said with gratitude. But Sandy wasn't looking at me. Instead her reporter eyes were riveted on Tito.

"Tito?" she exclaimed, shaking Tito's hand vigorously before he even knew what happened. By the time I introduced everyone, Sandy was sitting on the bed next to me, a pen hovering over her notepad. I gestured toward Tito, who had already started writing something on his own pad. Sandy watched, fascinated, as Tito scrawled his words out on paper and his mother read them aloud.

"It was nice meeting you Sun. I shall call you Sun because you have that shine on your smile."

"Thank you, Tito," Sandy replied. "How do you like the United States so far? Is it very different than India?"

"They are equal," Tito replied.

"What do you like about it here?" Sandy asked.

Tito quickly responded, *"The people. They are accepting me and I crave for it."*

Sandy nodded in understanding. "Tito, if I were writing something about you, how do you think it should start?" she asked.

I was thrilled that Sandy was thinking of writing an article about Tito. What none of us expected was that apparently Tito had given considerable thought to the idea of an article being written about him.

"Introduce me in a dialog with you with my calling you Sun," he started out. *"Then you can introduce my poem the Mind Tree and relate it to my nothingness condition of my body. I also think you can include Portia's coming to know about me and the conference of last year and then continue with my tests."*

Sandy wrote all of his words down, nodding in agreement. When she was done, she asked Tito, "Is there anything else?"

"And the desire to be a gypsy tree."

"A what?" Sandy asked, perplexed.

I didn't know what Tito meant either. "Is that one of his poems?" I asked Soma.

"He wrote about the gypsy tree," she replied. "It is the tree that can roam."

I was more confused than ever. "I don't understand," I said to Soma. But then suddenly in a flash, I got it. "Tito's poem 'The Mind Tree'—it's about a mind that is stuck in one place and can't move—so the gypsy tree—is that a mind that can move around, and be independent?"

Tito started to rock like crazy in his seat. "*Yes,*" he typed.

Soma reached down into her tote bag and pulled out a children's school journal with a black-marbled cover. She ruffled through the pages, which were filled with Tito's crude handwriting, until she found "Gypsies." "Here," she said, "Let me read it to you."

It looked as though the winter days that year had become warmer than usual. It was then that I had wished I got the ability to walk. And my dreams followed my wish. I could dream of being a gypsy-tree, walking beyond and across anywhere and everywhere.

Since it was not something to happen everyday, I could dream many people getting frightened of me and running away. I could dream myself walking on a busy market of some town and causing a great confusion on the road with some panic, some fear, some astonishment, some amusement and some disbelief.

I could dream myself walking with the crow's nests or perhaps with the group of monkeys. I could dream and dream as there can be no boundaries for a dream. And I could sense that there was no boundary for the gypsy either. The earth was as limitless space as any dream for him.

Yet the limit of the winter was bound to time. They left the field with their smell, with their laughter, with their drum beats, with their unfamiliar songs, with their quarrels and with their fading and still fading out happiness.

Yet my dream remained with their unfading memories, unbounded with the trap of time, for all my lonely moments.

Soma closed the journal and looked up expectantly.

Sandy took a moment to respond to Tito's poem. "Wow," she said, in awe. "That was beautiful, Tito."

"He has written hundreds like this," Soma said, beaming proudly.

"Really?" Sandy asked. "That's amazing." She reached out to Tito and put her hand on his shoulder. Tito stopped rocking for a moment. "Tito, you are a very talented writer."

At this Tito jumped up and stood by the door. Soma excused herself and Tito and then took him for a little walk up and down the hallway while I continued talking with Sandy about Tito and the testing we would be doing in Merzenich's lab. Soon they returned. Tito was getting anxious and wanted to go, Soma told us. But before we left, Sandy wanted to ask Tito a few more questions. "What are you hoping the tests will do?" she asked.

"Do something to show that I have a single channel," Tito answered, referring to his ability to process only one sense at a time. *"I am keen on turning the view of autism from a complex nature to a simple nature."*

"I see," said Sandy. "Tito, I'm going to be around for the next couple of days, while the testing is going on. I would like to see what happens." Tito rocked anxiously and did not respond. "Is there anything you'd like to ask me?" Sandy asked him.

"Do you have a degree?"

"No, I don't," Sandy replied. "I trained at *The New York Times*," she explained.

"I want to be introduced," Tito replied. *"I am seeking work."*

"I'll do anything I can to help you," she promised.

Tito jumped up again and began to pace around the room in an agitated manner.

Sandy was worried. "Does he need something?" she asked Soma. "Tito, do you need something?"

Tito stopped pacing and forced out a few strangled-sounding words which none of us could understand.

Sandy asked Soma, "What is he trying to say?"

Soma shook her head. "It's nothing," she replied.

At this, Tito looked directly at his mother, and uttered the sounds again, this time more urgently and loudly. It was obvious Tito was trying to communicate something else to Sandy. I asked Soma, "Can you get him to write down what he's saying?"

Soma tapped on the chair next to her. "Tito, sit!" she demanded. "Here!" Tito sat down and Soma quickly shoved a pad of paper onto his lap and a pencil into his hand. "C'mon!" Soma urged.

"*The publisher, very badly,*" Tito stated.

Sandy was confused. "What does he mean?" she asked.

"You asked if he needed something," Soma reminded Sandy.

Sandy laughed. "Oh, I get it," she said, smiling. "You're saying you need a publisher, very badly."

Tito replied, using his voice, "*Yes.*" This time we all understood.

For the next three days Sandy hovered nearby. I caught glimpses of her wherever we went, standing in a doorway or out in the hall, always within earshot and scribbling away in her notebook. And later, to my delight, she would write a fantastic article about Tito that appeared on the front page of *The New York Times* Science Times section.

As always seemed to be the case with senior scientists, Mike Merzenich was nowhere to be found when we arrived. Instead, a man who didn't look much like a scientist greeted us at the entrance of the cement behemoth that housed Merzenich's lab. Yoram Bonneh was wearing a black leather jacket and a faraway look. He had pale blue eyes and a lower lip that jutted out slightly, giving him the look of a handsome gangster. It was only when he spoke that I realized he was Israeli. His voice was quiet and gentle and his eyes stared off to the side as if he were always thinking about something. Yoram informed us that he was a psychologist and a neuroscientist and he specialized in the study of vision.

Inside, we took one set of elevators and then another and turned here and there down some hallways, until suddenly we stood facing a great steel riveted wall, with buttons and a speaker box and written directions. It was the entrance to a section of the building that looked more like it had landed from another planet than the mere addition that it was. Some pretty important top secret stuff must go on behind this highly secured entrance, I thought. Good, because this was where Mike Merzenich's lab was located, and I found it exhilarating to know that his ideas were so ingenious they had to be guarded behind these impressive, high-tech security doors.

Yoram punched some buttons, then spoke to someone through the speakerphone and this caused the steel doors to part silently at the center. Inside he flashed a badge at a woman behind a small plateglass window and gave a sweeping gesture that encompassed the rest of us. We stuck close behind Yoram as we wound our way through another set of corridors that led us to a group of gray-carpeted testing rooms.

At last we arrived at our destination: a small gray waiting room furnished with a red leather love seat and not much else. Gesturing for us to sit down, Yoram unfolded what appeared to be a printed schedule.

Today, he announced, raising one finger, he and Francesca Pei would be testing Tito's ability to integrate auditory and visual stimuli. Tomorrow, he continued, elevating the finger even higher, Tito's tactile sense would be investigated. During lunch, we would go next door to see Bruce Miller, the behavioral neurologist, who had met Tito at my ill-fated dinner party in Los Angeles. And tomorrow afternoon, Tito would be interviewed by John Houde, a pioneer in the study of how a person hears their own voice. On the third day, Houde would be testing Tito in an attempt to understand how, or even if, Tito perceived his own voice.

It was beginning to dawn on me: Mike Merzenich had assembled a team of experts to study Tito—bright young scientists, each of whom specialized in a different sensory modality. At last, someone was taking Tito seriously.

Soon we were crowded into one of the small testing bays. These rooms were all the same, with soundproof walls, a jumble of wiring, some electronic boxes and panels, a computer monitor and headphones, and other gear lying on a tabletop with a few rolling chairs parked in front of it.

Yoram listened as I explained that Tito could not see and hear at the same time when he was concentrating on something, and that the way Tito was tested must take this into account. Whether the choice of possible responses was presented as words or pictures made a huge difference in Tito's ability to give the correct response. Tito was primarily an auditory person and therefore he did very poorly when given a choice of answers in the form of pictures. Yoram was new to autism research, but he'd read enough of the literature to know that the prevailing belief was that autistics were visual thinkers. It was true that most autistic people, or at least the ones who could speak, described themselves that way, I admitted, but Tito was quite the opposite. I confided that I had developed a hypothesis that there could be two types of autism: a visual type and an auditory type. Yoram looked at me askance. Whether my hypothesis was true or not, Tito relied on his auditory system to the exclusion of his vision, I insisted again. Yoram could find out for himself when he tested Tito, I suggested.

Even though at first he didn't believe Tito's sensory processing could be so profoundly abnormal that he could not be tested in the usual manner, Yoram honored our request and adapted the experiments to accommodate Tito.

There were so many questions to answer. Did Tito see and hear completely separately? If so, was there an actual lag between his experience of two senses? And if there was a lag, how long was it and did it vary? And if it varied, under what conditions did it vary and why?

Yoram's background in computer programming allowed him to rapidly develop the appropriate experiments that could characterize Tito's unusual perception.

The basic setup of the first experiment was quite simple. Tito sat in a small, soundproof room wearing headphones and watching a blank computer screen in front of him. Suddenly a green patch would flash in the center of the screen at the same exact moment that a tone was heard.

"Did you see something, did you hear something, or both?" Yoram asked. There were three index cards taped to the table in front of Tito with the choices written out: SEE, HEAR, BOTH. Tito tapped HEAR.

In every trial where Tito was presented with the flash and the tone simultaneously, he heard the tone but failed to see the flash.

The next question was: If Tito couldn't see and hear at the same time, how long did it take him to switch from hearing to seeing or the other way around?

Yoram started out by separating the flash and the tone by one full second in time.

Tito, as Yoram discovered, could never see the flash at all, except when it appeared alone, without the tone. But what did that mean?

Yoram expanded the time separating the flash and the tone to 1.5 seconds. Still Tito could not see the flash if he heard the tone.

Yoram expanded the test to 2 full seconds between the flash and the tone, and Tito started to get the flash. He pointed at the answer, BOTH, but he said the effort was "painful."

When the test was expanded so there was a full 3 seconds between seeing the flash and hearing the tone, Tito was finally able to experience both 100 percent of the time, without discomfort.

I glanced over at Yoram. His forehead was scrunched up, and he was rubbing his chin and looking off to the side. Yoram admitted this was incredible. He didn't know what to make of this. He'd never seen anything like it before—ever.

"I wonder if the order matters?" Yoram asked aloud. "Would it make a difference if the flash or the sound comes first?" Yoram set up this test and tried it out on Tito.

As it turned out, Tito did better when the flash came first. He was able to shift more rapidly from seeing to hearing than the other way around. In fact, although it still took some effort, Tito was able to both see the flash and hear the sound when there was only 2 seconds between them, without it being a "painful" experience.

Why was it, then, that when the sound came first, Tito still needed a full 3-second interval between the sound and the image to perceive the flash at all? I suspected it was because Tito's hearing was the sense he used almost exclusively and so it tended to suppress or override his vision when he concentrated on something.

Next, Yoram reversed the order so that once again, the sound came first and the flash came second. He tried running the test again with 2 seconds between the sound and the flash.

"Can you see the flash?" he asked Tito.

Tito tapped on the NO sign. Then he spelled out: *"No. The sound is getting fixed."*

"When you say the sound is getting fixed, what do you mean? Do you keep hearing it?" Yoram asked.

"It registers with a lag," Tito replied.

This seemed to impress Yoram. "Like a long sound?" he asked.

"A sort of rest time," Tito replied.

"What do you mean?" Yoram persisted.

"It rests for a while. I like the three seconds better." Sound held Tito's attention longer. At least that was what I thought he was telling us.

"When visual came first was it different?" Yoram probed.

"I think so—I needed less time to get prepared."

"Do you actually need to switch over?" I asked, amazed.

"Of course I need to, don't you? Like a flash of lightning prepares you for thunder."

But unlike the arrival of thunder after lightning, what Tito was experiencing had little to do with the laws of physics. What Tito was experiencing was probably the result of years of adapting to his environment as best he could with his abnormal sensory system.

"Suppose you try concentrating on only the flash and try to ignore the sound?" Yoram asked.

"*It is painful,*" Tito answered.

"What do you mean?" Yoram frowned.

"*To switch too fast from ear to eye,*" Tito explained.

"How exactly do you do it?" I asked Tito.

"*I need time.*"

I realized Tito meant this quite literally—he needed 3 seconds to switch comfortably from ear to eye, not the 2 seconds we were asking him to attempt.

"Was it always like this?" I wanted to know.

"*Chaos is the name of it,*" Tito replied, cryptically.

"Tito!" a sweet voice suddenly called out, startling us. A tiny Italian person with a pixie face, short brown hair, and big glasses appeared in the waiting room, balancing a tray of drinks and a bag of sandwiches. Yoram introduced Francesca Pei and explained that her area of expertise, like his, was vision and that she would be helping with some of the testing. Francesca Pei's adorable appearance belied the fact that she was a fast-rising young neuroscientist. Her voice was angelic, pure sweetness and serenity. Her Italian accent drove the two *t* sounds in Tito's name like a pair of cheerful rivets, so that it sounded as if she were glad to see him every time she spoke it.

Throughout the afternoon, Yoram administered test after test to Tito in an attempt to characterize Tito's remarkable delay in auditory and visual integration as Francesca attended to Tito minute by minute, coaxing and cajoling, playfully teasing, empathizing, soothing. She crouched tirelessly for hours next to the computer monitor so she could watch Tito's gaze and see whether or not he was fixating on the screen, and she would direct his attention toward it, again and again, all the while giving him constant encouragement.

By four o'clock, the first day of testing was finished and so was

Tito. Yoram informed us that he had called a cab for us and it would arrive in thirty minutes. Soma and Tito sat and waited on the red leather love seat. Tito was at the end of his rope and wanted nothing more than chicken nuggets and a quiet bed to sleep in. I was amazed at how long he had lasted and how well he had held himself together throughout this first day. We watched as Yoram paced back and forth in front of us, rubbing his chin in that way he did when he had an idea. Sure enough, Yoram stopped abruptly and stared off to the side, which I now knew meant he was about to state the idea.

"Is the vision fragmented? Do images break into pieces?" Yoram asked. Tito stopped rocking long enough to jot down his answer.

"The perception is sometimes a tail of a cow and sometimes the horn. I fill in the gaps. But I need time."

"Do you look at the cow?" Yoram continued, scrunching up his forehead more than ever.

"What cow?" I asked.

"I want to understand, how does he perceive," Yoram said, shooting me a look that said, *Please shut up*.

"I get the essence of bovine expression and its peace and that is more important," Tito answered.

"Does that mean you don't actually see the parts of the cow simultaneously?"

"It does not matter whether the flower is big or small, but I see the delicacy and the fragile petals."

"He is studying adjectives," Soma chimed in.

Yoram pressed on. "You say you need time. The parts, the tail, the horns—are you scanning from one thing to the other, or are the two things separate, individual visual experiences?"

"Time to integrate. I look for the inner aspect, like what does the cow think about man."

"After you get the whole, does it break again?"

"The synthesis is irreversible," Tito replied.

Yoram was rubbing his chin again. Soma sat quietly. What in the world did Tito mean? It sounded like Tito only got fragments of a visual scene and that it took an extraordinarily long time for these to come together in a meaningful whole. If it took that much time and that much effort for Tito to perceive things, how could Tito navigate his way around in the world at all? Not that he did that very well, I reminded myself. If his senses were this fragmented, how did Tito process the environment—a room for example? There were thousands of visual items in a room.

Just then a phone, which I hadn't even noticed in the room, rang loudly, jangling all our nerves.

The cab was waiting. Yoram would walk us out.

"I will eat," Tito said suddenly in an almost unintelligible voice as he jumped up and ran out the door. *Me too,* I thought, as we trailed behind him. I was starving.

Back at the hotel, Soma invited me to take tea with her in their room. We piled two plates high with scones from the tearoom, and, balancing two cups of tea, we stepped into the shaky old elevator. Soma was talking about her idea of a school for auditory type autistics. I thought it was a good idea, I told her. But I wasn't really listening; I couldn't stop thinking about the tests that Yoram had given Tito that afternoon. I was determined to get another detailed description from Tito about how exactly he experienced the environment. In their room, I sat down on the floor next to Tito, who was sitting cross-legged, making his way through the first plate of scones. What could I ask him about? I glanced around the room. Nearby, a closet door was standing open. Taking care not to specify any particular mode of perception such as seeing or hearing, I asked Tito to describe exactly how he perceived the door that was standing partially open before us.

"The colour comes and then the shape and then the size, the whole thing needs time to get integrated. To be described as a door, there is the position, the open or closed."

It seemed as if Tito was perceiving a fragmented visual picture. The human brain actually does process images in the very components Tito described, namely color, shape, size, and so on, but we are unaware of these separate elements that our brains seamlessly combine into a smooth whole, incorporating all the elements. Tito, it seemed, was actually seeing these individual visual elements and then having to fit them together into a mental picture. What a tremendous amount of work to see a simple door!

"What happens if the position changes, if, say, we close the door?" I asked.

"*It may disrupt the whole thing, and you may need to start once again,*" Tito replied.

I wrote down his words and continued. "From what you're telling me, it seems like the visual information comes in parts, many different aspects that have to be put together to get the whole. Is the auditory sense more of a whole when it comes in?"

"*There is less classification in sound,*" Tito explained.

"You mean fewer elements?"

"*Yes.*"

"What do you think it would it be like if you could suddenly see and hear and feel your body all at once? Can you imagine that?" I asked.

"*Can you imagine what happens to a blind man when he suddenly got his vision.*"

I was taken aback by the sophistication of Tito's answer. He was right. If the brain had no experience, the mere ability to perceive sensory input could not impart meaning to the brain.[21]

I couldn't sleep that night as I tried to fully grasp Tito's description of how he perceived a door. He described seeing perceptual fragments, the color and shape and position, even before he could get that it was a door. I was trying to reconcile it with a description Tito had given me a few weeks earlier when I was interviewing him on videotape. Tito had been extremely anxious and agitated about being taped that day and he kept jumping up and running out of the room. When Tito finally answered my question about how he perceived things, he said that he "took a snapshot" and ran out of the room to study it and that was why he jumped up and ran out so often. This answer shook my confidence in Tito's self-reporting. I didn't know what to make of it. It was completely different from what he'd reported at other times. In fact it was the exact opposite of the fragmented visual experience he reported when he sat looking at a door today.

Later it made more sense to me; sometimes Tito did get only the parts and sometimes he did get only the whole picture. The important point was that he never got the parts and the whole picture together, at the same time, which is how the rest of us see the world.

One might think of this as "local" versus "global" processing. It is thought that the left hemisphere provides local information, or parts of the whole, while the right hemisphere supplies the global picture. When integrated together, the local and the global views combine so that we are unaware of either. I wondered whether Tito's polar opposite ways of seeing meant that his hemispheres were operating somewhat independently of each other.

The second day of testing began unofficially in the green-lacquered tearoom on the first floor of our hotel. Soma looked relieved to see me. She'd been having a hard time keeping Tito away from the pile of croissants that was temptingly displayed on the buffet table.

I wanted to ask Tito more about the things he was telling us yesterday. Would he mind? I asked. No, he replied verbally. I was starting to understand Tito better now when he tried to speak, at least I could get what he meant when he uttered simple words like yes and no. Tito's voice sounded just like Dov's, very low and throaty, with little control over volume and almost no ability to enunciate sounds that required a coordinated effort from tongue and lips, such as the t, or sh or d sounds.

"Tito, you said when you were a little kid it was 'chaos'—what did you mean?" I asked.

"I think that I automatically started to screen some inputs, such as when you have a migraine you turn off the sounds."

I knew what Tito meant. We all do it, but to a lesser extent than Tito. For example, if you're in an airport and having trouble hearing someone, you will automatically and unconsciously begin to lip-read, shifting your attention toward the visual modality in an attempt to get as much information as you can. Dom Massarro coined the expression "fuzzy logic model of perception" to explain the automatic sensory shifting we do in order to extract optimal information from the environment.

"Can you tell me what it was like?" I continued.

"I could not get at anything including the recognition (of things), so things were limited for me."

I remembered what Tito had said to me about this before. When he was very young, sometimes things "went together" that shouldn't. If he saw a cloud and heard the word "banana," they might go together from then on, and he couldn't get them apart. This overassociation between images and words made it so that Tito could not understand or identify things in the environment. He couldn't make sense of the world around him. He didn't realize that voices and people went together when he was very young and he couldn't understand why the voices stopped when people left the room. I thought this was probably what he meant now when he wrote, *"I could not get at anything including the recognition."*

But why did things sometimes "go together" that shouldn't, and yet at other times Tito described seeing only fragments like "a bit of the horn and a bit of the tail"?

The only circumstance I could connect with this was that Tito seemed to see the parts when he was calm and in a state of low arousal and he seemed to see the whole, or to take a "snapshot," when he was agitated and in a state of high arousal.

Suddenly an image burst into my mind of the Zoetrope. The Zoetrope was the earliest hand-cranked movie projector. If you cranked the Zoetrope at just the right speed, a series of still pictures would become transformed into the illusion of perfect natural motion. But if you cranked it too fast, all you saw was a single trembling image. And if you cranked the Zoetrope too slowly the illusion of motion disintegrated into fragments. Imagine if you had to crank the Zoetrope to make your senses "go together." Tito's arousal was like the Zoetrope, only Tito seemed to have little control over the cranking mechanism.

Soma was gently tapping me on the shoulder to get my attention. Tito was writing more.

"*But I think I tried to concentrate better on the sounds, which I heard around. It became a habit.*"

A habit? Was the delay Tito experienced between hearing and seeing caused by years of listening but not looking? Had Tito inadvertently trained his senses to operate separately? Is that what Tito did to try to lessen the "chaos"?

I looked up only to realize that Tito had run over to the pastry display and was stuffing pastries into his mouth as fast as he could. Soma was trying to pull him away. I rushed over and began tugging on Tito's other arm along with Soma.

"Tito!" I yelled.

Tito dropped the croissant from his hand and looked at me as if awakened from a dream.

"Tito, did you get better at 'concentrating on sounds' over time?" I asked, ignoring the stares of other hotel guests and the ruffled expression on the face of the Chinese gentleman as he approached with a broom. Tito allowed himself to be led back to the table by Soma. He sat down and she placed the pad of paper in front of him again.

"*Yes. The process was gradual,*" he wrote.

"Do you think your senses were normal in the beginning and then became overwhelming?" I asked.

"No, I think autistic from the beginning because I would shut off the world by shouting and yelling when I was two or three months old."

Tito had described these very early memories to me before. But further discussion would have to wait. Our cab was outside. My brain was running a hundred miles a minute and it wasn't even 8:00 A.M. I couldn't wait to get started at Merzenich's lab.

Yoram was waiting in front of the building when we pulled up. He led us through the maze of halls and past the security barriers until once again we arrived at the little red leather love seat. I could only imagine what that little red love seat, sworn to secrecy by virtue of its voiceless existence, might have witnessed over the years. A bearded researcher wearing shirtsleeves and a vest poked his head out of the testing room and introduced himself. Chris Moore told us he was almost done setting up the tactile experiments for Tito.

That morning we all crammed into the little testing room and we began to understand what was happening to Tito when he tried to look at something and feel touch at the same time. He could not. Nor could he hear a sound and feel touch simultaneously. There was a lag of at least 1.5 seconds in both situations.

Chris also wanted to test Tito's tactile sense by itself. First, he wanted to find out if Tito could feel where touch sensation was coming from on his body—this test was called tactile localization. Soma covered Tito's eyes and Chris touched Tito's forearm with a probe that was made out of a thin hair. He had a whole kit of these probes in all different diameters. Then Soma removed the blindfold and Tito was supposed to answer by showing where he had been touched on his arm. Tito could crudely approximate where he was being touched, but only when touched with the thickest probes.

In this, Tito was no exception; autistic kids usually could not point to their body parts. If I asked Dov to point at his nose, he might point at his mouth, or if I asked him to show me the top of his head he might tap his shoulder. I had noticed something else that was hard to explain about Dov—he couldn't close his own eyes when I asked him to. I once asked the pediatric neurologist and autism expert Margaret Bauman about this. She told me that the majority of her autistic patients over the years could not close their eyes when she asked them to. Like me, she found this very strange.

One of the first and most astonishing things Tito had ever told me was that he couldn't feel his body. Tito said he got a "scattered feeling" and he had to rock and flap and spin to feel his body, and that restoring bodily sensation in this way calmed him down. It was true that people did hallucinate when they were in sensory deprivation tanks. People went a little crazy when they couldn't feel their own body.

Tito had described how he experienced his own voice similarly. *"My voice comes from my stomach, it is centrifuged."* It seemed that he was getting a vibratory sensation from the trunk of his body and little feedback from his larynx, tongue, or lips.

I wondered if Tito's sense of his body had atrophied like his vision—from sheer lack of attention to that sense from the time he was very young—in favor of his auditory sense. I questioned Tito about this and in response he wrote a story about losing the sense of his body, "Pathway of Darkness." This is the fifth stanza:

How dark can be the dark?
There is no bound to that
For anything around that I saw
Was bounded by a darker black
I was slowly walking my way towards the darker side.
There was no turning back.
There was no reason what so ever to turn back.
The other side of the transparent wall must have been lit up by
another new day. I was not a part of it any more, for there was
nothing else left for me on that side.

So I walked with my own loneliness towards the darker side, along with many others like me.

Did I know who they were?
I do not think so.
There was no reason to know any body. There was no curiosity.
This side of the transparent wall has no bonds or relationships.
And that is a rule.

No one asked for any rule. And no one told us to follow any rule either. We just knew that it is a rule.
It is a rule to travel the dark side all together, but alone.

I was nearer to the darker side now.
Rows of people were entering it and slowly getting dissolved with the darkness.

I knew that there was no need to hesitate and ask anyone what was happening to those who were entering the dark side, which slowly revealed to me now as a path way. A tunnel like pathway.

I would get my answer once I was inside it.

So must be the others who were entering and who were waiting for their turn to enter.
No one had questioned anyone.

And my turn had come.

When Chris had completed the battery of tactile tests, he thanked Tito and Soma profusely for their assistance and bade us farewell.

It was almost noon when we walked over to the building next door to visit my friend Dr. Bruce Miller. Bruce was a behavioral neurologist who, among his other specialties, was an expert in ideomotor apraxia, a condition in which simple acts cannot be performed because the connections between the cortical centers that control voluntary action and the motor cortex are interrupted. I was convinced that autistic people like Tito had apraxia, and I wanted Bruce to test him for it.

"Yes, of course I remember you," Bruce said, shaking first Soma's, then Tito's, hand. He invited us to sit down in his office and began by asking Tito a series of questions. Then he proceeded to the actual testing. First, he asked Tito to pretend to comb his hair. "C'mon!" Soma prodded Tito verbally. Tito lifted his hand in the vague direction of his head, but he could not approximate combing his hair. Then Bruce handed him a comb. "Try again," he instructed Tito. But Tito could only move the comb toward his head, eventually bumping it against his forehead. Bruce administered a number of other tests to Tito while we stood by and watched.

When it was time to go, Bruce took me aside. "I thought it was just his mother typing," Bruce admitted, referring to the dinner at our house when he originally met Tito. "But this is as bad as any acquired apraxia I have ever seen in an adult, even the worst cases of dementia." Bruce explained that this was the failure of a circuit involving the frontal, opercular, and parietal areas of the brain. The opercular area was a component of Broca's area, the part of the brain involved in speech. People with opercular damage could write better than they could speak, Bruce said, glancing over at the piece of paper on his desk, which was covered in Tito's scrawled handwriting.

When we arrived back at Merzenich's lab, Yoram told us he wanted to repeat some of the auditory and visual tests from the previous day. Tito felt he had done badly on these and he was not looking forward to doing them again. Yoram repeated the first set of experiments, but Tito was becoming impatient and irritable. He started sniffing some papers on the table and ignoring the test.

"Why are you sniffing?" Yoram inquired.

"You are not sniffing—why?" Tito retorted.

"Pay attention!" Soma snapped.

"Is the test difficult for you?" Yoram asked Tito.

"No."

Yoram explained that the small plus or a minus sign that appeared at the center of the screen indicated whether Tito had given the correct answer or not.

"I know it, three mistakes," Tito said.

Yoram stared at Tito.

Tito was learning from the feedback.

"So you get better with practice?" Yoram asked.

"Yes."

"That's good, that's really good," I said, encouraging Tito.

Yoram was thinking.

"That means we can help you," Yoram said suddenly.

I shot a look at Yoram. Did he really mean it?

Yoram had begun to notice something strange. Tito was performing better on the auditory and visual integration task. Yoram checked the data. Yesterday Tito needed a minimum of a 2-second delay between the two stimuli in order to perceive both. And even that was difficult—"painful," as Tito described it. Yet today he was getting both the sound and image with only a 1.5-second delay between them.

Tito was rapidly learning through mere exposure, a phenomenon referred to as "perceptual learning."[22]

When we took a break, Yoram motioned for me to follow him out into the hall. There was good news and bad news, he told me. The good news was the auditory and visual integration testing had unexpectedly resulted in training Tito's brain to be able to process the two inputs closer together in time. This meant that Tito's sensory integration abnormalities had a chance of being improved through further training. The bad news was that it might be impossible to publish a paper on Tito because the initial results could not be reproduced. As Tito improved, the original data Yoram collected became invalidated. Shit.

Back in the waiting room, I found Soma reading aloud to Tito from Damasio's book *The Feeling of What Happens,* which I had given to Tito. When Tito saw me he began writing at once.

"What did the Israeli think? I could sense disbelief."

Tito was worried that Yoram didn't believe he was answering the test questions honestly, and thought Yoram and I were talking about him out in the hall, Soma explained.

"How about if you talk to Yoram yourself when he gets back?" I said.

"Why should I?" Tito shot back.

"To find out what he's thinking," I stated simply.

But when Yoram returned, Tito did not confront him, or perhaps it was Soma who preferred not to initiate such an exchange. Soon, Tal Kenet joined us; she was a pretty girl with oval glasses and long wavy hair reminiscent of the '60s, whom Merzenich had described as his "brilliant new postdoc." There was more cognitive testing planned before the John Houde interview. With Tal helping out, the testing room would be crowded. Did I mind waiting outside? They didn't really need me this time. I hesitated for a moment, and then agreed.

I watched as Yoram and Tal led Soma and Tito down the hall, and the four of them disappeared around a corner. Everything would be fine, I told myself as I curled up on the little red love seat and sipped a cold cup of coffee, unfolding the *San Francisco Chronicle.*

Not more than fifteen minutes had passed when Tal appeared in the doorway, looking tense. "I think you should come. Soma is upset." I followed Tal down the hall to the room where they were testing Tito.

It was as if I had walked into the scene of a crime. Looking very small, Soma sat on the other side of an enormous teak conference table, her face was dark and tense, the energetic light gone from her eyes. I hadn't noticed until now that she was wearing an uncharacteristic gray sari. Tito stood nearby, flapping and rocking like crazy, his eyes bugged out and his cheeks filled with air, holding his lips in a shape used for playing the tuba.

What had happened in the short time that I had let them out of my sight? The examiner, Raj, a tall, thin Indian student with long delicate fingers and kind eyes, looked guilty and sad. Yoram and Tal would not meet my eyes.

"We read him a story with Soma out of the room," Raj explained quietly, avoiding my glance.

"He couldn't answer a single question about it," Yoram mumbled, trying to sound sensitive but only succeeding in making his thick Israeli accent even stronger.

Soma stared downward, clenching her jaw. She had made it a point to protect Tito from this sort of inquisition. She had taken a risk; she had trusted these scientists to do whatever testing they thought would be useful. Now they had put her son on trial and the verdict was guilty. Guilty of being retarded. In which case Soma must be guilty too, of deception, of lying, of cheating—guilty of using her poor retarded son as a puppet.

Everyone felt terrible—Yoram, Tal, Raj. They were profoundly embarrassed to have exposed such a terrible lie. And even worse—as scientists—to have been fooled by it. For what else could it mean if when his mother left the room during the reading, Tito could not report one single fact or idea from the story that was read to him—not to anyone, not even to his mother?

I felt terrible too, but for another reason. I had let Soma and Tito down. I had promised this would never happen. I had promised to protect them from being put on trial, from being humiliated and shamed.

I was also furious. Whose idea was this anyway?

When I asked Raj what happened, he said Tito could not tell them what the story was about at all, even when Soma prompted him. And when they gave Tito hints by asking specific questions like "What color were the cat's pajamas?" Tito would give answers that were technically correct but not specific, like, "A color of the rainbow." Soma made excuses for Tito, suggesting that he was being a contrary teenager, playing a game with them. But I didn't buy it. I had never seen Tito exhibit any behavior even remotely like that. In fact, I didn't think Tito was capable of purposely manipulating people.

I decided to see if I could get Tito to answer anything at all about the story. What kind of story was it? What category did it fall under? Was it a newspaper article, a poem, a short story? Tito could not answer. I stepped out into the hall with Tito and Soma and quietly explained that if Tito was kidding around and really knew the answers, he should say so because this was very important. I asked Tito if he understood, and he said yes. But still, he could answer nothing.

I recalled when we were at Courchesne's lab and I'd watched in fascination as Bill Hirstein and Tito carried on a lengthy conversation about philosophy. I remembered noticing how Soma was sitting across the room. Soma would urge Tito on, with abrupt verbal prompts and sweeping gestures. But there was no way she could have signaled Tito to produce the kind of complex, unpredictable, naturalistic conversation he had with Bill Hirstein that day. So why couldn't Tito answer a single question about a simple story that had been read to him now? It didn't make sense.

Raj slipped out and the rest of us returned to the waiting room. Nobody was saying much. Yoram hung nearby, looking despondent. Tal sat in a metal folding chair and spun a strand of her long hair around her finger. I looked over at Soma and Tito. Would it always come to this—whether Tito was for real or not?

Soma looked betrayed as she slumped against Tito, who was stimming his brains out. I imagined they wished they were back in India.

My own depressed mood soon gave way to feeling impatient and irritated as I reran the events of the day through my mind. I was getting mad. If Tito couldn't tell us about a story that was read to him, why stop there? What *could* he tell us? How far would it go? Could he answer questions about a paragraph? A sentence? A single word? We were going to find out, I decided. We were going to do some more investigation, right there in the waiting room. What exactly could Tito remember and what couldn't he remember?

Soma and Tito agreed to my idea and Yoram and Tal said they would help. Yoram had a watch with a second hand, which was all we needed besides pen and paper. I asked Soma to leave the room. I read a single sentence from a magazine to Tito and asked him if he had heard me and whether he understood it. He nodded and made a sound that approximated the word yes. I signaled Yoram to start clocking the time. After three minutes had passed, Tal signaled Soma to return.

Soma sat down next to Tito and asked him what the sentence was about. Tito's only reply was to start rocking, bug out his eyes, and flap his hands.

We tried shorter and shorter attempts, until finally we were down to one lousy word: *hat*. Tito acknowledged he had heard the word and that he understood it. He even wrote the word down. We whisked away the legal pad, so Tito wouldn't see the word. We were down to one minute now. Still, when Soma returned, Tito could not tell her that the word was *hat*. But he could tell us something else. Curiously, he wrote down a long list of other words: cowboy, ears, wind, cerebrum, head—words that were related to hat. But not the word *hat*. This was one of the oddest things I have ever witnessed. Tito clearly knew what we were asking him for and somewhere inside his own mind he knew the word was *hat*—how else could he spontaneously produce a string of associated words? And yet he could not produce the word *hat* itself.

In the end, Soma stayed in the room and we let Tito keep the paper pad in his lap. "The word is ocean," I said. "You got it?" Tito nodded and said yes. Then he wrote the word on the legal pad in his lap.

Yoram checked the stopwatch; this time we were giving him only fifteen seconds.

"Okay, Tito. What was the word?" I asked.

We watched in amazement as Tito began to write directly below where he had scrawled the word *"ocean,"* which he had written only seconds earlier. He wrote the following words: *sea, fish, blue, wave, water, surf, swim. . . .*

"Tito," I said at last, "you wrote the word at the top of the page." Still his eyes stared off into space. I knew he understood me, yet somehow my words did not trigger any kind of visual search in Tito or cause him to look at the paper and read the word he had written seconds earlier. Finally, I tapped on the word *ocean* he had written. "Here, look here, Tito. You wrote it here." The tapping sound reflexively drew his visual attention to the location where he had written the word and he instantly saw it. Excitedly, Tito simultaneously said the word "ocean" aloud and wrote it down. What kind of mind was this? What kind of unimaginably deep absence of visual attention was this?

"Go ahead," I said to Soma, handing her the pad of paper.

"C'mon!" Soma alerted Tito. "The word is *box*," she told him as we watched. "Say it!" Soma commanded.

"*Box*," Tito said aloud.

"Now write it!" Soma instructed, tapping on the pad of paper. Tito dutifully wrote *"box."*

"You got it?" she demanded, throwing a glance my way to be sure I knew she was making fun of the way I had previously questioned Tito.

"*Yes*," Tito said.

Soma began to pace back and forth as if waiting for a soup to cook. Yoram raised his finger to signal that a minute had passed and Soma stopped in front of Tito.

"What was it?" she demanded.

"*Box*," Tito confirmed, writing the word without hesitation.

Soma's eyes narrowed and then she crossed her arms and stood there.

"Hello," Francesca Pei's lyrical Italian voice broke the intensity of the moment.

"What's going on?" she asked, looking around.

"Maybe the gentleman is thinking that I am fooling," Tito wrote.

Francesca looked puzzled.

"I performed badly today," Tito continued.

Francesca looked at Yoram inquisitively. But Yoram was deep in thought, turning his wedding band round and round on his finger, his brow furrowed in a pained expression. At last he spoke.

"I believe you, Tito," he said, his blue eyes now riveted on Tito.

There was another uncomfortable silence.

Then Tito began writing. Yoram looked at the pad in Tito's lap and read the words aloud.

" 'What do you think of Gaza?' "

Yoram looked up, confused. Then suddenly he got it: Tito was trying to make small talk. Yoram cracked the biggest smile I've ever seen. "I can come to lunch and talk about the Gaza," Yoram said effusively. "Would you like that?"

"Yes," Tito replied.

Yoram took Tito's arm and we followed behind them with a sigh of relief as we headed out for lunch. This time it would be Tito's choice, which was McDonald's, of course. And we would try to talk about anything but autism for a change.

When we returned after lunch, John Houde was waiting for us. He wore wire-rimmed glasses and a black goatee that gave him a distinguished, scholarly look beyond his years, which, like his academic accomplishments, belied his young age. In a seminal paper entitled "Sensorimotor Adaptation in Speech Production" published in *Science* (1998), Houde demonstrated that what we hear has a direct and powerful effect on how we speak. In his innovative experiment, Houde used an auditory feedback loop, in which certain vowel sounds were altered, to train subjects. It turned out that with only brief training, the altered feedback dramatically changed the way subjects spoke the sounds they heard. Not only did it change the way they spoke specific words, but remarkably, the effect generalized to other words containing the vowels which had been altered. I was impressed that Mike had assigned John Houde to study Tito's speech production and Tito's perception of his own speech. In fact, I could not imagine anyone better.

And yet, I was more nervous about these tests than any other. What could a person who cannot talk want more in this world than to find his voice?

Tito had never given up on talking. He continued to try to make the right sounds, to form words and sentences, every single day of his life, in spite of the fact that all his attempts failed. People who knew Tito could only understand his spoken language to a limited degree and even Soma often had to make Tito spell out his spoken words so that she could understand him. What made him keep trying? Was it because his scrawled handwriting and even his pointing and typing required such enormous effort? Or was it because writing and typing imposed such a different timing that they were simply not a satisfactory substitute for human conversation? Whatever it was, this testing would be the most emotionally sensitive for Tito—because he had the most to lose, namely his hope of ever being able to speak.

John Houde pulled up a chair and started his interview with Tito. The testing of Tito's voice would take place the next day.

"What do you hear when you are speaking, Tito?" he started out.

"*I don't pay attention to my own speech,*" Tito answered

"So do you know when you are speaking?" John asked.

"*I know it,*" Tito replied.

"Is it possible to pay attention to your own voice, even for a couple of minutes?" John wanted to know.

"*I will try,*" Tito promised.

"Can you tell if you are talking too loud or too soft?" John continued.

"Mr. John, I think I cannot," Tito responded. "*It happens to get different pitches at different times.*"

Tito told me before that his voice got louder sometimes and softer other times and that it wasn't under his control.

John took down a few notes and thought for a moment. "I can see he can phonate continuously," he said, turning to Soma. He meant that Tito could physically produce a series of tiny sound bits called phonemes to produce words and sentences, even though they were not very intelligible.

"*You are the first person who is appreciating my speech,*" Tito wrote.

"I can see he can imitate," John told Soma.

I knew what John was thinking—or at least suspected it—that if Tito could produce a series of sounds and if he could imitate, he could learn to speak.

"Tito, when you start to speak—do you then hear your own voice and it makes you stop speaking?" John asked.

"*I am not sure,*" Tito admitted.

"Is it easier to repeat after someone else has said the word?" John asked.

"*Imitation is less concentration,*" Tito responded.

John decided to give Tito's vocal imitation skills a try. "So say 'truthfully,'" he requested.

Tito repeated the word, but his enunciation was extremely poor and it sounded more like three similar guttural sounds instead of the three syllables of the word.

John wondered aloud, "What if I show you a word on paper?" He scribbled down the word *truthfully* and showed it to Tito.

Tito read it aloud. It was a little better, but he still spoke poorly. "*I need a prompt to start my next word,*" Tito explained.

"Say 'hopefully,'" John requested.

Tito repeated the word.

"Let's try it slower this time," John suggested.

Tito tried again, and John commented to Soma, "He does better reading out loud than when he speaks without reading."

"I am concentrating on the next word and so my own voice gets closed to my hearing," Tito explained.

"So you start to say word one but then you start to think about word two and word one is gone?" John clarified.

"Exactly," wrote Tito.

"So you don't know that you have finished word one?" John asked.

"I don't bother," Tito replied again.

"Why don't you bother?" I asked.

Suddenly Tito grabbed the pen out of Soma's hand. Soma tried to pry the pen away from him, but Tito wouldn't let go. He started marking his hand with the pen, as fast as he could.

"No!" Soma yelled.

Then Tito replied loudly, and verbally, *"Yes!"*

Soma glared at Tito and then decided to ignore him. Instead, she began to tell John Houde the story of how she first got Tito to speak.

I already knew the story; Tito had written about it in his "Memories and Beyond . . ." document.

I had no idea where my voice was hiding. Was it there somewhere in my stomach? Or was it there in my mouth? I had cried and surely I had cried loudly not even aware that I was listening to my own voice.

Mother wanted to help me because my volume was increasing with time and surely I could not stop easily. She brought my communication board in front of me and asked me to point and tell what was wrong. I told her that perhaps I was crying because I did not find my voice.

I remember that mother had pushed me suddenly without even giving me any warning from behind. It was so sudden and so unexpected that an 'uh' sound came out of me.

'That was your voice,' mother said.
'Now I shall push the voice out of you.' She pushed and I did the 'uh' sound again and again slowly doing it voluntarily with every push.

She kept a glass of water and told me to ask for it with my voice.

Then she started giving the pushes on my back once again, while I said, 'uh wah tah dah kah wah tah.'

I heard my voice say 'I want to drink water.' I continued my speech while mother continued the pushes.

I was not impressed with what my ears heard as my speech and with mother pushing my back to push out the speech out of my mouth.

'Are my lips moving like theirs?' I was constantly worried.

Somehow my speech or rather using my voice kept going with me in my therapy sessions and at home. My speech therapist, Mr Kant would give me a list of words to read. Words looking like bitter tablets. Bitter tablets waiting to get their completeness in my voice. And since everyone around me became so appreciative, at my producing those sounds, and when Mr Kant was rewarding me generously with a piece of chocolate every time for saying those words, I had no other go but keep my voice busy by reading those words out. As if I did a big favour by saying those words aloud.

That was the beginning of my speech.
 —From the "Memories and Beyond . . ." document

. . .

On the third day of testing, we met in the hotel tearoom for breakfast once again. Tito was ready to start communicating right away.
He had been doing a lot of thinking about the previous day, Soma
told me.

"I thought about it last night," Tito wrote, "that it is very difficult to
change the view of the scientists. Yesterday I heard one of them telling
about 'concentrating disorder.' It was the view which I totally disagree and
he said that he is in the process of discovery."

What was Tito talking about, I wondered to myself. "Discovery of
what?" I asked him.

"The small concentration disorder," Tito explained.

"In autism?" I questioned.

"In autistic disorder," Tito confirmed.

"And who was talking about it?" I asked, still trying to get at what
Tito meant.

"The speech person," Tito clarified.

I now realized that Tito was referring to something he'd heard
John Houde say the previous day. Houde had speculated about
whether autism might be an extreme version of Attention Deficit
Disorder, perhaps because Tito reported that he couldn't pay attention to the sound of his own voice.

"You mean John Houde?" I said. " He was just thinking aloud."

Tito appeared agitated, rocking and making clicking sounds.

"Tito, are you worried about that?" I asked.

"I am, because I know that he is going by the overt behavior," Tito
replied.

I knew that Tito meant he was worried that John would judge
him by his behavior instead of by his ability to think, as had happened so many times before. This was also what he meant when he
had said, "it is very difficult to change the view of the scientists,"
when I first sat down. And I agreed with Tito. If scientists only mea-

sured his "overt behavior," there was no point, because they would just arrive at the same wrong conclusion again.

"I think John Houde was just comparing autism to other disorders he knows about, like Attention Deficit Disorder," I explained, trying to allay Tito's rising anxiety.

"The trouble is that everybody tries to become psychologist," Tito replied.

"Tito, you just described the biggest problem in the history of autism! Thank God you are here to help change that!" I truly was grateful.

But now Tito was rocking and flapping wildly in his seat, his eyes bugging out like he was going to explode.

"Soma, ask him what's going on," I said.

Gulping down the rest of her tea, Soma patiently returned to Tito's side with paper and pen. Tito stopped rocking long enough to write another sentence. *"I concentrate best in the morning. I had trouble pointing at the word 'both' and that made a sort of disbelief."*

"Who disbelieved you?" I asked, suspecting Tito was referring to the testing from the day before.

Then I saw that Tito had started to pull the pen apart—cap, barrel, spring, ink—it was disassembled in a flash, and now the greasy black ink, the disastrous kind that leaks from cheap ball point pens, was getting everywhere, on his hands, the tablecloth, his shirt. Soma tried to grab the pen from Tito, but he held on to it with all his might, and a small scuffle between mother and son ensued while the gaggle of croissant-munching hotel guests looked on. Soma managed to wrest the pen and its parts from Tito's inky grip and we all sat down again. Then Soma wiped Tito's hands with the white cloth napkin, admonishing him all the while, as the Chinese gentleman looked on in dismay.

Tito had told me to ignore his behavior, yet at least in this instance it seemed related to what was going on in his mind. He was angry and disenchanted with the scientists, especially Yoram and John Houde. Tito felt he was being misjudged, and he was afraid of being labeled retarded again. I couldn't blame him.

"Who disbelieved you?" I repeated.

"The Israeli gentleman is not believing me," Tito replied.

"What's not to believe?" I asked him. I thought Yoram and Tito made up, but apparently Tito was still feeling defensive.

"I am a big observer of people and I realize that he thought that I am making up according to choice and so he thinks that I am outsmarting him, when if I want to I can, but I will not, because Portia, you trust me."

Tito thought Yoram didn't believe that he was responding to the tests to the best of his ability.

"I'm glad you know that I trust you," I reassured Tito. "And I appreciate that, because it is really important to test your perception," I said. "Your perception is different but that doesn't mean you're not intelligent. If we can understand more about your perception, maybe it can help other people with autism who have the same problem and who are intelligent too. That's what we are trying to do. Does that make sense?"

Tito responded, *"That does not mean that you have to become a lawyer for him. I will not misbehave. You can count on that. I will cooperate and try to forget it."*

Inside, I was chuckling, though I kept a very solemn expression on my face since I knew that Tito was serious. He was saying that I didn't need to defend Yoram so much and that he would try not to hold a grudge. "Thank you, Tito. I really appreciate it," I said.

"That's my 'Merchant of Venice' background coming through," he added.

Just in case I hadn't noticed his fine intellect, impressive education, and wry sense of humor coming through, or worse yet, if I hadn't even made the connection at all from his remark about my not needing to be a lawyer for Yoram, Tito was reminding me now. It was a double entendre: he was alluding to the fact that my name, Portia, was also the name of the lady lawyer in Shakespeare's play *The Merchant of Venice*. Truthfully, I hadn't made the connection until he pointed it out.

When we arrived at the lab, I took Yoram and John Houde aside and explained Tito's concerns. How he felt they were drawing conclusions based on his overt behavior and not his mind, and how Tito still felt Yoram did not believe him. Yoram seemed shocked. Yoram resolved to be more careful about what he said around Tito. John Houde was amazed when I told him Tito was upset by his speculation that there could be an element of Attention Deficit Disorder involved in autism, and Tito thought he was wrong about that. "He heard that?" John asked with obvious surprise.

Perhaps Tito was more correct in his assumptions than I'd given him credit for. I thought John Houde realized that Tito heard and understood everything that was going on around him. Yet I knew it was hard for people to keep reminding themselves that regardless of his overt behavior, Tito had a fully present mind. Perhaps if a person acted as oblivious to others as Tito did, it was counterintuitive to think that they were aware of the reactions of others. For if they truly were aware of what others said and did, why would they behave in such a socially unacceptable manner? And yet Tito *was* aware.

"Yes, he did understand," I replied to John Houde.

John looked perplexed and embarrassed.

"Well, that's good!" he finally said.

I knew from talking to John Houde that he was a compassionate person and I knew his remark was sincere. He literally meant that if Tito was that amazingly and unexpectedly aware and mentally intact, it was a very good thing.

Into the lab buzzed Al, the resident tinker, inventor, and, literally,

TV-repairman-turned-brain-repairman. He looked every bit the egghead inventor I'd been hearing about, with thick glasses and a noggin big enough to hold two brains. They told me he was a genius at jerry-rigging together the little devices and gizmos that researchers needed to try out their ideas. John Houde needed a device that could increase the volume of Tito's speech feedback in a very controlled way. He also wanted to introduce a variable delay in the feedback of Tito's voice and to control and manipulate the frequency of the sound of his voice, to see if any or all of these alterations might help Tito hear himself speaking.

If Tito *could* hear himself speaking, he might be able to learn to speak, John Houde postulated.

"Sorry, I had to wait till Radio Shack opened," Al said, producing a small device from his shirt pocket that looked like a transistor radio. Al had altered the device minutes earlier to do all the things John Houde requested. Houde thanked him and, after fiddling with the settings, he connected the device to a large pair of headphones.

Once again we all crammed into the tiny testing room. John Houde handed the headphones to Soma and asked if she would try to get Tito to wear them. And though Tito would wear headphones for hours on end while listening to reggae music, Tito hated wearing headphones for testing. After Tito's bad reaction to them on the first day, Yoram had tried to avoid using headphones, but today there was no choice. When Soma tried to put them on Tito, he rebelled. I managed to catch his eye and shot him a look that said *"You promised!"* And although he never looked right at me, I saw that he was smiling and I could have sworn he took some delight in our secret moment. After that, Tito wore the headphones without any fuss.

John Houde adjusted the earpieces over Tito's ears.

"Is that okay?" he inquired.

"It is fine," Tito answered verbally.

"Could he hear himself?" I asked Houde excitedly.

"It's not turned on yet," John Houde said patiently. "Is that okay?" he asked again.

"*It is okay,*" Tito replied.

First he would be getting some baseline data, John explained. What would simply wearing headphones and getting Tito's own voice piped back through them do? John wanted to know.

Soma suggested that Tito read something; it would be easier for him to talk that way, she explained, pulling out a copy of *Alice in Wonderland* from her tote bag. She held the book out in front of Tito and prompted him to read aloud by tapping along each sentence while making a little guttural sound to prompt each word. As Tito read aloud, his voice became progressively louder and faster, as if he could not hear himself. He began flipping his collar rapidly between his fingers and then alternated between sniffing his fingers and his collar as he kept reading. Then his pace slowed down and his volume diminished and he stopped reading. He yanked the headphones off and stood up.

John took the headphones from him. "That was good, Tito. Excellent."

"*I was paying attention to the next word . . .*" Tito broke off in midsentence and stared into space, frozen, his pen suspended in midair. "C'mon!" Soma commanded, tapping on his hand. Tito resumed writing and completed the sentence he had started. " *. . . and not my speech.*"

John wrote this down. "That's good to know. It's good to know those things."

John began adjusting the gizmo Al had created; he told us he was going to introduce a slight delay in the auditory feedback, a delay of 23 milliseconds. He placed the unit in Tito's shirt pocket and connected it to the headphones. Again Tito read from *Alice in Wonderland* and again his voice sped up and grew louder. Suddenly, Tito's voice changed, shifting into a lower register. It sounded as if he were possessed. He tore off the headphones once more.

"Can you hear yourself?" John asked again.

"*I think I cannot,*" Tito replied.

John Houde adjusted the device once more; this time he was altering the frequency feedback,[23] he said, which was expanding the range of sound.

Soma put the headphones back on Tito.

Once again, John trained his eyes intensely on Tito. "Okay, let's try this."

"*I want to drink water,*" Tito stated.

Seeing our perplexed looks, Soma explained, "That's his test question."

It took me a minute to realize what Soma meant. I couldn't believe it. That was the sentence Soma had given Tito when he was six years old and she had pushed his voice out of him and called his attention to it. Tito was using the first sentence he had ever spoken.

"Could you hear that?" John quickly asked.

"*Yes,*" Tito said.

John's eyebrows shot up.

"*But I could not hear you,*" Tito said, adding, "*It won't support communication.*"

"So you could hear your voice, but it sounded strange?" John asked.

"*Yes,*" Tito answered.

"The change in frequency produces a weird, high-pitched sound. It's not as useful as feedback for learning to speak . . . but it shows we *can* get Tito to hear his own voice."

John Houde sounded excited. "Now if we can just do that again, but keep his voice in a normal frequency range. . . ." He was wracking his brain. "Let's try setting the frequency back to normal. We'll keep the 23-millisecond delay." He fiddled with the device. "And we'll crank the volume up twice as high. Maybe that will do it." Soma nervously glanced at me. I nodded that it was okay.

Soma put the headphones back on Tito and prompted him to

start reading. Tito's voice became lower and lower as he slowed down his pace. Tito ripped the headphones off and looked around wide-eyed.

"What is it?" John Houde asked Tito.

Tito grabbed the pad of paper, something I had seen him do only once before, and started to write.

"*I do talk badly,*" he wrote, eyes still wide.

"How do you know that?" I blurted out.

"*I heard me,*" Tito replied.

I stared for a moment at Tito and then I looked over at John Houde. He was smiling.

"Differently than usual?" I continued. "Did you hear yourself more than usual that time?"

"*Yes, I feel ashamed,*" Tito answered.

"Why?" I asked, confounded.

"Tito, did you hear yourself speak?" John Houde asked Tito, wanting to confirm.

"*Yes,*" Tito said.

"What did you hear?" I asked.

"*I heard the echo,*" he told us.

"Did you hear something different than what you usually hear with the headphones?" I asked, insistently.

"*Certainly. I heard myself. I don't hear it otherwise,*" Tito confirmed.

"So without the headphones, you don't hear it?" John asked.

"*I don't take the trouble of hearing it because mother speaks it out,*" Tito replied.

"Tito, were you paying more attention to your voice, or did the headphones help you hear yourself?" I wanted to know.

"*It assisted me,*" Tito confirmed.

John Houde and I talked over each other as we tried to explain to Tito the incredible significance of being able to hear his own voice and how it not only could allow him to control the way he spoke but how it was essential to being able to speak at all.

John Houde wanted to repeat the last trial immediately with the same settings—the slight delay of 23 milliseconds and the volume at twice normal—to see if he would get the same results. We all wanted to know whether Tito would hear his own voice again or not—whether such a simple adjustment had really worked, as it seemed to have.

Tito was rocking in a standing position which looked like repeated bowing, while he flicked a pencil in front of his eyes. But he was also smiling, and even though his eyes were riveted on the flickering pencil, I thought he looked happy.

Headphones in place once again, Tito was ready to start.

"Go ahead, Tito, you can start reading," John instructed him.

Soma held up the book and got him going and Tito read aloud, excitedly. He was smiling a lot. Then he stopped.

I turned to John. "Was that enough reading?" I asked him.

"Yes. I want to know if he had the same experience or not," he said, looking at Tito.

"*Same*," Tito stated.

"Great!" John exclaimed, beaming.

But Tito wasn't finished answering. "*I think I should stop talking,*" he continued.

"What do you mean?" I asked, confused.

"*I talk badly,*" Tito said.

"But you talk very well for all the difficulties you've had!" John quickly countered.

"And you will get much better," I said, trying to be encouraging. "I love to hear your voice," I added, my own voice quavering.

"Me too," John chimed in. He sounded quite emotional.

"Don't you love to hear his voice too, Soma?" I asked her, hoping she would encourage Tito too.

Soma looked very serious, but I could see she was blinking back tears.

"Yes," she said simply.

"The fact that you can hear your own voice and know it sounds different than normal shows it can improve just by that. It's not something to be ashamed of or feel bad about. It's just . . . it's just neurology!" I finished, not having found the right word.

But Tito seemed to be getting more and more upset. He jumped up and started pacing. Then he started pulling off the tape that had been used to repair the plastic upholstery of his chair. Then he ran out to the waiting room and came back again. He stood there a moment.

"I heard that I speak very badly and I know it," he said, rocking furiously.

"Were you surprised?" I asked him.

"Yes," he replied. Then he went tearing off down the hall.

Soma and I followed close behind. When Tito was a little calmer, we sat on the little red leather love seat together and I tried to talk some more.

"I feel so different," Tito wrote.

He started to jump up again, but Soma pushed him back into his seat.

"I found that I talk so badly," Tito continued.

"Could you tell that you got better?" John asked him.

"No. I am not at your level." I knew Tito meant that he could not speak as well as the rest of us.

John put his hand on Tito's shoulder. "Tito, I study speech and my professional opinion is that you got better." Always the scientist at heart, John couldn't help but add, "I was also wondering if you could hear it—that you got better?"

"I may," Tito admitted reluctantly.

This made John Houde light up again. "Okay, you pick the next word, Tito!" he offered.

"What can be dearer than your name?" he wrote, vaguely turning toward me.

"Are you trying to embarrass me?" I asked. Now I was smiling too.

"*Yes.*"

"Try saying it," John instructed Tito.

"*Portia,*" Tito said, using his voice.

Yes, it was definitely more understandable!

"Could you hear the change?" I asked Tito, trying to contain my excitement.

"*I think that every word on the dictionary has to be dealt with for ten years.*"

Tito was overwhelmed by the enormity of the task at hand. He thought he would have to learn to say every word in the English language, one by one.

John jumped in, saying, "There are only forty different sounds you need for the English language, Tito. Once you get them you can say any words!"

Tito did not reply.

"You spoke and I could understand!" John said emphatically, trying to get through to Tito.

"*Does it matter?*" Tito responded.

"You don't have to take my word for it—you could hear it yourself," John said.

"*Will you stop calling me autistic?*" Tito asked.

I knew Tito was asking the profound question that was in the back of everyone's mind: if he could talk, would he still be autistic?

John thought for a moment. "Hard to tell—but being able to speak would make a big difference," he said honestly.

Again there was silence.

"I feel like you are a bottle of thoughts and ideas. Being able to speak, you could let your thoughts out easier," John said, struggling to express his own thoughts.

"*I think the neck should be broken,*" Tito stated.

"Break the bottleneck?" I asked, suspecting Tito's meaning.

"*Yes,*" he concurred.

I was right. It was a triple entendre. To break the neck was a metaphor. It meant to break the bottleneck, the bottle being the bottle of thoughts and ideas John Houde was alluding to, and the expression *bottleneck* being both literally and figuratively—that which was stopping the flow of information from getting out—and possibly the physical neck, which was the origin of the voice itself. At least that's what I thought Tito meant. Tito had an extraordinary ability to condense an amazing number of meanings into his words.

Wanting to encourage Tito, John continued. "You have normal sentences. You would not be called autistic if you could speak," he ventured.

"I need this flapping thing."

Yes, even if Tito could speak, his autistic behaviors would still be there. But maybe his stimming would decrease if he could talk. If Tito could talk, he could stay in contact with people in real time from moment to moment, and that certainly should have a calming, modulating effect on his arousal and his attention, perhaps even on his perceptual organization and his sensory processing. "Tito, you told me yourself that reading and writing help you get organized, didn't you?" I lobbied.

"Certainly," Tito agreed.

"Then talking should help you get even more organized," I argued.

"That may be a distant possibility," Tito conceded.

I looked up and saw that Mike Merzenich had been standing just outside the door, listening. For how long, I did not know.

Mike Merzenich looked exactly as I remembered him from when we first met at the Innovative Technology for Autism conference nearly a year ago. In fact, he appeared entirely unchanged; his glasses were still slipping down his nose, his shirttail was still half tucked in, and he still had that warm, charming grin. "Hello, Tito. I am Dr. Merzenich," he said, entering and shaking Tito's hand.

"Pleasure to meet you," Tito responded politely.

Mike turned and shook hands with Soma, thanking her for coming to his lab. Then, turning to Tito, he asked: "Tito, when you talk, can you feel yourself talking—can you feel it in your neck, can you hear it?"

"*I know I am talking, but I do not bother how,*" Tito explained, re-iterating that he did not attend to his own voice whether it be the feeling or the sound.

Mike continued, "Tito, when you say a word—what's in your mind? Are you thinking of a letter or a meaning, a word, sounds?"

Without hesitation, Tito once again explained, "*I am thinking of the next word.*"

Mike pressed on, "Do you sometimes think of the meanings of more than one word—like a sentence?" he asked.

"*The next possible word that will go with the one I thought before,*" Tito explained.

"Is it the same with writing as when you speak? Are you thinking of letters, sounds, or the next word?"

"*I think of the next word,*" Tito repeated.

"When you were hearing yourself on the headphones could you think of the next word?"

What an interesting question: if Tito could hear himself, did it interfere with his ability to think and use language?

"*I sort of got stuck,*" Tito said.

Mike was right.

"*So disgusting,*" Tito said, judging himself harshly.

"Tito, it's not disgusting at all—you just aren't used to it," I said, trying to convince him.

Mike stood up. "Tito, you are a fine young man," he said, shaking Tito's hand vigorously.

Mike announced that we were all invited to his house for dinner that night. His poor wife, I thought.

I knew it would be too late for Tito. And if Tito couldn't come to the dinner, that meant Soma couldn't either. I wished they could stay in the United States longer. If they did, I would find an aide, a one-on-one companion for Tito to buy Soma some freedom.

By the time I got Soma and Tito back to our hotel, it was teatime. The Chinese gentleman greeted us with a cold look and soon we were comfortably settled in with our tea and pastries. Soma told me that in the two months they'd been in the U.S., Tito had been exposed to more people than during his entire life in India. Tito's communication had changed radically, I realized. The language Tito used when I first met him was dense and cryptic and he often rhymed his words. But now Tito's sentences were becoming more natural and conversational. He was starting to bring up his own ideas, instead of just answering questions. *"What do you think of Gaza?"* I loved it.

That evening, my cab dropped me off at the top of the street where Mike Merzenich's house was located. The street itself was so short and steep that the cabdriver declined to enter the cul-de-sac.

Mike's wife, Diane, was pretty and energetic with a short brown bob and a friendly face that had a perpetually amused look on it, which I suspected Mike was partially responsible for. She appeared to be in a good mood despite the fact that her husband had sprung a dozen dinner guests on her just a few hours earlier. By the time we sat down, I also knew that she was a fantastic cook. Something told me this wasn't the first time Diane had to pull off one of these impromptu dinners. How *did* these men get these fantastic wives I wondered?

That night, I found myself surrounded by some of the best and brightest scientific minds in the world and they were all talking about autism and I felt that I had arrived somewhere. Something good was starting to happen.

13.

Dreaming
in Sound

Back in Los Angeles, we had a very dull, boring, and yet necessary job to do: We had to prove to the scientific establishment once and for all that Tito was autistic. It was a hot sunny day as Dr. Sarah Spence trudged up the cement stairs to Soma and Tito's apartment carrying a large briefcase full of paperwork including the two gold-standard autism diagnostic tests: the Autism Diagnostic Interview (ADI)[24] and the Autism Diagnostic Observation Schedule (ADOS).[25] After the thrill of San Francisco, this was the last thing on earth any of us wanted to do. And yet I knew we had to do it. If the things we discovered about Tito at Merzenich's lab were ever going to amount to anything, we had to make sure there was no question about whether or not Tito really was autistic.

Sarah Spence was a child neurologist at UCLA who also worked with CAN's Autism Genetic Resource Exchange gene bank visiting hundreds of multiplex families in their homes. She was tall and thin and probably prettier than any doctor Tito had ever seen. Instead of a white coat and balding pate, Dr. Spence wore a long flowered skirt and kept her sandy, shoulder-length hair tucked neatly behind her ears. She had a formal, businesslike manner about her, but she spoke to Tito with a gentle kindness and respect.

The ADOS was designed to assess, among other things, social behavior and language, perhaps the two biggest perceived deficits in autism. There was no question that Tito was impaired in the social and communication domains. But there was a problem when it came to assessing Tito's language—the ADOS test was not designed for someone who could not speak and yet had language.

Sarah Spence explained the tests to Tito and they began.

Did Tito have any friends, Sarah asked.

"I am autistic so how can you expect me to gather friends?"

Tito had changed since we were at Courchesne's lab only a few weeks ago when this very question about friends had hurt his feelings. Now he was matter-of-fact about it. Next Sarah asked Tito why being autistic kept him from having friends.

"You know I cannot initiate," he replied. I sensed that Tito was growing impatient. I couldn't blame him.

"Do you want to have friends?" Sarah inquired.

"I do but I have to accept it because that is the law of the universe."

After several more questions along this line, Tito seemed to be getting exasperated and he tried to make a point about his talents instead of his deficits.

"But do you think that I could write better with a gregarious attitude?" he asked Dr. Spence.

Sarah took Tito's cue and segued briefly to other subjects such as how Tito asked for things and where he went to school. Then she asked him if he had a girlfriend.

The fact that Tito could not possibly have a girlfriend made his answer all the more heartbreaking.

"Be realistic," Tito said. *"I don't expect that to happen. More or less I don't like those giggling girls. I like older women and all of them are married."*

"Would you like to have friends?" she persisted.

"*Why should I answer something which I have not experienced?*"

I could see that Tito was getting fed up with this line of questioning and then he did something I had never seen him do before: He was blatantly sarcastic.

"*Okay I can tell caring got, and bla, bla, bla,*" he wrote.

I knew what he meant. "*I can tell caring got*" meant "I can say I care," if Dr. Spence insisted.

The ADOS took about three hours to administer. When at last the test was over, Sarah thanked Tito and Soma for their participation and Tito disappeared into his room.

Although she had administered the ADOS to hundreds of children, Sarah Spence admitted she had never come across anyone like Tito before. It was going to be hard to score the language module of the ADOS, because Tito contradicted every assumption about autism and language that the ADOS was based upon.

She was certain, however, that Tito met the diagnostic criteria for autism on the ADOS, Sarah Spence told us as she packed up her bag to go. She said Tito was fascinating and she wondered whether there were others like him.

That, of course, was the very question that loomed in the back of my own mind.

The psychiatrists in England who diagnosed Tito as autistic at age eleven were certain that he was one in a million. But could it be that it was Soma who was one in a million? After all, she was the one who taught Tito to communicate.

Could there be other nonverbal autistic people who looked and acted just like Tito, but were without any means of communication?

Tito was autistic but he did not fit any description of autism that I'd ever read or heard about. Autistics were supposed to be visual thinkers, they were supposed to have problems with language and communication. But Tito was the opposite of a visual thinker. Tito was an "elective blind" person.

I thought back to one afternoon when Dov was almost three and I was sitting in the kitchen, thrilled to be talking on the phone with Temple Grandin.

Temple was perhaps the most famous autistic person in the world. Oliver Sacks published his book *An Anthropologist on Mars*, in 1995, which featured Temple Grandin and catapulted her into public awareness worldwide. Temple herself had published several well-received books related to the topic of autism as well as numerous books reflecting her professional career as a consultant and designer of livestock handling facilities.[26] Remarkably, Temple had earned an advanced degree in animal science and conducted a very successful career in the field. Recognized as a popular speaker on the autism lecture circuit, Temple often spoke about her experience as an autistic person.

"Autistic people are visual thinkers," Temple told me over the phone. "Always give the autistic child a visual representation," she advised. "They just can't get it from spoken words alone."

After I hung up, I sat thinking about what Temple had said as I watched Dov running around the kitchen wearing only a diaper. The therapists had already advised us to use more visuals and less language with Dov. He was not understanding language, they said, and that meant he probably never would. But pictures didn't seem to help Dov either.

Standing with his back to me, Dov reached up, pulled a dishtowel from the kitchen counter, and threw it on the floor. "Pick that up, Dov!" I said crossly, just for the hell of it, knowing that he could not see me, much less understand what I was saying. To my astonishment, without turning around, Dov picked up the towel and put it back on the counter. I couldn't believe it.

After a moment, Dov pulled the towel down, and again I asked him to pick it up, which he did, all while never turning around to look at me. It seemed as if he understood the words I spoke. How was that possible? What I had just witnessed went against everything I had been told about Dov and about autism.

Now, six years later, I was beginning to understand what I had seen that day. I realized that there was probably another type of autism, one that no one knew about because those who had it could not speak—the auditory type. From what Tito and Temple had told me, it seemed there were two major types of autism—a visual type, like Temple's and an auditory type like Tito's. Temple said that she experienced sensory overload early in life—very much like the "chaos" that Tito described. What if it were as simple as that? One type adapted by using their ears almost exclusively, the other by using their eyes.

In fact, Tito had stated this idea exactly in an earlier e-mail:

> . . . each Autistic person tends to develop one particular sense organ through which he tries to perceive the situation.

> I have developed my hearing better than my other senses. I have learnt to be comfortable that way because trying to use all the senses turns into a total chaos.

According to this hypothesis, the visual autistic child, precisely because of his preferential use of vision, would have a distinct advantage when it came to imitating motor skills and behavior, especially the ability to produce speech. But this advantage would come with a high cost: the preferential use of vision would diminish development of auditory processing with catastrophic results in language development.

The auditory autistic child, on the other hand, *would* develop language. But he would have a different price to pay for exclusively listening and not looking. Because of greatly decreased visual activity, the auditory autistic child's ability to imitate would suffer, severely diminishing his motor skills. This would impair his ability to produce voluntary actions and behavior, including spoken language. This type of child might always be perceived as cognitively low functioning, even if he was not.

But why did some children adapt by preferentially using their vision while others adapted by preferentially listening? I wasn't sure, but I had a hunch. It was already known that vision was not normal in autism.

Perhaps at the more severe end of the autism spectrum, vision was simply too overwhelming to be useful and actually got in the way of understanding the environment as Tito described. This could result in avoidance of the use of vision, or, in effect, a kind of developmental blindness. Decreased use of vision from an early age would curtail development of activity-dependent visual processing.

Perhaps at the higher-functioning end of the autism spectrum vision was overwhelming but not to the degree that it was entirely detrimental. A child with a markedly superior capacity for visual processing could come to rely on vision too much, even become captured by it and mesmerized to the exclusion of using the auditory pathway. Decreased use of audition from an early age would curtail development of activity-dependent auditory processing, resulting in a deficit in capacity for language.

Both types of neural processing adaptation would result in abnormalities in neural representation, memory encoding, and retrieval, and interfere with pathways involved in communication. To put it mildly, none of this would be good for developing social skills.

Dov was nine years old now, and I hadn't talked to Temple Grandin in a very long time. I wondered what Temple would have to say about an autistic person like Tito—or if she would even believe me if I told her that such a person existed. Tito contradicted some of Temple's most firmly held beliefs about autism, and her own experience of it.

"You're hard to get ahold of!" a cranky voice complained over the phone. It was true; we'd been exchanging phone messages for over a week.

"I've met a very unusual autistic person and I'd like to get your take on him," I began. I explained that Tito was nonverbal, appeared retarded but had a high IQ, could read and write, and had written a book of poetry. "Tito relies on his auditory system the way you rely on your visual system," I told her. Tito must not be autistic, Temple insisted. Tito was definitely autistic, I told her, adding that he had been diagnosed with autism, using the gold standard assessment tools like the ADOS. Temple didn't buy it.

How I wished Temple could meet Tito in person! But for now, I had to be content with asking Temple some questions—questions I'd never thought of asking her before. I wanted to find out how Tito's perceptual experience compared to Temple's and if there were any parallels.

Tito had trouble seeing and hearing at the same time, I told Temple. Had she ever experienced anything like that? "No," she replied without hesitation, she didn't recall ever having that problem.

What was it like when she watched a movie, I asked next. Temple said she had no problem watching movies. But there was one thing—the plot; she had trouble getting the plot. When I asked Tito about going to movies, he said he didn't see the point in paying money to sit in a dark room listening to a story.

Then I asked Temple about her dreams. She said her dreams consisted of "full-color pictures" and that they were "mainly visual." "The auditory," she said, was "not the main part." She said she "couldn't remember the audio." And that it was "hard to talk in a dream."

I had asked Tito about his dreams too.

How do I dream?
My dream is an extension of my waking system of stimulus and
my interpretation of world with those stimuli.
My most widely used sense organ system is my auditory sense.

*Like my real life experience, as I hear the world, I hear my
dream, with very few 'associated' images in it.*
*Like my waking experience, where I gaze at a mark and listen to
music or voices, my dream happens to be the same.*
*However I recognise the voices in my dream and can tell that it is
Portia's voice, and the words are not coming from the point, at
which my dreaming eyes are looking.*
Did you ever wonder how a visually impaired person dreams?
Or if a hearing impaired dreams in silence?
*Well an Autistic person dreams in whichever mode of recognising
the world he is capable of, he uses that.*

Tito dreamed in sound. Later he described seeing colors in his dreams, but never images, except once when he dreamed of a frightening fire, just before a terrible bout of mania descended upon him.

And what about faces? I asked Temple. Temple said she was "bad at faces" and that she could not talk to a person and look at their eyes at the same time.

Tito told me he recognized people by their voices. When I asked Tito about faces, he said, *"Faces are like waves, different every moment. Could you remember a particular wave you saw in the ocean?"*

And when I asked him why he didn't focus his eyes on people's faces, Tito replied: *"Why should I see and miss out your words?"*

Temple told me she learned to read in third grade, using "Look and Say, Dick and Jane books," and by sounding out words. Soma had also used a phonics approach to teach Tito to read. When Temple's mother read to her, Temple said she saw pictures in her mind, while Tito said he "couldn't get the picture."

Once Temple had learned to read, she began to convert words into pictures and eventually it became automatic. "Now I just directly convert words to pictures," she said. She wanted to show me how she did it and began reading aloud from a magazine over the phone, explaining the process as she went.

"CD (I see CDs) pirates (I see a pirate ship) beware, the music industry (I see a bunch of mucky-mucks, corporate types in suits) has a new weapon (I see a gun) up its sleeve (I see a gun up a sleeve)."

How did she get the meaning? I asked. "How do I encode?" Temple rephrased my question. "I know this is an article about people copying CDs illegally. This is what the article is about," she stated, demonstrating that she understood the meaning, but she left the question of how unanswered.

Temple was concerned about something else: "I need to find an article that doesn't have pictures," she stated, concerned that pictures could influence her. The thought hadn't crossed my mind, but she seemed intent on proving she could convert words to pictures instantly, without any pictures to help her along. Finally, she dug up an issue of *Feedstuffs*, which she described as "a boring livestock magazine." *Feedstuffs* did not have pictures, Temple told me before she began to read from it, converting words to pictures instantly, as promised.

In his book *The Mind of a Mnemonist*, the Russian psychologist Alexander Luria presents the case history of his patient Shereshevsky. Luria explores Shereshevsky's cognitive style in depth over a thirty-year period. After reading Luria's account of this patient, I was struck by the remarkable similarity between Shereshevsky's method of converting words into pictures and Temple's. "For when he heard or read a word it was at once converted into a visual image corresponding with the object the word signified for him." And "When S. read through a long series of words, each word would elicit a graphic image."

Temple had produced an incredible video for CAN in which she explains thinking in pictures. Temple explains that she has no generalized concept of things, such as the concept of "dog." Instead, she has to search through her memory files of dog pictures—every dog she had ever seen in her life. She shows us a picture of a hairless Mexican Chihuahua and asks, "How am I supposed to know *this* is a dog?" Then she shows us a picture of a cartoon dog, the character Marmaduke, and asks the same question again, this time even more confounded.

Temple talked about trying to use rules to identify "dog." For example, a dog has four paws, two ears, a tail, fur, and so on. But these sorts of rules weren't specific enough because they worked not only for dogs but for cats and a number of other animals as well, she said. The inability of a rule-based strategy to detect or assign meaning is strikingly similar to the formidable problems that have been encountered historically in efforts to develop artificial intelligence. In fact, it wasn't until I read Hubert Dreyfus's book *What Computers Still Can't Do* that I really began to gain an understanding of the cognitive style of the autistic mind.

I thought of Tito and how it seemed that he got the meaning of things by looking through other words in his mind, the same way Temple looked through pictures in her mind.

Dear Portia, one word can radiate so much. It is like a chain reaction getting bigger as it collects more and more words to it, Tito wrote to me.

Today, Temple's mind might be more aptly described as Google image search, while Tito's mind might be described as an online thesaurus.

The two types of autism, auditory and visual, was a great hypothesis, but now what? Even if the idea was correct, it did not answer the question of whether or not there was even one other person in the world like Tito.

14.

A Galaxy Is a Group of Stars

You sit down to dinner and life as you know it ends.

—Joan Didion,
The Year of Magical Thinking

The phone was ringing. It was 6:00 A.M. according to the blurry clock on my nightstand. Who could be calling this early, I wondered? Probably some East Coast parent who forgot the time difference—that happened a lot because of CAN. A voice filled with alarm startled my senses awake. "Portia, have you turned on the TV or the radio? They're bombing New York right now and they're headed for the White House!"

My sister can be a very dramatic person. She used to be an actress. But what could she possibly mean by "bombing New York"? I got up and turned on the TV as she continued talking.

I experienced a rising wave of physical anxiety as the images that blinked onto the television screen seemed to confirm her words.

Outside, everything looked as it always did. A trillion phosphorescent green leaves filled our bedroom windows and trembled in the morning breeze. My sister kept talking. No words could exaggerate the situation, or explain it.

I told the children they were staying home from school today, and no TV.

I didn't want to see it. But I couldn't tear my eyes away because without watching, my emotions began to spin out of control. By midmorning we knew that the relatively calm, peaceful chapter of recent history in which we'd been privileged to exist was over.

Worried, I phoned Soma and Tito only to find Soma calm, preparing a pot of curry and listening to Dolly Parton. Life in India had exposed her to religious and political upheavals, war, and natural disaster with a regularity I could not imagine. Why didn't I have Dov come over? Soma suggested, when I told her I'd kept the kids home from school.

The day wore on with no beginning and no end, a timeless blur of urgency without any apparent road toward resolution, a day filled with fear and sadness. The kids played around the house and Maria took Dov to Soma's apartment for a session. He had been seeing Soma once a week for about six weeks.

The house was dim and quiet when Maria and Dov arrived back from Soma's. Maria helped Dov take off his backpack and shoes and prompted him through the steps of washing his hands and then guided him toward the kitchen where we were gathered for dinner. "Portia," Maria said, smiling as she picked up her purse to leave, "you should see what Soma's doing. Today she didn't touch his arm at all and he was pointing."

Her words took a minute to register. "What do you mean?" I asked as I set down a pot of rice back on the stove.

"Dovie's really doing good," Maria replied. "You should see it."

"See what?" I inquired, following her to the front door, still clutching a pair of potholders.

"She's just pushing on his knee and he's doing it," Maria said, beaming with pride.

"Doing what?" I asked impatiently.

"Communicating!" she answered, waving over her shoulder as she closed the door behind her.

Frustrated, I watched as she crossed the lawn toward her car and drove away. I wondered exactly what Maria meant by "communicating" and I made up my mind to take Dov to Soma's the next day to find out for myself.

I woke up earlier than usual the next morning as the sudden recollection of what had happened the previous day flooded my mind. I turned on the TV and watched the continuous footage of the attack, dissected into a thousand horrific sound bites and images. Jon was awake and sitting up beside me staring at the screen.

In truth, Jon and I had not awakened to an ordinary day since Dov was diagnosed with autism.

When I checked my e-mail, I saw that this morning mail from Soma had arrived at 6:40 A.M. It was Soma's custom to rise at 5:00 A.M., say her prayers, meditate, prepare Tito's breakfast, and then write her e-mails. Each morning she would dutifully write to her husband, her mother-in-law, and her mother. I felt honored to be included in this group, but I still wondered why I was included today.

> Portia,
> I would love to show you something new with Dov.
> Dov and I are progressing quickly.
> I would love to work with someone else too before I go back.
> And I am not afraid of any challenges.
> Talk to you later,
> Soma

In spite of Soma's ambitious nature, I knew she could be very polite when it came to describing her own accomplishments. So I took her words to mean that she'd had some kind of breakthrough with Dov and it gave her the courage to want to try her method with other autistic children. At least I hoped this was what she meant. But I wasn't going to let myself get carried away—not yet, not until I saw what Maria and Soma were referring to.

After Dov had a bath, was dressed, and had eaten breakfast, we drove to Soma's apartment. Gabriel came along too, because there was no one to watch him that morning. At four, Gabe seemed more like a giant baby with the chubby physique of a toddler, with Dumbo-style ears and big brown eyes. At least he had hair now, I thought, as I kissed his head and buckled him into his car seat. Today Gabriel and Dov wore matching blue-striped shirts, as any brothers might, and for a moment they looked like two ordinary boys. Yet how different they were, I thought, as I slid the seat belt across Dov's skinny rib cage, while he stared out the window, seeming to not notice me.

As we drove toward Soma's, I couldn't stop the flood of disappointing possibilities that was racing through my mind. Probably Soma would be holding Dov's hand or at least his elbow. Maybe she would be moving the alphabet board around under his hand. It's not that I doubted Soma, but there were a thousand ways to do this wrong, a million ways to confer unintended influence. I was prepared for disappointment, but I packed along the video camera anyway—just in case.

Soma opened the door and greeted us with her usual cheerful smile and brisk movements. The apartment looked pretty much the same as it did the day they moved in, except that the silk floral arrangement that had been on the dining table and every other nonessential item had been crammed into the closet, out of Tito's reach. Tito was stalking around the apartment, looking bored and agitated. I wondered if he was jealous—his mother had never worked with anyone else before.

Wasting no time, Soma marshaled Dov over to the couch. A spiral notebook and a few colored markers were on the coffee table, along with a textbook and a piece of cardboard with the alphabet

printed in lowercase letters, the same kind Soma often used with
Tito. Dov sat cross-legged on the couch next to Soma, looking
toward the window where vertical blinds split the sunlight into irre-
sistible stripes of light. Yet he *did* sit down next to her and he *was*
staying there, I noted to myself, trying to be positive.

Soma opened the textbook and began to read out loud at an incredibly rapid pace: "A galaxy is a group of stars. . . ." Why was she
reading to him about the solar system? How could she expect Dov to
understand her when she was reading so fast, not to mention in that
heavy Indian accent? I popped a tape into the video camera and
turned it on anyway.

Gabriel stuck his face into the lens, crossing his eyes, hoping to
get some attention. "Stop it!" I hissed under my breath, not wanting
to disturb Soma as she worked with Dov, even though he seemed to
be paying no attention to her as he continued to stare in the direction of the blinds.

Soma stopped reading and without pausing a millisecond she demanded: "Okay! A galaxy is? . . . C'mon, show it!" Dov turned
toward the board Soma suspended in midair in front of him. I held
my breath. "C'mon! Show, show, show!" she commanded, prodding
his knee with her thumb as she urged him on.

Then, in a moment that remains more clear in my mind and
more astonishing than any man walking on the moon, Dov raised
his hand—by himself—glanced tentatively at the board, and
pointed to the letter G. Was it chance? I didn't have time to wonder
as Soma forced ahead.

"Okay, 'G,'" she said, simultaneously writing it down. "Good,
good! You can do it! C'mon, show it!" Again, Dov glanced at the
board, looked away, and pointed, this time to the letter R. "Go, go,
go!" Soma kept up the animated urging.

G-R? What was G-R? It didn't make sense. I looked through the
camera lens to be sure I was getting everything anyway. I saw that
Gabriel had crawled up behind them on the couch. "Gabe! Get out

of there!" I whispered fiercely. Ignoring me, he moseyed in closer to them. "C'mon!" Soma continued.

One by one, Dov pointed out the letters as Soma wrote each letter down and urged him on. "'G-R-O-U-P!'" she spelled out triumphantly. "Yes, we are getting it! Very good!! C'mon, show!" she continued, never letting up. Finally there were three words: *"Group of stars."*

Group of stars? Of course—a galaxy *is* a group of stars! Had Dov actually answered that question? Was it possible? It seemed true. How could a boy who could not spell his own name be spelling out an answer like that? Soma read it again, "'Group of stars!' You are right! Keep going!"

For the next half hour, I watched in awe and fascination as Soma read other science facts to Dov and questioned him about what she'd read. It seemed crazy, absurd. Dov didn't know his colors. He didn't know the alphabet or numbers. We'd been trying to teach him these things since he was three years old and he had made almost no progress at all. It didn't make sense.

Yet again and again Dov pointed at a letter, then another, some-times missing one, sometimes hesitating, but always continuing until he answered Soma's questions. Dov seemed to be demonstrating a level of intelligence than I had never suspected or dreamed he might possess.

I watched Soma closely. What *was* she doing?

She was talking nonstop, in an intense, loud voice; she wasn't holding his hand, she wasn't even touching his shoulder. She was prodding his knee with her thumb. Beyond that, I could detect no other clues as to how she was so miraculously getting Dov to point and to answer questions I didn't even know he was capable of under-standing.

I could barely begin to comprehend what this meant. It meant that Dov was intelligent—far more intelligent than we'd dared to hope or than he'd ever been able to show us. It meant that he was not retarded. It meant that he'd been in there . . . all these years. I could barely keep from crying.

The world can be changed forever in a day. Yesterday, my world as I knew it was destroyed. And on this day, an entirely new world was born.

Everything I thought I knew about Dov, about learning and intelligence, about language and speech, about development and behavior, about thinking and being, was turned upside down.

Driving home that day, with Dov and Gabe in the backseat, I was glad they couldn't see my face or the tears that were streaming down it. For the first time, I knew that Dov could understand every word I said. How long had he been able to understand us? I could not know, but now, perhaps I could learn from Soma how to ask him. He had understood us all along. And now, after so many years apart, I didn't know what to say. I glanced in the rearview mirror at Dov. He looked exactly the same, distant, removed, isolated, staring at some thread he was flicking in front of his eyes, yet I saw him differently now.

What was he like? After all these years, I had a thousand questions to ask him and a million things I wanted to tell him. And yet I couldn't think of what to say. "I love you," I blurted out. My words hung strangely hollow in the interior of the car. I glanced back and saw a slight furrow of confusion in Gabriel's chubby forehead and Dov just kept staring at his twirling thread.

Would I be able to communicate with Dov? I couldn't wait to try. Soma would teach me how.

A sudden, loud crackling sound startled my senses back to the moment. "What was that, Mommy?" Gabe asked, frightened.

I looked out at the sky, which I now noticed was unusually dark. "That was thunder, Gabriel," I told him, only half believing it myself. "Don't be afraid, it's just a thunderstorm," I said, looking back at Dov. Was he afraid? I hesitated and drew in a deep breath. "Dov, do you remember when we took you to the Jersey Shore when you were just a little boy and it stormed the whole vacation?" I checked in the mirror again. Dov appeared impervious.

"Was I there?" Gabe asked.

"No, you weren't there," I said, smiling to myself, "you weren't born yet." Gabe always asked this question, even if we were talking about dinosaurs.

The first heavy drop of rain struck the windshield with a loud plop. Then came another, and another. And it was raining. It never rained in L.A., especially not in the fall. For once the weather was on my side, I thought, as the heavy drops splashed down like big tears of happiness and remorse.

As we drove toward home in silence, I recalled when Jon first saw Soma communicating with Tito and he tried to do it with Dov. He placed his hand over Dov's and urged him to type. This seemed to produce a few words sometimes, but not very often or not very reliably. When I tried to do it, it felt the same as when we tried facilitated communication. I was skeptical and I wasn't sure who was actually communicating.

I also recalled one night when I was away at a CAN conference, and Jon was at home reading *Harry Potter* to Gabe and Miriam and Dov. Dov was puttering around the bedroom stimming as usual, but as Soma pointed out, he never left the room—and he could have.

When Jon closed the book and said it was time for bed, Miriam ran down to the kitchen and brought back a laminated place mat that had the alphabet printed on it. "Here, Dov!" she said sweetly, "What did you think of *Harry Potter?*" They waited and nothing happened. "Did you like it?" she persisted. "Point at Y for yes if you liked it and N for no if you didn't." Jon placed his hand over Dov's and Dov seemed to point at the letter Y.

"What did you think of it?" Miriam continued, delighted. Again,

Jon placed his hand on top of Dov's and Dov pointed out the letters "S-C-A-R-Y." Miriam and Gabe laughed at this.

"Okay, what was so scary?" Jon asked Dov, still holding his hand firmly under his own. "D-E-M-E-N-T-O-R-S," Dov seemed to point out.

Jon had called me that night at my hotel to tell me the good news, that Dov was communicating. But when I returned home a few days later, I saw that it was the same hand-over-hand method. "No one is ever going to believe this," I told Jon after he held Dov's hand to type out a word. "The way you're doing it, it's impossible to tell who is actually communicating," I said, instantly regretting what sounded like an accusation.

Now I couldn't wait to tell Jon about what I'd seen at Soma's apartment. "She's not touching his hand or his arm, not even his shoulder." I told him breathlessly as soon as he walked in the front door from work.

But Jon didn't even smile. Instead he just went upstairs and got undressed and started reading *Variety* on our bed, wearing only boxers and wool socks. What was wrong with him?

"I don't believe it," he said, putting on my reading glasses, which made him look both skeptical and ridiculous. "I want to but it's just wishful thinking."

"I wasn't exactly a believer myself until today, when I saw it with my own eyes," I said, still trying to convince him. "Not that I ever doubted Soma or Tito for even a minute. But I just didn't see how it could work with Dov," I added.

I had to get Jon over to Soma's apartment.

Jon and I didn't speak as we climbed into the car the next day and headed toward Soma's apartment. Maria was going to meet us there with Dov, after school. Jon had to see Soma working with Dov. I could tell he was holding back, trying not to get his hopes up—after all, they had been dashed a thousand times before.

As we climbed the cement steps, we could hear Soma's voice as her words floated through the window and down the steps toward us. Her words, made all the more strange by her intense Indian accent with its curt British overlay, poured through the slatted blinds and fell upon our disbelieving ears.

"'Whether it was meant to arouse our slumbering souls or as a clarion call to war against the worst part of our natures, the primitive sound of the shofar blast stirs something deep within us.'"

The door was open when we reached the top of the steps and we entered to find Soma on the couch reading out loud to Dov from a book titled *The Jewish Holidays* as Maria looked on with a pleased expression. We smiled at Soma and quietly sat down as she continued.

"'On its most basic level, the shofar can be seen to express what we cannot find the right words to say. The blasts are the wordless cries of the people of Israel.'"

Tito came out of his room and stood at the door making urgent sounds and looking at his mother, clearly trying to get her attention. "Later, Tito. We'll go for a walk later," Soma said without looking up. Tito just stood there. "Tito, sit down and color!" She commanded, tilting her head toward some crayons and paper on the table. But Tito went back into his room.

"'The shofar is the instrument that sends those cries of pain and longing hurtling across the vast distance toward the Other.'" Soma closed the book and looked up at us expectantly, her eyes filled with pride.

"Dov," I began hesitantly, glancing over at Jon. "How did you like going to Temple last night?"

Without missing a beat, Soma continued. "C'mon!" she urged him, prodding his knee with her thumb. Dov lifted his hand and pointed at *I*. "'*I*,'" repeated Soma. There was a pause, Dov's hand faltered. "'*I*'... don't get less!" I thought she must mean don't slow down.

Dov raised his hand again and kept going. "*E-N-J-O-Y-E-D-I-T*."

"I enjoyed it," Soma read out his words. "Oh, you enjoyed it? Very good!" Now Soma looked at us. There was a look of pride in her eyes. She had a lot to be proud of.

"Dov, can you remember the name of the holiday?" I ventured. Again Dov began to point as Soma's voice urged him on with a continuous stream of verbal prompts and encouragement. "*R-O-S-H*"— then Dov's hand dropped again.

"The next letter is *H*," I said in a near whisper as if we were on *Password*.

Dov threw himself down on the couch and let out a frustrated cry between grinding teeth. "You see how upset he gets," Soma said.

Was he really getting upset because he couldn't spell the word? I wondered. "You know Dov, Rosh Hashana is a hard word. I was trying to look it up on the computer today and I couldn't spell it."

Now Dov sat up. He seemed to calm down. "Yah! C'mon. We can do it!" Soma urged him on. Again he pointed at the letter *I*, then *L-I* and then *J*.

"'*L-I-J*'?" *What's that?* I thought.

"I'll take it for a *K*," Soma said without hesitating. The *J* was right next to the *K*. Well, all right, let's see . . . I thought. Then Dov pointed at *E* and *D* and then *T-O*.

"'*I liked to*,'" Soma spoke the words he had pointed out. *G-O* came next and then *T-H-E-R-E*. "'*I liked to go there!*'" Soma exclaimed.

"How did you feel? What did you feel when you went there?" Soma asked to my surprise, since she usually stuck to academic subjects and avoided emotional topics. "*C-L-O-S-E*."

"Excellent! See, it can be anything!" Soma exhorted. "C'mon!" she urged him. He kept pointing, "*T-O*."

"'*Close to,*'" Soma read out. "C'mon! You can do it!" "G-O" "'*Go*'! Yah! Very good!"

Suddenly Soma's expression softened and her voice trailed off. Dov pointed to one last letter, *D*, and then dropped his hand. Soma looked up at us silently, with an almost embarrassed look, her eyes looked a little teary. "'*Close to God,*'" she said in a quiet voice.

Close to God? What was this? I wasn't even sure I believed in God anymore. We didn't talk about God around our house much.

It was Jon's turn to speak now. His voice trembled slightly as he formed his words. "You felt . . ." His voice cracked and he paused to recompose himself, clearing his throat loudly. "You felt . . . close to God?"

Soma quickly recovered her chipper demeanor. "Good, you're talking so much!" she encouraged Dov, waving the board in front of him again. Dov lifted his hand and began to point again. "Good, good, very good!" she extolled as Dov continued to point. He was pointing faster and better now. "*I-H-O-P-E.*"

"'*I hope*' . . ." Soma echoed his words out as he continued to point. "*T-H-I-S-Y-E-A-R-I-S.*" "'This year is . . .'" "*A-N-E-W.*" "'*I hope this year is a new* . . .'" I could not imagine where this sentence was going.

Dov was getting frustrated again, leaning over, making distressed sounds. Maybe he had reached his limit for the day. There was no need to push him. He could tell us more later. It was okay if this didn't make sense. We'd seen enough today to last a lifetime.

But Soma pressed ahead, urging all the more insistently. He bared his teeth at her and made a movement with his head that I knew came right before head butting began, something Dov did when he was really frustrated or angry. "It's okay," I said to Soma, hoping she would stop while she was ahead and before he blew up.

But she just kept going. "C-A", he pointed at. "'C-A,' c'mon! Try it! Okay I'll take it for an *L*." Then he tapped on the *L*. Power of suggestion, prompting, cuing—whatever, he was learning! I thought to myself.

"*Call*—okay I'll take it as '*call*'!" Soma continued triumphantly. "*F-O-R-A-L-L-L-I-K-E-M-E.*" "'*For all like me.*'"

"Can you read us back the whole thing? I lost track," I said to Soma.
"*I hope this year is a new call for all like me.*"

We sat there in silence trying to absorb what we had just witnessed. Finally Jon broke the silence. "That was very thoughtful of you, Dov"—Jon sounded like he might cry—"to think about others." His voice trailed off.

But there was more. "*T-O-F-I-N-D.*" "'*To find . . .*'" "*S-Q.*" "'*S-Q*'? Try it again! C'mon! Good! Do it!" "*S-O.*" "Good, good! You are doing it! '*M-E Yah!*' C'mon, do it!" "*H-O-P-E.*" "'*Hope. To find some hope.*'"

"Soma, please—read it back," I again implored. She read back the words she had written down in her little notebook as she'd been reading them back to us.

"'*I hope this year is a new call for all like me to find some hope.*'"

"Oh, that's so nice, Dov," I said. Now it was my turn to have my voice break up. "I am going to write that down and save it, okay? That was such a nice thing to say." I looked over at Jon and saw that his face was buried in his hands.

Soma looked uncomfortable. "See, you started communicating," she said to Dov cheerfully, trying to restore a lighter mood to the room. "Now some other children will start coming. Won't that be great?"

Tito burst out of his room and began pacing around the tiny apartment. "Okay, Tito!" Soma said, jumping up suddenly. "Now we will walk!"

As in previous years, I regretted not prepaying for valet parking at the Temple. Jon would have to drop us off for Rosh Hashana family services and meet us inside.

Jon, Gabriel and Miriam knew some Hebrew, but Dov and I did not. Inside the Temple, I was on an equal footing with Dov as we sat together and listened to the prayers and songs being sung in a language we did not know. It made some sense, since God didn't actually have ears, and it was not the words themselves that wave of intention from the heart that we call prayer. What language did God understand? How could anyone get a message through to God? I wondered.

And so with Dov at my side, we rode the waves of glorious sounds that humans utter when they are together and hoping they are in the presence of God. And it was true, Dov and I could be with God as well as anyone in the congregation, whether we understood Hebrew or whether we were mad at God or even believed in him.

I saw Jon making his way toward us. Evidently he had experienced the miracle of finding a parking spot. Miriam and Gabriel hugged their father as he joined us and together, Jon and I sang, we intoned, we implored, we prayed, while the children alternately daydreamed and joined in. At least I thought Jon and I were praying together, until I heard him whisper to Dov, "What's this letter?" pointing at the Hebrew letter aleph in the prayer book.

Dov pointed to the letter A on his alphabet board. Jon shot me a look. "Show me *gimmel*," he said, holding the prayer book in front of Dov. Dov pointed to the Hebrew letter *gimmel*. Jon hesitated, baffled and amused.

"Okay, what does this word mean?" Jon asked, pointing to the word *Adonai* in the prayer book. Dov pointed on his board: "G-O-D." Jon just stared at his son with a bewildered smile. "I don't know. . . ." he said finally, shaking his head.

But to our surprise, Dov continued to point at letters on his board. Slowly, effortfully, he produced a sentence.

"Why must you doubt everything I know?"

Jon and I stared at each other, oblivious to the singing voices that rose and fell around us. Suddenly I heard the voice of the rabbi, who had begun to speak. His words floated into my consciousness with a sudden clarity. "Rather than focusing on whether God hears us or not, we should concentrate on *koleinu*, our voice," he said. "For the essence of prayer is the uplifted voice, the voice that is lifted in longing or song, in guilt or anger, sadness or despair."

I stared at Dov, who stood beside me, clinging to my arm; here was a boy who had no voice at all. How was he supposed to cry out to God? I wondered. Just then a terrible blast of sound ripped through the solemnity the temple.

It was the sound of the shofar blasting—the long, spiraling ram's horn that is blown at the end of the first day of services on Rosh Hashana. It is a sound not easily described, at once moving and alarming, riveting and unsettling, primitive and transcendent. It is a call to the present moment that cannot be ignored.

As the piercing blasts of the shofar rang out I stood frozen. The eternal light above the altar shone as it always did and the white marble lions guarded the Ten Commandments as they always did, and yet everything was somehow different. Something had become transformed, something I could not see with my eyes or name with my voice, and yet I knew it.

That night after we tucked Miriam and Gabriel into bed, Jon and I sat at the edge of Dov's bed. "Ask him how he learned Hebrew," Jon said, handing me the alphabet board.

I held the board in front of Dov. "C'mon!" I extolled, trying as hard as I could to sound like Soma. But Dov's eyes just kept staring down at the string of shiny beads in his hands. "C'mon! You can do it!" I continued, feeling stupid. I remembered Soma prodding Dov's knee. I continued to urge Dov on, and began to poke at his knee. I felt disconnected and ridiculous. Jon looked away; perhaps it was too humiliating to watch, I thought to myself. This wasn't working. What was Soma doing? Without thinking, I put my hand on Dov's shoulder.

To my surprise Dov lifted his hand. "C'mon!" I resumed excitedly, ratcheting my voice up another notch. "Good, good!" I exclaimed as he pointed at the letter *P*. "Keep going!" I implored as I tried to keep up a stream of rapid urgings while prodding his shoulder. I didn't know what I was doing, but as long as it produced the next letter, I kept doing it. He pointed again and then again, the letters *R-E-S-S*, then his hand fell down and he stopped. I stopped too. I was exhausted. How did Soma do it? I wondered.

"*Press?*" Jon asked, shrugging. "That doesn't make sense." He looked away again, perhaps this time in disappointment. It seemed like nonsense, a chance string of letters, I had to admit.

"What does '*Press*' mean, Dov?" I asked, trying to rev up my Soma imitation again as I prodded his shoulder and shook the board in front of his face. I was struggling to keep it up, when Dov began to point again, first at the letter *M*, then *A*, then *N*. And then his hand fell back down and his fingers returned to the shiny beads. I sighed and put the board down.

"'*M-A-N*, man'! Very good, Dov! You spelled the word 'man'!" I hugged him tightly, smiling. I wanted to encourage him, even if the words didn't seem to mean anything, or at least not to me. The important thing was he had pointed to some letters, he had formed two words, or at least it seemed like he had. It was a start, I told myself, even if it didn't make sense.

"Wait a minute!" Jon shouted, suddenly standing up. "Pressman!" he yelled, throwing his arms around Dov. "Pressman Academy! He means Pressman Academy!" It took a minute to register. Dov had attended the Pressman Academy preschool at Temple Beth Am for two years—when he was three and four years old; he went with an aide. Had he really picked up some of the letters of the Hebrew alphabet way back then? The nursery school classroom flashed into my mind. There were posters everywhere: posters of the Hebrew alphabet, posters of simple words in English and Hebrew with pictures. Posters of words like apple and girl and boy and God. Was it possible? Had Dov learned some of these while he was there, just by being exposed? And even if he had, how would he remember them now?

I felt as if I must be going off the deep end. A boy who could not count to ten, a boy who didn't appear to know his ABCs, or say a single word—how could a boy like this *know even one single letter of the Hebrew alphabet, much less from five years ago?*

For what seemed like the hundredth time in recent days, tears once again filled my eyes, as I leaned down and embraced Jon and Dov. And like a heap of human confusion and imperfection, a lump of bewilderment and wonder, we slumped there like that, Jon's arms around Dov and my arms around both of them. I felt crazy, ecstatic, frightened. Miracles, I was learning, not only brought joy but by their very definition must shatter your world, casting everything you thought you knew to the four winds.

15.

Handsome in
a Jacket

What have you been doing all these years?

—*Jon Shestack*

Listening.

—*Dov*

brought Dov to see Soma every day after that, and I watched in awe as she taught Dov about the world—about colors and shapes, about plants and animals, about the ocean and mountains and the weather, about grammar and math, and about the human body—as Dov sat beside her and listened and then answered her questions. It seemed that Soma was trying to rapidly fill the holes that Dov's isolated experience had left in his repertoire of knowledge. She was building a world in his mind, facts connected by facts. A literal framework that explained the world as we know it.

Dov's aide, Maria, was one of the very first to succeed at getting Dov to type out single-word answers and short phrases. Perhaps it was because Maria had been brought up a strict Catholic and believing in miracles was not a problem. Maria kept a log of what happened every day at school and in the first days and weeks after Dov began to communicate with Soma, Maria wrote about that too.

September 12, 2001

Maybe if Miss Karen could see Soma working with Dov she would change her mind and see that these kids are smart enough to learn.

I've been using the board at school but with me he just starts to play. I know he will do it. I need to practice it with him.
—Maria Lopez

It so happened that Dov's annual meeting to update his individual education plan (IEP) was scheduled to take place only a few weeks after he began to communicate. I brought Soma to Dov's IEP meeting to show that coven of "experts" what we had discovered about Dov. He would need a radically updated IEP with all new goals, many of which jumped years ahead of where he was when they last tested him. Dov sat next to Soma and typed out short answers to some of the simple questions they asked him.

"I'm sorry," one of the school psychologists blurted out, pushing back from the table and visibly rolling her eyes, "but I don't buy it. I don't believe the language he's demonstrating is functional."

It took me a minute to grasp what she meant. "You mean you think he's just using words like . . . like a parrot?" I asked incredulously.

"Exactly," she replied.

"Dov," I said quite clearly to be sure they all could hear me. "What are we here for today?" I could not suppress the tiny smile that crept up at the corners of my mouth as he typed: *"For my IEP."*

During this period, I awoke each morning with a rush of excitement. I would open my eyes and suddenly remember that Dov was communicating. Every day was a new adventure as I discovered yet another new thing about Dov and I began to piece together what he knew and began to get an inkling of the person he truly was.

And every night as I lay in bed, new questions flooded my mind. I'd snap on the light and jot them down to ask Dov the next day at Soma's.

What did he think of his brother and sister? Did he know how to read? How long had he been understanding us? Could he tell time? What kind of music did he like? What did he want to be when he grew up? Which did he like better, cats or dogs? Did he like to take a shower or did he like to take a bath? What was his favorite color? How did he learn to add and subtract? There were a million things I wanted to ask Dov.

I photocopied the alphabet board and laminated it and distributed it to everyone who came into contact with Dov—his one-on-one aide, Maria, his therapists, his teachers, our baby-sitters, and Miriam and Gabe, everyone. I demanded that they use the alphabet board with Dov or at least try.

"He's intelligent and he understands everything you are saying," I told them. I showed them how to position the alphabet board in front of Dov. I insisted they visit Soma and observe her working with Dov and try to learn from what they saw her doing. I ignored the fact that I was not very good at it myself, at least not yet. We would all learn together, I told them. We would get better at it, and we would be able to do it like Soma—someday—if we just tried hard enough.

When I brought Dov out to meet his aunts and uncles, he held on to my arm, clutching his favorite marble, looking down, squeezing his eyes shut, curling his fingers under his tucked-down chin. I knew he was feeling very shy and probably overwhelmed. I'd told my sisters and brothers that Dov had begun to communicate and now they had come together to experience it firsthand.

Even Billy had come. I was surprised to see him; I didn't think he'd come. I gave a little wave and smiled. It was all a bit much for Billy, I knew. I hadn't seen him for quite a while, months in fact. Billy was grown up and had his own life now. I hadn't been able to get him over to the house since Dov had started to communicate. Maybe he was afraid it wasn't true. Billy had been hurt in so many ways by his brother's autism. First when he was just a kid himself. "Dov doesn't love me anymore," he told us, brokenhearted when his adored baby brother no longer looked at him or smiled. And then all through his teenage years when we were too busy battling autism to notice his problems in school or the fact that he needed our attention so badly. I felt sorry for that.

We sat down and I shook the board in front of Dov and urged him to point. How I hoped he would be able to type out even just a word or two to show them that he understood what they said, that he could think, and that they could get to know him, and that there was a real person inside.

Everyone was waiting. After several false starts, Dov pointed to a series of letters and spelled: *"Hi Aunt Sarah."* My sister began to cry. My other sister, Lenore, the doctor, looked tearful too. My brother Lloyd was filled with so much empathy and compassion and such a strong desire to make contact with his long-lost nephew that he grabbed the board from Dov and began typing a message to him. "Lloyd," I said gently, not wanting to embarrass him, "he can hear you fine." Lloyd turned a little red. "Oh, yeah," he said, smiling. Then he spoke the words he'd typed to his nephew: "Hi, Dov, I love you." We all started to laugh, and then cry, and then laugh some more.

One of the first things I wanted to know was whether Dov could read. When he picked up a book, which he did often, he would just rapidly flip the pages in front of his eyes. He couldn't really read a book that way, while he was stimming on it, but still, maybe he *could* read. He seemed to have learned so many things just by pure exposure.

So one day I picked up a piece of paper and, saying nothing, wrote the question: "What color is a lemon?" and I showed it to Dov. I had no idea what size to make the letters or how complicated a sentence to present, but I knew that if Dov answered, he must be reading. Then I held up the alphabet board. "*Yellow,*" came the answer. Yes, he was reading.

"When did you learn to read?" I asked him.

"*Six,*" he spelled out. Dov was six when we began using Nina Lovaas's sight-reading program with him. At the time it was the first hint of success we'd had after years of no progress, and we were thrilled. After two years, when he was eight, he seemed to have learned to identify about twenty sight words. This meant he could choose the correct word from two choices and place the card in the empty space in the sentence strip. But this learning did not generalize to other sentences or choices of answers—in other words, sight-reading was not leading to language and communication as quickly as we hoped it might.

We'd now been using picture cards with Dov for several years and we were still using them when I met Soma and Tito. These were small Velcro-backed cards with pictures of favorite foods, water, and stim toys. There were hundreds of these picture cards in Dov's binder, but he rarely used more than three or four of them. Now I suspected they might have played a role in his literacy as well. We'd always written the word at the bottom of the picture cards hoping that somehow Dov might learn to recognize the words. Maybe he had.

Now that I knew Dov could read, I realized that I had no idea what his reading level was. I didn't really know how to test him either, so I made something up. First I showed him the simplest kind of reading book, the kind created specifically for beginning readers, with only a few words on each page, in large type. I took his index finger and ran it along the words as I commanded, "Read! Read! Read!," sounding foolish even to myself.

I watched his eyes in my peripheral vision and saw that every time I said "Read!" he would fleetingly glance at the page. Then I tested him and indeed he could give one-word answers about the sentences he had apparently read. Then I moved on to picture books with a few sentences on each page in normal type size, with a wider range of vocabulary words. Again, Dov seemed to be able to read the words silently and then answer questions.

I continued to work our way up through more and more advanced reading material until finally we reached a fourth-grade-level chapter book about the life of Helen Keller. He could read this too. I proceeded to increase the number of sentences from a few to a whole paragraph and then to the entire page. And he could read it and answer questions.

It turned out that Dov had been absorbing information from all kinds of sources. A couple of weeks after the terrorist attacks on the World Trade Center, our art dealer friend John Lee visited us from New York. We'd told him that Dov had started communicating and seemed to have normal intelligence. We couldn't wait for John Lee to see Dov.

We were sitting around the kitchen table when John arrived. I put the board in front of Dov and asked him if he remembered John Lee from New York. "Yes," Dov spelled out. John Lee smiled. "Hello, Dov," he said gently.

"Is there anything you want to say to John?" I asked Dov, hoping he would be able to point well tonight. Everyone's eyes were on Dov as he began to point. "Did you know anyone who died?" he asked John Lee. The room was quiet for a moment. "Yes," John replied, staring down at his hands in his lap.

"Dov . . . how did you know about that?" I asked, amazed. I held up the board and again he typed *"N-P-R."* "That's not a word," I said gently, laying the board down.

Jon started laughing. John Lee and I looked at him blankly. "Yes, it is a word." He chuckled. "National Public Radio." It was true. We always had the radio on in the kitchen and we always listened to NPR.

Oddly enough, Dov's best subject, at least when it came to communicating answers, was math. He pointed correctly at numbers better than anything else. That was fortunate, because perhaps hardest to accept or understand was Dov's actual ability to do math. In school, he was not known to have any math skills at all. Dov's academic goal in math was to learn to count from ten to twenty. He had already spent five years working on counting from one to ten.

Yet at Soma's, I saw that Dov could do basic addition and subtraction, and he knew his times tables up to the sixes.

Ever since Miriam had started getting homework in the first grade, she and our sitter had been doing her homework together in Dov's room at a little table. Dov could not be left alone and so he bounced on his bed, spun his beads, and seemed oblivious to what they were doing. There, each school night, Miriam practiced her weekly list of vocabulary words out loud, and it finally occurred to me: They had been practicing the multiplication tables out loud for months. Miriam had memorized her multiplication tables up to the sixes. And so had Dov, I realized with a sense of shock followed by relief. At least I had found some rational reason for how he had learned them.

One evening soon after Soma had taught Dov long division, I was driving home with Dov and Miriam and two of her friends who were coming over for dinner. The girls were complaining bitterly in the backseat of the van about their Hebrew class. "Dov doesn't have

Hebrew at his school," I commented, knowing they'd be envious and making a mental note to myself that I was going to have to find a Hebrew tutor for Dov if he was going to have a bar mitzvah someday.

"*He* goes to school?" said one of the girls incredulously. I cringed. I felt bad for Dov because I knew he understood the implications of her statement. I knew she did not mean to be cruel; she simply didn't realize that Dov could understand her. "Of course Dov goes to school," I answered as evenly as I could. "He can read and he can type and he understands everything you are saying." We rode the rest of the way home in silence.

When we got to the house, I tried to lighten things up. "Hey, come on and see this—Dov is really good at math." I grabbed an alphabet board that had a row of numbers from one to ten across the top and symbols for the basic mathematical functions. The girls gathered around as I held the board in front of Dov. "Okay, Dov," I began. "Let's do some long division." I smiled brightly at the kids. "Does anyone here know long division?" I asked innocently, knowing that Miriam's fourth-grade class had been miserably struggling with it all year.

There was a moment of silence followed by some mumbles: "Sort of," "Kinda," and "It's hard." "Dov, can you show us how you would do this problem?" I asked, jotting down the problem. "One hundred sixty-eight divided by twelve is? . . ." The girl's eyes widened.

"What do we do first?" I asked Dov. I thought I saw a trace of a smile as he pointed out the first operation: "Twelve into sixteen goes one time," I said as I wrote it down. "Are you following?" I asked the girls. "Kinda," "Sorta," and "Huh? I don't get it," came their respective replies.

"Then what?" I asked Dov. Now he really was smiling. We continued like this for the next several minutes with Dov pointing out the next steps of the problem and me writing them down until finally he came to the answer. "That's right! Twelve goes into one hundred sixty-eight fourteen times!" I glanced around at the girls' dumbstruck faces.

"Did everyone get that?" I asked, barely concealing my glee. "Not really," "Huh?" and "We didn't study that yet," they confessed. Then the girls ran off to play before dinner. I hugged Dov and gave him a big kiss. "I am so proud of you!" I said, wishing I could think of a less ordinary way to express how extraordinary I thought he was.

Even though Dov had picked up an amazing amount of information by listening and through sheer exposure, there was a lot he hadn't been exposed to and what that consisted of was totally random. For one thing his academic education had been largely confined to the hour or so a day he'd spent listening to his sister do her homework in his room. All the while at school he was being taught at the pre-academic level. I could hardly bear to think of the endless hours he'd spent failing at tasks he could not do, like counting from one to ten by manipulating colored cubes, when he already knew basic arithmetic. In fact this was the sort of activity he had been engaged in all day, every day, his whole life.

I now saw Dov in another new light: instead of seeing him as uncooperative or uninterested, I saw him as infinitely patient, never giving up.

If there were holes in Dov's academic repertoire, there were even bigger gaps in his social knowledge due to the diminished level of interaction he'd had with people most of his life. Surrounded at school by other students who could not speak or control their behavior and teachers who had no way of knowing that he could understand language, Dov had limited opportunities for social learning.

Now, for the first time in his life, Dov was beginning to ask for things. One day at Soma's he spelled the word "toy," when asked what kind of toy, he spelled "doll." I asked what kind of doll. "Barbie," was his answer. I was thrilled, I didn't care if Dov was autistic *and* gay—that was all right because for the first time ever, he wanted a toy. We drove straight to Toys "R" Us after our session with Soma.

Inside, we went directly to the rather formidable Barbie aisle and picked out a doll. I found myself throwing a Ken doll into the cart for good measure.

When we got home I tried to figure out how to play with these dolls with Dov. He had such poor motor skills and coordination and he wouldn't look at anything. I held one doll in each hand and made them talk. "Hi, Dov!" Barbie chirped. "Nice to meet you!" Ken said. I watched for any sign of a reaction. Dov's eyes were squeezed shut and his chin was tucked down on his chest. I couldn't tell if he liked this game. I guided Dov's hand to hold Ken. I spoke for both dolls. I acted out some more dialogue between the dolls and after a while I put them away in a plastic box, which I put on a shelf across the room.

A few days later, I sent Barbie and Ken to school with Dov for show-and-tell. A week later, our baby-sitter bought another Barbie doll for Dov and I suggested he take it to school to show his classmates, but he pushed it away. "What's wrong?" I asked. *"Dolls are for girls,"* he typed, to my astonishment. Some of the kids had laughed at Dov when he brought his dolls to school last week, Maria told me.

Not only was Dov starting to fill in the holes in his education but he was also learning about social rules.

Dov continued to exhibit a surprisingly rapid rate of social learning over the coming weeks and months, even showing us that he had a sense of humor. One morning at the breakfast table, I handed Dov his board and asked if he had anything to say. The kitchen was crowded and noisy, as it always is before school in the morning.

"Be quiet! Dov is trying to communicate!" I yelled until the kids finally settled down and waited expectantly. "C'mon, Dov! You can do it!" I commanded, trying to sound as much like Soma as I could. "What do you have to say?" I demanded of Dov, at which time he suddenly farted loudly. This sent the kids into hysterics.

Gabriel rushed over and grabbed the board. "Dovie, what did you mean?" he asked, barely able to choke the words out through his laughter. *"Joke,"* Dov typed. Apparently Dov was rapidly developing what passed for a sense of humor in our family.

Another change I noticed was that Dov began to stay in his chair at the dinner table long after the other children ran off to play. Before he could communicate, Dov could barely sit for ten minutes at the dinner table. Now Dov seemed to like to listen to grown-ups discuss politics or trade gossip. It seemed to me, now that Dov had some form of interface with our world, his interest in it was growing in direct proportion. Slowly he was beginning to join the culture of humans, perhaps simply because now *he could.*

I didn't realize just how culturally deprived Dov was until one day when I was watching Soma as she was teaching him the concept of where we live, a person's home, their community, city, and so on. "What are some of the things a tourist or visitor might like to see in Los Angeles?" Soma asked, to which Dov replied: *"K-mart,"* *"McDonalds,"* and *"beach."* It was true, these *were* the places Dov liked to go. I vowed that Dov would start to visit museums, see movies, and go to cultural events around Los Angeles more often.

One night I took Dov to an outdoor mall, where he stopped in front of an electronics store and we sat down on a bench there. "What?" I asked him as I pulled out his board from his backpack. "Is there something you see there that you like?" I held the board in front of him and waited as I watched the tube of flashing lights race around the edge of the store window, illuminating the dozens of miniature screens that flickered in unison there. What was Dov seeing? How did it look to him? I wondered.

"C'mon!" I implored, placing my hand on his shoulder and lightly prodding him. *"Jacket"* was what he typed out. My eyes scanned over to the Brooks Brothers store next to the electronics shop. "A jacket? You want a jacket?" I said, delighted. "What kind of jacket? For cold weather? Or for special things, like going to Temple?" I asked him. *"Everywhere,"* he replied. "You mean like a suit jacket, like Dad wears?" I asked, my heart pounding. "Yeah," he said audibly.

I looked at my watch; it was thirty minutes before the stores would be closing. "Come on!" I said, pulling him up. We went into Brooks Brothers and Dov tried on a shirt and a navy blazer. I pulled him by the hand toward the three-way mirror. "Look!" I said, "See how handsome you are?" Dov had the habit of never looking up when he walked and so I gently tilted his chin upward with my hand until he could see himself. When Dov saw himself in the mirror in that jacket, his eyebrows shot up and his eyes popped open, as if to exclaim, *"Wow! I am handsome!"*

There was just one problem: the jacket's sleeves were way too long. I found the store tailor, a short, dark man in his sixties with the stoic look of one dedicated to such a meticulous profession. Yes, he could alter the sleeves. The jacket would be ready for pickup in one week.

"One week?" No, that would not do, I told him in a desperate voice. "You don't understand, my son has never asked for anything in his whole life before. This is the first time. We have to leave this store with this jacket, tonight." The man looked at me as if I were crazy, yet with a degree of compassion in his eyes as he glanced over at Dov, who stood with his head down and his eyes closed, still in the jacket with the sleeves that were too long covering his hands.

The tailor checked his watch and told me he was sorry, but it would be impossible, the store was closing in fifteen minutes. "Please," I begged him, on the verge of tears. "Look!" I said, pushing the board in front of Dov, not knowing what, if anything he would say. Slowly, laboriously, Dov typed out the words: *"Thank you."* The man looked shocked and deeply moved. Somehow, miraculously, the alteration was made in those remaining fifteen minutes before the doors of Brooks Brothers were locked for the night.

"Come and see for yourself," I told my friend Marianne Toedtman. She'd heard all about Dov's new ability to communicate, his hidden intelligence, and Soma. Marianne was an extremely practical, down-to-earth person; she was also the main family recruiter for CAN's gene bank, the Autism Genetic Resource Exchange, and she had an autistic child herself. Like most parents, Marianne was also wary of the "next miracle" for autism.

Marianne sat and watched as Soma read to Dov and then asked him questions. When Dov began to point at the board, spelling out words and sentences, I saw her mouth drop open, but no words came out.

"Of course, Tito and Dov are two in a million," Marianne blurted out finally.

I stared at Marianne blankly when I realized she was not kidding. Then I looked at Soma. Suddenly the three of us burst out laughing. That simply couldn't be true. Dov and Tito could not be two in a million—could they?

In the back of my mind, a frightening thought was taking shape—a perfectly logical thought that I had been suppressing because it was so huge and so terrible. If Soma's method did work with other autistic children, then the unthinkable was probably true—it was likely that there were many more of these so-called lower-functioning autistic children and adults who possessed an intact mind but had absolutely no way to let anyone know about it.

I had to tell someone.

I picked up the phone and once again I called Mike Merzenich at his lab in San Francisco. Shocked to hear his voice at the other end when he answered, I didn't know where to begin. Would he even believe me? I told Mike that Soma had tried her method with Dov and it worked. Dov was now typing, pointing at letters, and communicating.

"That is wonderful news! You must be so happy," Mike said without hesitation, to my enormous relief. Could I bring Dov up to San Francisco with Tito next time we came to do more testing? Mike asked. You bet I could!

I e-mailed Yoram at the University of San Francisco, and he replied at once.

Dear Portia,

I am very excited to hear about Dov's progress. Is it like having a new son? The real Dov that you had no idea of his existence? Somehow it reminds me of the split-brain story (e.g. the work of Sperry and Gazzaniga). It is as if there are 2 people there and you can only communicate with one of them (the one in the talking hemisphere). It is not that you couldn't previously communicate with Dov—you couldn't communicate with the other Dov. It fits with the "fragmented mind" description of autistic people. However, the apparent split-mind of autistic people does not need to go with the hemispheres as you suggested (although it might). I will try to think about a way to test this experimentally.

Do you think Dov could do the experiments we did with Tito?
—Yoram

Yes, in fact, I did.

16.

Beneath
the Silence

There were few things that made Jon more proud than knowing his annual CAN letter was posted on refrigerators around the country. Every fall since we started CAN, Jon had written the year-end appeal letter. And every year he procrastinated until the very last minute. Perhaps it was precisely because the letters contained such a heartfelt and sometimes agonizing personal message that writing them was such a torturous process for him. The process started in early September with sincere promises of getting the letter done on time, followed by sessions of late-night pacing that escalated throughout the month. With October came the perpetually miserable expression, the sudden bouts of swearing, the bourbon, the cigarettes. And then finally, sometime in November, about the time we thought it was probably too late to mail anything out, Jon would always come through with a beautiful letter.

This year would be no exception, I suspected, despite the extraordinary news we had to deliver. But to my surprise, by the end of September, Jon had already written the first half of his letter.

Dear Friends,

Something miraculous has happened at our house this last year. We always said there was a boy in there. We always believed or tried to believe that Dov understood us, even though he had no way to show us it was true.

While still nonverbal, and unable to control most of his behavior, Dov has learned to point to letters on an alphabet board. It turns out that all this time he has been taking in so much. He can read and he can spell, and he has begun to tell us about himself. He has told us at a very basic level that he thinks and understands. For the first time we know that red is his favorite color. School is "boring." His little brother is a "spoiled rotten kid," and he's worried when I take a plane trip. Beneath the silence he is intelligent and emotional.

This revelation has turned our family upside down. We can't talk to Dov like he's two anymore, or treat him like a baby. We have to talk to him like a nine-year-old boy. He is a boy—full of understanding. He's intact. He has a sense of humor. We are so glad to finally meet him.

But on the other hand it just confirms the cliché, horrible but true, that he is trapped. And he knows that he is trapped. He knows how alien he appears to everyone else, and he doesn't yet have a way to use his voice or command his body to do what he wants.

And so our great joy is mixed with some sadness. . . .

One night, just a few weeks after our first trip to Toys "R" Us, I looked around Dov's room as I sat on the edge of his bed. The baby toys and books were gone and in their place were other kinds of books: books about the weather, architecture, and religion, and books about famous people like the polar explorer Shackleton and Abraham Lincoln. There were books of folktales and Greek mythology and books about birds and insects and rocks and gems and the solar system. There was so much to teach Dov about the world now that we knew he could understand.

But there were no new toys. Dov still couldn't play with toys. Lightheartedly, I inquired why he hadn't played with his dolls lately. *"Can't,"* he typed. "Why not?" I asked. *"I feel mad because I can't get my dolls,"* he replied. I thought I knew what he meant—he still couldn't organize any kind of purposeful behavior on his own at all. I told him how sorry I was about how he felt and I could imagine how frustrating it must be—things like that, I sympathized, things he couldn't get or do that he was frustrated about. He looked at me with an expression I had never seen before. A wave of anger and hurt crossed his face. He looked as if he were about to cry. *"Everything,"* he replied, pushing the board and me away.

I began videotaping Soma's sessions with Dov and I watched the tapes over and over in the hope that I might begin to understand what she was doing. I needed to get better at communicating with Dov and become less dependent on Soma. I also knew that what Soma had discovered was too important to remain a mystery, locked up in one person.

When Dov was with Soma their communication just flowed. Not that it was easy—it was very hard for Dov and nonstop work for Soma. But Soma was a master at keeping the flow going, and Dov would type out several sentences in succession with her—much more than I could get from him.

Soma moved faster than any human being I have ever witnessed, her voice never stopped; it rose and fell in a continual volley of staccato sounds as she read facts in short bursts immediately followed by questions, all the while reassuring Dov while she simultaneously urged and cajoled the next letter and the next word out of him.

Her hands never stopped moving—they flew through the air, one hand waving the alphabet board in front of his face, the other prodding Dov's knee, and then with what seemed like a third hand, Soma would somehow dash off quick sketches and diagrams for Dov, on the fly, all the while jotting down every letter, word, and sentence as Dov pointed them out. In this way, Soma inadvertently created a kind of record of the academics they worked on and their conversations.

It was hard to keep track of everything Soma was doing, much less to begin to systematize it. I felt as if what I was left with was the impossible task of imitating Soma, which truly I could not.

It took every ounce of Soma's energy and dynamic presence to keep Dov's attention under her command, and to stay attuned to his responses and shifts in his attentional state. Literally, from the moment he entered through her apartment door, Soma established a seamless flow of interaction with Dov, a second-by-second rapport. If she broke the flow, she would have to start again. This meant Soma could not talk about what she was doing while she was doing it. My questions would have to wait.

I continued to interview Soma every chance I could. I wanted to know everything about how she originally developed her method with Tito, in the hope that this would shed light on what she was doing now.

But it quickly became apparent that although Soma was a genius at what she did, she could not describe what she was doing or why it was working. And among the many things she'd tried with Tito over the years she wasn't always exactly sure which ones had really contributed to her success with him.

Yet from the beginning, I noticed that there were a few things that Soma did consistently.

Soma's sessions with Dov were always about thirty minutes long. She worked with him for about ten minutes at a time, with short breaks in between. These ten-minute "on" periods were intense, high-energy drills with absolutely no downtime and no chance for stimming or any other distraction. Soma captured, commandeered, even kidnapped Dov's attention. And just as with Tito, Soma did not care what Dov did during those breaks between teaching sessions; he could stim his brains out, for all she cared.

"You have to outpace the stim," she explained to me once, in one of her rare moments of doling out a gem of wisdom about what seemed to come completely naturally to her. What did she mean? You had to look at how the child stims, she said, observe the pace of it. And you had to go faster. The autistic child is constantly distracted, so *you* had to be the biggest distracter of all.

"You have to *become* the stim!" Soma declared.

And in polar opposition to everyone else who worked with autistic children, Soma completely ignored behavior. In fact, she never referred to it at all. I noticed she always allowed Dov to hold his favorite beads or whatever he had been stimming with in his left hand while she worked with him.

Soma never pressured Dov to perform. Instead she intensely urged and prompted, all the while encouraging and reassuring him. She never used a reward system. Instead, she proclaimed that the accomplishment itself and being recognized as intelligent were the autistic child's greatest rewards.

That Soma always sat on Dov's right side was something I also noticed.

And Soma always shook the board in front of Dov's face, sometimes she even brought it right up to his face and tapped him lightly on the nose with it and then quickly pulled it away again. What was she doing? "Yah, the attention!" she exclaimed. She must be doing that to capture his visual attention and to orient him, I thought.

These things were all I had to go on at first. These, and the impossible requisite: act like Soma.

Maybe an expert would be able to see something that I was missing. I invited my friend Dan Gillette to come down from northern California to observe Soma working with Dov. Dan was chairman of CAN's Innovative Technology for Autism program, and in my opinion, a genius, though he looked about sixteen, rode a scooter, and preferred talking about his dog, Cricket. Dan had a background in psychology, communication, education, and technology; maybe he could figure out what Soma was doing.

"Dov never looks when he's pointing," Dan whispered about five minutes into Dov's session. "He glances at the board and then looks away," he continued. "Soma stops moving the board each time Dov looks away." I stared at Dan. Then I watched Soma some more. He was right.

Soma shook the board in front of Dov's face, Dov would glance at it and look away. As soon as Dov looked away, Soma held the board still. That way, Dov could point without looking, because he knew that the letters would be exactly where they had been when he looked.

"Thanks, Dan," I said, as I jotted his brilliant observation into my notebook.

"I think she's using his knee like a 'think pad,'" our friend Rob Lemelson, the UCLA anthropologist, said after seeing Dov point with Soma for the first time.

But this meant he thought Soma was signaling Dov where to point on the alphabet board by pressing on his knee. "Really?" I asked, incredulous. If Soma was actually signaling Dov through an imaginary alphabet on his knee, I'd like to know about it, because I'd never been able to signal Dov in any way at all, his whole life.

Even if Soma had devised some sort of "think pad," it should be studied seriously, I suggested to Rob, because no other method had ever worked before.

After Rob left, I thought more about his doubt that Dov was truly communicating. It was true that Soma preferred educational exchanges over personal interactions, even though she used the terms *education* and *communication* interchangeably. Yet there was a big difference between academic education and natural communication.

One usually assumes that communication is necessary to answer questions and therefore a prerequisite for receiving an education. But it turns out that getting information in and getting answers out about factual subjects is a completely different and far less complicated operation than what we casually refer to as communication. Communication requires rapid processing of complex information in real time, it requires initiation, spontaneity, and flexibility. And unlike facts, the meaning of communication can be changed by unpredictable variables such as mood and emotion.

Given this, it was not actually surprising Soma preferred academics and that they were her pride and joy. Soon after Dov began to point with her, Soma began to gradually increase the academics. Within a couple of weeks, she had Dov doing thirty math problems at a sitting and he was becoming agitated and irritable. "Maybe after so many years of being alone, he doesn't want to be a human calculator!" I joked with Soma, who did not find this the least funny. "He has to increase his endurance," she said impatiently, but with a polite smile.

"Endurance for what?" I inquired.

"For tests!" she replied, shooting me a look like I was quite dense.

Tests. Of course, tests. Soma had trained Tito to take tests. Tests proved you were intelligent. Tests proved you weren't retarded. But I also wanted Dov to be able to interact with people. Soma conceded to some degree, and from then on her sessions with Dov ended with five minutes of open-ended conversation. Despite the amazing ability to learn academics that Dov was demonstrating now, it was those last five minutes I looked forward to most. I had a million questions I wanted to ask him. I wanted to communicate with him. I wanted to be with him in a shared mental and emotional space, thing they called joint attention.

I had also begun to notice that Soma did not like to communicate with Dov about anything that she did not already know. She preferred to ask him questions about information she had taught him, things she knew the answer to. This bothered me and even caused a flicker of doubt to cross my mind, which I instantly felt guilty about.

Soma loved facts and information. She loved them for themselves and also for the validation and the prestige they brought. I remembered her telling me that Tito could not always accurately report facts about ordinary things that had happened to him, even the same day, such as what he'd had for lunch. Instead he would indicate a food he *could* have eaten that day—a logical but nonspecific answer to the question. As if he were unable to recall the actual details of the event. How odd, I thought. Understandably, this frightened Soma when Tito was little, because people were already skeptical about his ability to communicate, and especially whether or not he'd actually written the poems she claimed he had.

And then there was the time when Tito was little that a speech therapist had quizzed him about why he "would not speak," and he typed out *"my parents are fighting."* Soma and R.G. were taken aside separately and reprimanded for their bad behavior, which the professionals said was the cause of their son's refusal to speak. Alarmed, Soma vowed to use her method solely to educate Tito and to avoid open-ended communication from then on.

I couldn't get Soma's statement, "We never talk anything personal," out of my mind, as I thought of the loneliness Soma and R.G. must have felt, confining their interactions with their son to the world of indisputable facts.

But at least Soma and R.G. had each other to share their ideas and thoughts and feelings with. Tito only had his mother. And Soma was determined to stick to facts and facts alone when it came to communicating with Tito. How lonely Tito must be, I thought sadly—even now. I wished I were able to communicate directly with Tito. But an occasional one-word, verbal answer was the most I could get without Soma at his side. I wondered about R.G. I knew he'd been a skeptic of Soma's methods when the newspapers and magazines were full of stories debunking facilitated communication as a fraud. But what about now? Could R.G. communicate with Tito when they were in India? No, Soma said. They did math problems together and that was it.

I wished it weren't true. But I had already begun to encounter the same problem with Dov. When it came to facts, responses came easily for him. But personal communication was a different story. Dov often couldn't answer simple questions accurately about what had happened to him, such as whether a therapist had worked with him at school or if there'd been a birthday party, or if he and Maria had stopped at McDonald's on their way home.

Even more upsetting was the fact that Dov still couldn't reliably communicate his wants and needs to us. Sometimes he could, but more often he could not. Despite being able to do math and answer academic questions and at times being able to tell us what he was thinking or feeling, when I asked Dov what he wanted to eat for breakfast, he might type out *eggs*, and then refuse eggs, then type out *pancakes*, and then refuse pancakes. Even a response of yes or no was not always reliable. And we often found ourselves frustrated, having to revert to the same old guessing games as before. In this respect, Dov had not changed very much.

We began to figure out some simple strategies, which helped. For example, we could verify Dov's intention by polling his responses to a question—a verbal yes, a nodded yes, and a multiple-choice yes meant yes. Two out of three responses being in agreement was usually a good indicator of what he meant.

I knew that Tito had this same problem when he was younger, but what about now? I asked Soma. Not as much, she said, but sometimes. That was why she "never talked anything personal."

But I had seen Tito reliably report things that had happened to him. What about that fifty-six-page document describing his early memories that he'd written and sent me? Soma explained that everything Tito had ever written about his past had been written spontaneously, "when it came to him." But when she asked him to write about his personal experience, even now, Tito usually could not do it "on command."

I decided to ask Tito about this. He explained that unless he was "paying attention," he could not remember things later. Why could he remember certain things and not others? How could he remember the new pair of squeaky white shoes that traumatized him at age three, but not what he had for breakfast this morning? *"Because the shoes made an impression and the breakfast did not,"* Tito answered.

I tried to think through how it was that any of us remember what we had for breakfast this morning. I could only remember what I'd eaten for breakfast for maybe the past three or four days. Further back, I was simply filling in the blank with something I might have eaten, an answer that was generally but not specifically true. It struck me that this was exactly what Tito did—he often gave answers that were within the realm of possibility, even probability—much like an answer we might give if asked what we had for breakfast a couple of weeks ago. Only Tito used this strategy to answer questions about things that had happened to him only hours, sometimes even minutes, earlier.

I must have brushed my teeth. I always did before going to bed, but tonight I didn't remember doing it. I didn't even remember getting into bed. Yet that was where I found myself as I turned the endless riddle of Tito and autism over and over and over in my head. If only I could think about it a few more minutes, a few more hours, maybe I could figure it out. It was like playing a slot machine—if I thought about it long enough, the answers had to start coming up.

I looked over at the empty pillow on Jon's half of the bed. He'd been in Washington for several days. Maybe when he came home tonight I would be able to stop thinking and go to sleep. I switched off the light, but the darkness of the room didn't help. Instead it was like a movie theater when the lights go down.

"Because the shoes made an impression and the breakfast did not."

Did that mean if Tito was made to pay attention to a specific event that he would be able to remember it later? Could you control what made an "impression" on Tito? Was that what Soma was doing?

Then it hit me—their arousal had to be externally modulated. It had to be activated, oriented, and maintained for input *or* output to occur. And Soma had figured out how to do just that.

Now suddenly I understood why Soma's method worked so well for learning information but not so well for learning from ordinary life situations, which meant not so well for recalling personal experience either. After all, what exactly should she call Tito's attention to in everyday life? It seemed so unnatural to narrate another person's moment-to-moment existence. And it occurred to me that this *was* sort of what Soma had done during those years that she had ferried Tito around town daily, describing everything in the environment to him.

It dawned on me that this is what the typical human mind does: It pays attention to the right things in the environment, moment to moment, in real time. Apparently we learn this very early in life, like paying attention to faces. But how do we know what the "right things" are in the first place? By the arousal level associated with them, which would determine not only what is remembered but also what will be noticed in the future.

Did that mean if I could get Dov to pay attention in a situation, say, for example, to what he was eating for breakfast, that he would be able to recall it later?

This must be what Soma meant when she referred to what she was doing as her "teach and test" method. So simple, yet so profound. She'd been telling me all along, I just hadn't understood. Information in, information out—both required modulating arousal and thereby attention. First to encode the information and then to retrieve it. Which would explain why Tito could not answer a single question about the story Raj read to him at Merzenich's lab when Soma wasn't in the room. They didn't know how to alert and maintain Tito's arousal and attention and so there was no memory trace to draw from when they questioned Tito about it.

I thought back on the arousal studies that Bill Hirstein and I did with Ramachandran a few years earlier when we studied forty autistic children using the Galvanic Skin Response (GSR) measure. What we saw was remarkable—the autistic children's arousal levels were off the charts, and not only the highs but the lows too. They had, on average, three times as many arousal peaks per minute as the control subjects.

Many people argued that these wildly abnormal arousal levels could be the result of the anxiety caused by the testing itself. I might have wondered if this were true had I not become obsessed with learning what was going on inside Dov. Until I saw Dov's GSR readout, I didn't know whether he was completely out of it or if he was experiencing an excruciating overload of stimulus, which caused him to look that way.

The GSR readout provided a window into Dov's inner state; it gave me a new understanding of him and a kind of connection to him. So I bought the equipment and watched Dov's arousal myself, at home in his normal environment, over a period of weeks. I saw that his arousal shot up and down like lightning bolts across the computer screen even as he sat quietly on the couch staring into space, and I became convinced that what I was seeing was not merely an artifact caused by the testing procedure.

But no one knew what to make of this, much less what to do about it.

If the arousal levels of autistic children were fluctuating so wildly, how did this affect what they were experiencing, and how did that in turn affect what they were encoding? And what about the retrieval of information that was encoded like that, coupled to irrelevant arousal levels? How would the brain know where to find things? Or what was important?

I began to understand how important it was for a brain like Tito's to deal in stable information, information that was not dependent upon arousal for its meaning—numbers, letters, facts, anything that could maintain stable meaning, in spite of careening arousal levels that could associate incoming information with irrelevant levels of arousal.

Whether Tito's arousal was soaring off the charts or bottoming out, whether he was experiencing an acute panic attack or he was attentionally blind to his surroundings, the meaning of numbers, letters, and factual information could be depended upon to remain the same.

Ramachandran had coined the term *salience landscape* to describe what people's brains encoded as important. He said he thought autistics had an abnormal salience landscape. I was just beginning to understand what he meant. You had to populate a young mind not only with information but also with the relative importance of that information. The autistic mind was not getting a reliable reading of the environment in terms of the relative importance, or as Ramachandran put it, the "salience of things."

Normal arousal activity was not something people learned by being taught. Typical patterns of arousal activity were driven and shaped by experience. But something had gone terribly wrong in the autistic brain and arousal activity seemed to be uncoupled from experience of the environment. Unless you could find a way to regulate arousal activity, the autistic person could not easily learn from the environment *as they experienced it.*

I remember when it dawned on me that Dov did not learn from the environment. The situation that made me realize this was the bathtub. We had lived in our house for about six years and Dov still did not seem to know the hot from the cold tap in the bathtub. A typical child would have learned this merely by experiencing the temperature of the water, if nothing else.

It was a circular system that fed back on itself: experience became memory, and memory continuously paved the way and predicted what would be noticed and experienced and subsequently stored, and so on. There was a tightly coupled relationship between what we experience in the environment and what we have experienced previously. And the two have to match up somehow. It was this stable relationship between internal and external worlds, between encoding and prediction, that seemed to be missing in Tito and Dov.

To a certain degree you could match information from the external world to information in our internal world by using rules—categories, classification, hierarchical relationships—but how did we just "know" something? Temple Grandin had a problm with this too; as she explained it, she didn't have a general concept of "dog," and instead she had to look through mental pictures of every dog she'd ever seen. She said she'd tried to use rules to identify "dog-ness," but rules such as four legs, tail, two ears, etc., were not specific enough or unique enough to distinguish a dog from a cat or many other animals.

So this "dog-ness" that most people seem to just automatically understand—matching the dog we see in the environment with the representation of a dog in our mind—must not rely on a set of rules or a catalog of specific correlated features. But if not, what then?

Donald O. Hebb proposed an answer to this question in 1949: ". . . any two cells or systems of cells that are repeatedly active at the same time will tend to become 'associated,' so that activity in one facilitates activity in the other."[27] Hebb was suggesting that our experience activates large-scale assemblies of neurons in the brain and the more frequently these neurons fire simultaneously, the stronger the connections between them become. This is why our cumulative experience of dogs, for example, lights up enough neurons at once for us to recognize everything from a miniature schnauzer to a Great Dane to the Peanuts cartoon character Snoopy as a dog. But imagine if every time you saw a dog, you were in a radically different arousal state. If that were the case, as it seemed to be in many autistic children, your neurons might not activate in typical assemblies and instead might form many more, much smaller-scale neuronal assemblies, each representing a distinctly separate and different experience of a dog—a kind of correlate to the pictures of individual dogs that Temple said she had to search through mentally in order to recognize a dog. My mind was racing as I recalled reading that vertical columns of neurons, known as minicolumns, had been found to be more numerous, but smaller and less compact in their cellular configuration in brains of autistic patients.[28]

A small group of neurons flashed in my own brain, drawing me back to an interview I'd conducted a few months earlier with Dr. Ivar Lovaas, the psychologist at UCLA, who first declared that autistics were capable of learning through operant conditioning. "Matching, matching, matching," Lovaas had said over and over. "Everyone is always trying to match to the environment. The autistic kids too." He described all human behavior as some variation of attempting to match interior and exterior worlds. "Matching is probably a primary enforcer," he said, implying that it is intrinsically rewarding and perhaps a basic drive underlying human behavior. He said autistic kids literally match things up, like lining up objects, because they are trying to match things too. "This puts autistic kids right into the continuum of human behavior; it is really not that different," he speculated.

It was true, Dov was always matching. He'd search through a bin of building blocks until he found two blocks that were the same size, shape, and color, or two rocks that were the same size and shape. I had asked Dov why he liked to click two rocks together and listen to the sound they made, and he typed: *"equal."*

Lovaas saw imitation as the human attempt to match the environment *behaviorally.* Lovaas believed that learning to imitate was the greatest indicator of a good prognosis in autism. "They rapidly improve once they begin to imitate," he said. "Learning to learn by observing their environment," was how Lovaas described it. The problem in autism was that their own senses could not be relied upon to provide accurate or even useful feedback about the environment. "When the kids begin to learn, they learn like typical kids," Lovaas added. He was probably right about that, I thought. Once Soma managed to capture Tito's attention, she taught him to read using a perfectly ordinary method: phonics.

Lovaas had told me about one of his first patients, an autistic boy named Johnny who he discovered tied to his bed in an institution to prevent his self-injurious behavior. When Lovaas visited him, the boy was eleven years old and could no longer walk because the tendons in his legs had shortened from lack of use. Lovaas took some index cards from his pocket and wrote the alphabet on them and showed the boy A and then B and explained what they were and showed him how to point at them. "Show me A," he demanded, just like Soma. "Show me B." To his astonishment, the boy pointed to A. And then to B. In the course of the next hour, the boy learned the entire alphabet. "I was flabbergasted at his speed of learning," Lovaas said.

How extraordinary, I thought. It sounded like what Soma did!

I was curious to know what Lovaas would think of Tito. But to my disappointment, he declined my invitation to meet with Tito. Lovaas said that he couldn't favor any one patient. But I suspected that Lovaas simply could not fit a person like Tito into his strictly behavioral paradigm.

I had no idea why these kids had such a roller coaster of an arousal system, but I knew it made matching their internal world to the external world almost impossible.

I spotted my laptop across the room and I jumped up and brought it back into bed. The room glowed blue as the screen came to life. There they were, the original graphs from our GSR study. I stared at the screen. Somehow what Soma was doing had to do with this. She was regulating their arousal and attention—second by second, moment by moment.

The graphs showed that the autistic kids' average amplitude was three times greater than normal. Their arousal was racing between extremes that most people rarely experience. And these peaks were occurring about twice as frequently. Their arousal was careening higher and lower than normal, and the arousal events were occurring more often. What would *that* do to perception, learning, and memory? I wondered.

When we did our study, we were going on the assumption that autistic people *responded* abnormally to the environment and we were trying to see what it was they were or were not responding to, and to what degree. We had recorded an autistic child's response to an object and then compared it to their response to a face. But what I realized now, looking at these graphs again, was that this was not a series of responses to stimuli—it was activity without a pattern.

The autistic children's arousal was erratic and seemed completely uncoupled from the environment. What did that mean?

It meant that stimuli in the environment were being perceived and subsequently encoded according to arousal levels that were not necessarily relevant to the stimuli itself.

I tried to think about what that would feel like. What happened when my arousal was too high? I remembered when I was in a car accident; I could still clearly see the watch I was wearing, how my arm looked, the steering wheel, the belt buckle of the sheriff—none of which were important. It seems that when arousal is cranked up, your brain captures everything with crystal clarity, including irrelevant stimuli, and stores it forever.

What happened when my arousal was too low? I thought about the times I'd missed my exit off the freeway because I was thinking about something else, like what color to paint my kitchen. Apparently when we are in a low arousal state, we sometimes fail to perceive highly relevant stimuli altogether.

I imagined rocketing up and down between these two states. This would mean that it would be very hard to predict what I might notice or store in memory. Sometimes I would be in a normal arousal state, encoding normally, and sometimes I would be hyperaroused and encode everything indiscriminately, and still other times I would be hypoaroused and encode nothing.

No wonder Soma had to teach Tito everything he knew by providing him with facts and information. His own experience was completely unreliable. *What he noticed and encoded spontaneously was unpredictable because his arousal levels were unpredictable*. Facts and information, on the other hand, were completely stable and predictable; they did not change according to your arousal state.

Soma had to conduct Tito's arousal activity like an orchestra, to keep it in a range where he could attend to the information she was presenting long enough to encode it. And no wonder she had to juggle his attention, like keeping so many balls in the air, to get that information out of him later. Soma's method worked well to recruit Tito's attention to information, but it wasn't clear how her method would ever be able to bring Tito's attention to focus on the moment-to-moment reality of his own everyday life.

Yet it was not as if Tito couldn't think on his own. He had ideas and opinions and feelings. But he always needed Soma to get the words out.

And yet, if Tito's mind had been populated only with facts and information, why wasn't Tito just a "walking encyclopedia"? How could he be capable of independent thought—which clearly he was?

The answer to this question held much hope and promise: although Tito's perception, arousal, and attention were abnormal, once information made its way into his brain, it became ordered and grew and connected as it would in any brain.

The problem with this sort of mind, though filled with not only information, but feelings and thoughts, was that it was not connected to the environment. It grew like an isolated island of humanity apart from our world; a world that was defined by interaction and behavior.

In spite of these profound limitations, Tito's drive to be a part of the world endured, he longed to be included, to have friends, to act "normal," and he never stopped trying to speak. Somehow, once Soma had furnished Tito's mind with enough information, a complex, thinking, feeling, reasoning person could live there, and not only live but grow and flourish, just as any human being's mind can thrive under the right conditions. It was just that for Tito those conditions were unique and it took an extraordinary person like Soma to figure them out.

I turned on the light and reached for my dog-eared copy of Tito's "Memories and Beyond . . ." beside the bed. I was looking for a passage I remembered reading, which now made sense to me. *"Abstract should turn to concrete. Because life cannot just feed only on abstract."*

This was how Tito described his first awareness of the connection between what was in his mind and what was in the world. He wrote about his first awareness that his own consciousness was separate from the world, that he had a mind that could not only react but could think on its own.

MY LEARNING . . .

Abstract should turn to concrete. Because life cannot just feed only on abstract.
So my beginning to learn and express myself is a turning point in my life.
I became aware that I was a part of my surroundings because I was a concrete thing in the world.
I was a part of it even if I stayed away from the banging door or made a clicking sound.
I was a part of it because the books told me so.

Tito could not feel his body; he had difficulty experiencing his own physical existence. Yet Tito knew he existed and he understood that his mind was embodied in the physical world, because Soma taught him this fact.

I closed "Memories." I felt so privileged to know Soma and Tito. I felt so lucky.

Finally, taking a deep breath, I shut down my computer. I would read my notes again, first thing in the morning. Whether right or wrong, I felt like I had figured something out.

I heard the front door open downstairs. Jon was home. A few minutes later, I heard each of the children's doors being opened and gently closed again. I knew he was going around and kissing each of them. He always did that.

Jon looked exhausted when he appeared in the doorway of our bedroom. After throwing off his clothes and getting under the covers, he asked how everyone was as his last words lapsed into a snore.

I couldn't wait to tell him what I thought I had figured out.

"I *am* listening!" he would swear every time I accused him of being asleep.

Babies could be tested at a very early age for signs of abnormal arousal activity, I explained excitedly. And if they showed signs of going off track, they could be given intensive intervention to help stabilize their arousal activity. There were even pharmaceutical agents that were known to "inhibit sympathetic outflow from the brain," I declared enthusiastically, feeling very hopeful. Could babies at risk for autism be fed a proper "salience" diet? I wondered out loud. But what would that consist of?

I looked over at Jon.

Maybe he *was* listening. You never knew when someone was listening. Dov taught me that.

When I awoke the next morning, Jon's side of the bed was empty. I found him downstairs, hunched over *The New York Times*, the radio tuned to NPR, clutching a cup of coffee. Without looking up, he shoved a piece of paper across the table toward me.

He had finished his letter for CAN.

> . . . *and so our great joy is mixed with some sadness.*
>
> *One day I asked Dov if he was looking forward to growing up. He spelled out "yes" and I asked him why. He typed out "I like girls." My heart did a flip. What a simple, normal little sentence. And such a handsome young fellow saying it. But then I looked at him a moment later stimming out on a bag of marbles, unable to stop*

giggling, and I thought it's going to be a long journey to get him where he needs to be.

And it's not only us. Portia and I know that there are hundreds of thousands of children and adults just like Dov, who cannot fully communicate, cannot fully control their bodies and their behavior.

Each year before I sit down to write this letter, before I tell you that we are getting closer every day, before I ask you to support our efforts to cure autism, I ask myself, "Is this false hope?"

I know the answer with perfect clarity. Last year who could have foreseen the blessings we were about to receive? And who can foretell the blessings already on their way?

There is no false hope, only hope.

—Jonathan & Portia

17.

How Many Others?

*I was in a whole new world of alphabet. I felt that they
were so much like me. So mute to look at. But so many
words and a whole language hiding within them. So much
sound and so much meaning. Every expression and
every understanding hid in their mute form.
And I began to consider myself to be like them.*

—*Tito*

t was a bright, windless morning when Tito, Soma, Dov, and I pulled into the Carousel School parking lot. Dov's school was in a bleak, featureless neighborhood near the airport where glaring heat rose off the streets and chain-link fence protected every property.

Tito wore a white shirt and leather loafers for the special occasion and Soma a saffron sari with gold embroidery. Dov's teacher, Miss Karen Spratt, welcomed them to her classroom, where nine autistic students, aged eight to eleven, sat with their one-on-one aides in a semicircle of plastic chairs along with occupational therapists and teacher's assisstants. Tito was flicking a pencil like mad in front of his eyes. "Sit!" Soma commanded, at which Tito surprised everyone by dropping to the floor and assuming a cross-legged position without ever interrupting the flicking of his pencil. I stood up in front of the class and read from the handout I'd prepared for everyone:

"'Tito is thirteen years old and has autism. Tito's mother, Soma, taught him to communicate by pointing at letters to spell words. Later, Tito wrote sentences and could say what he was thinking. Now Tito can use a laptop computer to write his thoughts and communicate. Tito writes poetry and has published a book. He has plans to become a professional writer. Tito and his mother are visiting from India.'"

I asked Tito to address the class.

"*I am humbled,*" Tito wrote in his notepad as Soma read his words aloud.

I asked Tito what he thought of the school.

"*I am very impressed how is it.*" Then, addressing the classroom again, he added: "*I think that you are getting restless.*"

This was an understatement: the children were squirming, making loud noises, yelling, crying, laughing, jumping, and crawling.

I thought I'd better move things along quickly while they could still be contained in one room. In the handout there were three of Tito's poems: "Red," "The Mind Tree," and "Forest Days," which I read aloud to the class. Tito chose "Red," which he had written when he was much younger, because he thought it was a poem that children would enjoy. I agreed, as "Red" was a kind of little fable.

RED

Red was sad and miserable
The earth had little of it,
It cried to be unable,
To colour the sky a bit.
For the sky was already blue,
Perhaps it suited best,
The waters of oceans too,
Loved the sky reflect.
The clouds of the sky also,
Were white or coloured grey,
The grass on meadow showed,
The touch of green shade.
'I'd love to be somewhere,

And show my brilliance too!'
The red colour's complain was,
From it's heart true.
The sun quietly burnt,
Up beyond the sky,
In hot fumes of gold,
It heard the red colour cry.
From that day on,
Every sunrise and set,
Begins and ends the day,
With the colour red.

When I finished reading Tito's poems, I asked if he had anything else he'd like to say.

"*I get very shy when it is recited,*" he wrote on his pad, followed by "*I love to write.*"

I asked Tito if there was anything he'd like to say to the children.

"*You are a very promising lot,*" he typed diplomatically.

The next instant before anyone knew what was happening, Tito bolted for the back of the room. What was he doing? "Tito! No!" Soma shouted, running after him. But it was too late. Tito had spotted a package of cookies in the snack area and was already on the floor, sitting cross-legged, rocking back and forth, having stuffed the entire contents of the package into his mouth by the time Soma reached him. "Tito! Get up!" she commanded, at which Tito rose obediently, cookie crumbs trailing behind as he followed Soma back to the front of the room and sat down cross-legged on the floor again. After wiping his mouth on his sleeve, he typed: "*I can not resist myself. I am very sorry.*"

It was time for my surprise now.

"Dov, would you come up here, please," I asked, motioning for Dov to join us in front of the class. Dov stood up from Maria's lap and she gave him a little push toward the front of the room. Dov clenched his fingers in front of his face and just stood there, before another push from Maria propelled him close enough that I could ferry him the rest of the way to sit in the small chair next to Soma. The room grew quieter. "Dov has a surprise for you," I said, beaming.

"Dov, which of Tito's poems did you like best?" I asked him proudly, as if this were just any talk show about poetry. Dov stared at the alphabet board, then glanced away. God, I hoped he would do it! Then, slowly, deliberately, he began to point, and with Soma's urging and her thumb pressing into his knee, he spelled out: *"I loved The Mind Tree."*

I heard Miss Karen and some of the other adults in the room gasp. I could feel myself smiling so big it hurt. "That was great, Dov!" I said, hugging him. "Thank you!" Then I gently helped him get up and go back to his place in Maria's lap. I didn't want to pressure him to do too much this first time out in front of a real audience.

"William!" one of the aides shrieked as a chunky boy of about nine who had suddenly gone mute at the age of three ran toward the front of the room. "William! Get back here!" his aide yelled, trying to catch him. But William had his own ideas. He plunked himself into the small chair next to Soma, nearly knocking it over. "Yah, it's okay," Soma said in a kind, understanding voice. The next thing I knew, Soma was waving the alphabet board in front of William's face and he was looking at it. He raised his hand and made a pointer of his index finger and began to aim it at the board. "Yah! You try it. You'll do it!" Soma said, encouraging William, clearly as happy about the turn of events as he was.

I stared, fascinated. What was William doing? Was he actually pointing at the letters? Was he trying to spell a word? No one was sure, but we were astounded that he was trying. Now two other children appeared next to Soma. Erica, a little girl with long dark hair and a worried expression who could not speak, and a little boy named Sammy who could not stop laughing—ever. And then I saw that almost every child in the class was making their way to the front of the room. What were they doing? One by one they sat in the little chair beside Soma as she waved the board in front of their faces and one by one they tried to point at the letters. Whether they were trying to spell anything was not half as astonishing as the fact that these children who generally could not sit for more than a minute or two, much less look at something or point at it, were doing all of those things completely of their own accord. Soma seemed to hold some kind of magical spell over them; it was as if she were the Pied Piper of autism.

Suddenly this eerie fairy-tale scene was pierced by a bloodcurdling scream and all eyes turned toward Maria, who was now holding her hand protectively and wincing. "He bit me!" she said in a pained voice. I rushed over to them, mortified. "Dov! Why did you bite Maria?" I asked, humiliated and bewildered by his behavior. But Dov only looked away, expressionless. Before I knew it, Soma was standing by Dov's side waving the alphabet board and he began to type.

"*It was my turn.*"

Indeed, it *was* Dov's turn.

But Dov, I now knew, was probably not the only one who was waiting. There were probably dozens, maybe even hundreds of others, who were waiting for their turn too.

What should I do? What *could* I do? The only thing I was certain of was that somehow I was going to have to bring this discovery into the mainstream. It felt like a moral obligation of the deepest kind. I had not felt such a heavy weight of responsibility on my shoulders since we started CAN. Today I had glimpsed something that, once seen, I could never turn my back on.

What I had been hoping, wishing, and praying might be true for Dov had come true: he had a mind. *How many others were there?*

Not long after Tito's poetry reading at Carousel School, I found another child for Soma to work with. One night a couple we knew only slightly came over for dinner and brought their three children, the youngest of whom is autistic. At four years old, Max was still not talking. He never stopped moving and he seemed to avoid direct contact with people. He was a beautiful little boy who reminded me of the main character in the book *The Little Prince*, with long curls and big eyes and the ethereal look of a fairy-tale child. I told Max's parents about Soma and asked if they would like to have Max see her once or twice a week. I explained that we'd seen great progress with Dov in a short time—in fact, Dov had begun to point and communicate after having seen Soma for only one thirty-minute session a week for six weeks. This was unheard-of for a child like Dov, for whom it could take years to learn the simplest things. Max's parents looked as if they wanted to believe what I was saying but couldn't quite, until I reached over and stuck the letter board in front of Dov, who suddenly removed a toy block from between his teeth and spelled out the word *"hi"* quite clearly. Yes, they said, they'd like to try Soma's method with little Max.

First Soma worked with Max, and then one by one others followed. They were all different. Some sat quietly and stared into space. Others leaped up suddenly and ran in circles screaming through the apartment. Most were nonverbal. A few could talk but their speech made no sense. Soma's method worked for them all.

Each new child's success was more thrilling than the one before. Soma and I were in a constant state of amazement, as her method seemed to work with one child after another. I recorded each new child's characteristics and tried to observe whatever variations in Soma's method I could detect. I videotaped each session and I took notes. Afterward, Soma and I would sit for long hours in her apartment discussing each child. We tried to figure out what was different about each one, what was similar, what worked and what didn't work, and why. I wrote down everything and then I watched the videotapes and thought about it some more in light of my conversations with Soma.

Soma's method had to be documented and studied. A knot formed in my stomach when I thought about going back to the CAN board to ask for a one-year extension for Soma and Tito to stay in the United States.

If they could just see Soma working with Dov, they would understand, I told Jon, confessing that I had invited Soma to give a demonstration with Dov at the upcoming CAN annual scientific meeting. I knew that many of the CAN board members would be there, I explained.

"You know, they think you're nuts," Jon reassured me when I told him my plan.

On the day of the CAN annual scientific meeting, we drove to the Loews Hotel in Santa Monica. Erika Karafin, one of Dov's therapeutic aides, was waiting for us in the lobby. Soma and Dov were scheduled to go on second, I told her, before she whisked Soma, Tito, and Dov off for a short, distracting walk on the beach.

The presentations were going to take place in the hotel ballroom, a large room with modern chandeliers and concentric rows of chairs. The room was already filling up when I arrived and I saw that several scientists and some CAN board members were already seated. My friend Gino, ever the auteur, with his black beret and charming Italian accent, waved from the front of the room, where he was setting up the video camera to tape Soma and Dov.

I didn't hear a word of the first presentation as I watched vigilantly for Erika, Soma, Tito, and Dov to return. At last, they appeared at the back of the room. Dov looked handsome in his navy blazer, and I was relieved to see that he seemed fairly calm.

When the lights came up, I stood up and introduced Soma and Dov as they made their way to the front of the room and sat in the two chairs Gino had set up for them. I took a deep breath and sat down myself. I felt as if my life were on the line.

"What do you want to say?" Soma started out, shaking the alphabet board in front of Dov.

Dov began to point at letters on the board and Soma read each one aloud. "'R-O-C-K'—Rock! Very good!" she exclaimed. "Yes! We have been studying rocks! What are the three kinds of rocks?" she continued, waving the board in front of him. But this time Dov did not respond. I saw he was gritting his teeth. Something was bothering him.

"C'mon!" Soma commanded, shaking the board again. But Dov did not type. Instead he growled and suddenly head-butted Soma. My palms were sweating. I was mortified.

"Yah!" Soma continued, as if nothing had happened. "We are nervous!" she said, speeding up her pace. "C'mon! You are doing it!" Now Dov was really mad but Soma kept pushing him until finally, between head butts, he began to point again. I breathed out.

Again, Soma read the letters as he pointed: "'I-G-N-E-O-U-S.'" Soma was beaming. "Igneous. Yes, we know it! Very good!" she exclaimed, "That is one of the categories of rocks. You are right!"

And in this way, going a million miles a minute, barely dodging Dov's head butts and pinches, Soma got an angry, growling Dov to spell out the three categories of rocks: igneous, sedimentary, and metamorphic.

I was relieved when it was over and Soma and Dov joined Erika and Tito and they left the room. I rationalized to myself that at least this was a demonstration of how even such an out-of-control, behavioral wreck of a person could still be intelligent. But I was not so sure that I had convinced the CAN board that Soma and Tito should stay in the U.S.

The room was emptying out for the morning break when Gino came over to me. "I found this under the camera tripod," he said, handing me a rock. "I think Dov dropped it on his way up to the stage." I turned the rock over in my hands. It *was* Dov's rock, the one he had been carrying around for days, a security blanket of sorts. "Thanks," I said, still staring at it.

I now realized that Dov spelled "rock" because he had lost his rock on the way to the stage. He wanted his rock; he *needed* his rock. But when Dov spelled "rock," Soma pushed him, until he spelled out what she wanted him to: the three main categories of rocks.

Maybe it was seeing Dov spell out the three categories of rocks, or maybe it was just the look of desperation they saw in my eyes; I would never know. But shortly after the CAN annual science meeting, the CAN board announced they had approved a one-year extension for Soma and Tito to stay in the United States, all expenses paid. And for that I would be eternally grateful.

Soma was ecstatic when I gave her the news that they could stay another year. But Tito was not. Tito was mad. He was feeling jealous and resentful. He felt left out. Tito picked up his pad of paper and pen all on his own in what was one of the only times I'd ever seen him do this. He was angry. His father, he wrote, would not have approved of what his mother was doing and she had not even asked his permission.

"*Mother is making a heroine of herself. I don't think she can manage it,*" he wrote.

I explained to Tito that his mother had a right to do whatever she wanted with her life; she could make her own decisions and needed no one's permission to do so.

Then, before my disbelieving eyes, Tito wrote: "*You may wear the pants but I am still the man.*"

And with that, he stalked out of the room, slamming the bedroom door behind him. Sexism was more pervasive than I'd ever imagined, I told Jon as I recounted the incident to him over dinner that night.

The next week, Dov's teacher Karen sent a note home with him. Soma could begin volunteering three days a week in Dov's class at

Carousel School. I knew we needed to hire a cameraman to tape Soma working with the kids at Carousel. We also needed a video camera and a hell of a lot of tape. But how could we afford it? The CAN board had not allocated any funds for such a project.

And there was another problem. If Soma was going to volunteer at Carousel School, we would have to hire an aide to help out with Tito while Soma was working. How could we possibly pay for all this? Maybe we could borrow some money, I thought, not really wanting to mention the idea to Jon. He hadn't wanted Soma and Tito to move in with us when I had suggested it as a way to save money for CAN. And he wasn't going to like this idea either.

As fate would have it, our friend Rob Lemelson, the anthropologist, happened to invite us to dinner around this time. Could I bring Tito and Soma, I asked?

The Lemelsons' house was a pleasant, welcoming place, situated on a street with white wooden fences and palm trees wrapped in twinkling lights and set on a hillside not far from the ocean. Inside, the teak furniture reflected their former adventuresome life in Bali and the walls were hung with exquisite oversized paintings done by Rob's wife, Sue Morse. Rob was an intellectual whose interests included anthropology, psychology, and neuroscience. His passion was the scholarly study of the perception of mental illness in different cultures. Rob himself had been working on a documentary about the cultural perception of Tourette's syndrome in Indonesia. In fact he had created a foundation that funded research on such topics.

I introduced Rob to Tito and explained that Rob was an anthropologist. *"I had the feeling that you are an engineer. Did you travel to meet the aborigines?"* Tito inquired. Rob smiled and tried to describe what an anthropologist was. Then he asked Tito whether India was mostly Hindu. *"That is right but personally I follow the Buddha, I also follow the Tao,"* Tito replied in scrawled handwriting.

Not unexpectedly, about halfway through dinner, Tito began to get agitated and Soma asked me to call a cab to take them home. I watched through the picture window of the living room as they waited outside for their ride. I was surprised when I saw Jon join them. How nice, I thought, until I saw him light up a cigarette. Then Jon began to pace back and forth, talking and gesturing, a stream of smoke trailing his words. Tito stayed glued to one spot, rocking and flapping furiously. Whatever Jon was saying, Tito appeared to be listening, though neither one of them ever looked at the other.

Over dessert, I told Rob that Soma was going to attempt to teach the other nine autistic students at Dov's school to communicate by pointing. It would be critical to document the experiment, I explained, hoping to appeal to the anthropologist in him.

The next day I visited Soma and Tito at their apartment and shortly after my arrival Tito typed out: *"I have joined the liberation."*

I had no idea what he was talking about and asked him what he meant.

"The women's liberation," he explained. *"I think Mr. Jon is a very good speaker."*

I couldn't conceal my smile. Jon must have been lecturing Tito on women's rights as they waited for their cab outside the Lemelsons' house after dinner that night. And Tito had taken Jon's lecture to heart.

Life was changing very fast for Tito. Soma used to spend every waking moment with him, but not anymore. Now she was working with other children in their apartment every day. This upset Tito. He often paced around the small apartment, stopping from time to time to loom threateningly over his mother and whatever child sat beside her on the couch. Eventually Tito would disappear into his room, slamming the door behind him. He would sit cross-legged on his bed, a pair of earphones shutting out the world, rocking and flicking his fingers in front of his eyes for hours. I knew something had to change. Tito needed a one-on-one aide, someone who could be a companion to him, someone who could escort him around town and free up Soma. Jon and I decided that somehow we would cover the cost of an aide for Tito.

Where Claude came from, I was never sure. I only knew that like so many others from that invisible army of saints who serve as a second body for those who cannot function alone, the elderly, the sick, the mentally ill, Claude was an immigrant seeking a better life in America. And as was usually the case with saints, Claude appeared at just the right moment in our lives.

9/26/01

Was it funny, was it odd?
That I went out with Mr Claude?
What is the matter that you ask?
Mr Claude is Portia's biggest reward.

And dear mother, what did I do?
Why should I reveal all that to you?
All I can say is I am looking forward
For my outing with Mr Claude.

Mr Claude from Phillipines
Is a great person, I earnestly mean.

Mr Claude, Mr Claude,
With broad a smile, and shoulders broad.
Mr Claude, Mr Claude,
Talking of heavens, the earth and God.

Mr Claude Mr Claude
Made me successfully to walk and jog.

And Mr Claude Mr Claude
A pleasant man with pleasant thoughts.

—*Tito*

For the first time in his life, Tito went out without his mother and roamed the city with his new friend Claude. And for the first time in her life, Soma was flying solo. Now, at least during the day, she could go places by herself, she could go to work, or to buy groceries, or even just wash her hair, without worrying about Tito.

And now that Soma and Tito would be staying for the next year, Tito would need to go to school. And with Claude at his side, he would be able to.

It was the day after Thanksgiving vacation in 2001 that Soma officially began her position as a volunteer at Carousel School. She would come in three times a week and work with the students individually. That same day, Gino started as the official cameraman, videotaping at the school once a week, thanks to Rob Lemelson, whose foundation had generously agreed to support the project.

We built a small soundproof booth in the classroom with a one-way mirror and a speaker system so that Soma could work in a controlled environment with each child and teachers could observe.

The teachers, aides, and therapists stood outside the booth and watched Soma. They were struggling to learn to work with the children the way Soma did. At the very least they were trying to find out what Soma was teaching them so they could bring the children's academic work into line with their emerging capabilities. But Soma was not in the habit of keeping a log or filling out forms. So the teachers had to go on the scribbled sheets that Soma generated on the fly to attempt to decipher what the children were learning.

Soma only wanted to do what she did best, and that was teaching.

But there was growing frustration among the teachers. They did not know how to teach their students anymore. And they felt like fools.

Only two months later, by Christmas, all nine children in the class were starting to point with Soma to varying degrees. Some were spelling simple three-letter words, while others were doing math and science and spelling out sentences. Every child could do some level of academics and all of them were demonstrating cognitive abilities far beyond what anyone had ever suspected they were capable of.

And there was something else that took a while to dawn on me. Although each child was now pointing and answering questions with Soma, no one outside Carousel School knew anything about the miracle that was unfolding there. *Not even their own parents.* How could this be? And yet I could see how it happened. The children could not initiate anything on their own. Most were transported to and from school in the school van and so their parents never saw them working with Soma. And there was no written record of what Soma was doing or what the children were learning.

As it turned out, the disconnect that we were beginning to see was a harbinger of what would turn out to be the Achilles' heel of Soma's method.

Dov's teacher began to contact the parents and invite them to come to the school to observe Soma working with their children. There were tears of disbelief, joy, and shock as one by one these parents saw their children spell out answers, revealing minds that no one had known were there. Once the parents discovered their children were capable of communication, they began bringing them to Soma's apartment after school, hoping that additional sessions with her would speed their progress.

Just after the winter break in early 2002 I was contacted by Miriam Weintraub, a producer from the TV show *60 Minutes II*. They wanted to do a story about CAN. We were thrilled. Miriam Weintraub came to our house, where she observed Dov pointing on his alphabet board. I told her about Soma and Tito and that we hadn't known how intelligent Dov was until he was nine years old. I told her about the nine students at Carousel School who had also started to communicate.

As the words left my lips, my mind told me to stop talking. We were not ready to go public with this, I quickly added. We could not tell parents that their autistic kids might be more intelligent than they suspected when we had no way of helping them get at that intelligence yet. And CAN was a scientific research foundation. Promoting unproven concepts and methods on national television could be destructive to the foundation's credibility. But this was the chance of a lifetime, to tell millions of people that autistic kids were intelligent, if only they could be given a way to show it, Miriam Weintraub argued, persuasively.

The *60 Minutes II* crew arrived at Carousel School one spring day in 2002 and taped for the rest of the week. Soon after, Carousel hired Soma full-time as a paid employee. Tito started attending a private day school in a classroom for severely autistic students and Claude went to school with him every day.

Claude was trying to learn to communicate with Tito, but he was still only able to elicit single words and short phrases from him without Soma's prompting. Tito was in the "life skills" program at school where he was learning to clean a bus and a toilet so that one day he could have a job. I was appalled. But Soma thought it was okay. "Jesus was a carpenter," she said. As far as Soma was concerned, it didn't matter much what Tito did during the day at school. Tito's education would have to wait until the evening, when she could teach him. This left little time for the writing he loved.

Now more than ever, I thought Tito needed someone to talk to. I asked my psychologist, Dr. Samuel Smithyman, if he would see Tito on a pro-bono basis and he kindly agreed. Dr. Smithyman managed to fit Tito in between his other clients—the Hollywood producers and their wives, the heads of studios and their wives, the famous actors and their wives. Dr. Smithyman was about to meet a couple like no other he'd ever counseled.

As it turned out the Smithyman sessions were more like group therapy. Soma was there to help Tito communicate, Claude was there to chase Tito and bring him back when he ran out of the room, Gino was there to videotape, and occasionally I was there to observe. From the beginning, it was Dr. Smithyman's goal to be able to communicate with Tito himself, without anyone else, especially Tito's mother, in the room.

At his very first session, Tito, with a strangely intense gaze, stared straight at Soma, who blanched as he spelled out: *"I hate you."* Ironically, Tito was totally dependent on his mother, even to spell out his feelings about her. And while perhaps considered a normal expression of adolescent rebellion in our world, Tito's angry sentiment toward his mother seemed anything but therapeutic to her. I was relieved when Soma agreed to bring Tito to see Dr. Smithyman again.

By summer, Soma and Tito had moved out of Park LaBrea and into a bigger apartment on Hollywood Boulevard. Soma announced that she was going to get her driver's license and buy a car. The fact that Soma had never driven in her life and now lived in one of the busiest cities in the world did not deter her.

"Come quick!" Jon yelled to me from the balcony of our house one day. "Look!" He smiled, pointing to the street below. There was Soma, in a bright blue sari, circling her new blue Honda like a gracious game show hostess, her face beaming with pride as she gestured at its many lovely features. "Wait!" I yelled, "I'll be right down!" But she just gave a toss of her head, got in her prized possession, and gleefully drove away. I caught a glimpse of Tito in the backseat as they sped from view. Soma's mantra, *"Find a way or make a way,"* took on a whole new meaning with Soma behind the wheel of a car on the streets of L.A.

The next week, I found an excellent immigration lawyer for Soma and Tito. They wanted to stay in the U.S. for good.

18.

Cogwheels

In dreams begin responsibilities.

—*Yeats*

On January 15, 2003, the thirteen-minute segment aired on *60 Minutes II* that focused on Soma's method, Tito, Dov, the students at Carousel School, and the Cure Autism Now Foundation. By 7:00 A.M. the next morning, CAN had received over one thousand e-mails. These were among the first I read:

My brother Alec is ten years old. He has severe autism. He is not talking and my mom is not sending him to school anymore. Someone comes to the house five days a week for four hours, but he is more of a baby-sitter than a teacher. Is there any way I can get Soma to help my brother?—Daniel

I am overwhelmed with joy for you and your family and all the families like us who want nothing more than to be able to communicate with their child. I have not stopped crying since I watched the 60 Minutes segment. I cannot believe that all the times I told my son Malcom how much I love him, that he hears me. My son

Malcom is four years old and reminds me so much of your son Dov. We want to use Soma's method, can you please help us?—Yvonne

We saw the CBS show on Tito Mukhopadhyay and would like to know more about Soma's method of teaching. We have a daughter who is seven years old and we would very much like to communicate with her.—Rose

My brother Leon lives in a group home. He is almost twenty-six years old and profoundly autistic. Looking into his eyes, I see a very deep emotional man who is begging for us to understand him. He still has violent outbursts and I cannot help but think that it has a lot to do with his inability to communicate. How can I learn Soma's method? I would do anything to be able to reach him.—Maribel

I have a nine-year-old autistic son who is nonverbal and also only makes sounds that are unintelligible and stims a lot. Dov reminded me so much of my son Brandon. I have always felt that he hears and knows everything we say. I know in my heart that he is smart. Are other children going to have the chance that Dov and Tito and the children at Carousel School have had with Soma's teaching method? I hope and pray so.—Kathy

Within the next month, CAN had received more than five thousand e-mails; the phones continued to ring and the daily flow of letters through the CAN office mail slot showed no sign of letting up.

It was clear to me that many and maybe even most nonverbal autistics could learn to point, and that pointing could be used to get an education and eventually to learn to communicate. I began to think of Soma's method as something really big, on the scale of sign language for the deaf or Braille for the blind.

The responsibility was enormous and the moral obligation weighed heavily on my heart and mind as I tried to figure out what to do next. I knew there must be thousands of people with autism who, if given the chance, could probably learn to communicate. Soma's method desperately needed to be disseminated. But we had nothing to disseminate?

People desperately wanted to bring their children to see Soma. What they saw on *60 Minutes II* gave them hope, and now they wanted their children to communicate like Tito and Dov.

Soma's apartment became filled with gifts from hopeful and grateful parents. But the flowers they gave her died in her bathtub and the soaps and the candles lost their perfume in the darkness of her closet. These were tokens of appreciation she didn't understand or desire. Less than two years ago, back in India, no one would even let Soma try her method with another autistic child, and now Soma had time for nothing else—she was seeing more than fifty children a week.

I thought back on Soma's first attempts with Dov, sitting on the grass with him in her lap, trying to get him to point at the alphabet board. By now, Soma had honed her method into an art, if not the science I wished it could be.

Soma's method needed to be described in writing, a kind of a manual. But a manual of what?

The only thing worse than ignorance is having to create an excruciatingly detailed description of something you don't understand. This was the job I now faced in attempting to coauthor a manual describing Soma's method. To say this was a labor of love would be to trivialize the agony of it.

Soma and I worked together one weekend a month. We holed up in a hotel, away from our work and our kids. Soma talked fast, pacing around our small hotel room, racing through her method and then moving on to topics she found more interesting, like astrology and husbands, while I typed away. We drank pot after pot of black tea, played Baroque music, tried aromatherapy and ginkgo—anything to keep our concentration going.

As we examined Soma's method, Soma and I identified some very interesting things about how her method worked. One discovery we made had to do with hemispheric laterality and could easily be translated into a therapeutic tool. The human brain has two hemispheres, each wired to the opposite half of the body. Soma always sat on the child's right side. She prodded the right knee, she tapped the right shoulder, she lifted the right hand, and she talked into the right ear. But it was the fact that she lightly held the child's left hand in place that tipped me off. Soma was signaling the child's left hemisphere through the right side of his or her body. And she was inhibiting the right hemisphere by lightly holding down the left hand. When his or her behavior was getting out of control, Soma would start doing math with the child, activating the left hemisphere.

When I went back and watched videotapes of Soma, my observation was confirmed. The child's right hand was almost always cooperating and the left hand was almost always disrupting. And although both hands often participated in stimming behaviors, it was almost always the left hand that *initiated* the stimming behavior. These observations ultimately led to a number of useful techniques that could help a child become more cooperative and they proved to be especially valuable when just starting to work with a child.

As I tried to describe Soma's method in writing, I realized that the pointing, typing, and communicating were something entirely different than what any of those words typically described. The pointing that Soma taught was not pointing in the sense of being a communicative gesture and it did not generalize to other situations. Typing was a better description of the activity; it was a tool that could be used for the purpose of communicating, but typing was not exactly the right term either because the typing Soma taught was much more than a mere mechanical skill—it was a bridge to our world. To say that the children were communicating was correct—

sometimes. Since the children seemed to be very dependent on prompts, especially in the beginning, and yet could produce some autonomous communication, it could be better said that they were learning to communicate by practicing communication.

As I tried to analyze Soma's method, an odd thing struck me. Autistic children could become literate long before they learned how to communicate.[29] By the age of six, Dov had apparently learned to read, but even now he still did not possess the functional communicative skills of a two-year-old. Because of this, Dov had also been deprived of the multitude of opportunities to interact with people that most children experienced during normal development.

From this perspective the communication problem in autism became twofold. First there was the problem of learning to communicate, and second, the cumulative deficit of communicative experience—the missing years of human interaction. It seemed counterintuitive that literacy could be used to build a bridge leading toward the ability to communicate, yet that seemed to be exactly what was occurring.

For nonverbal autistic children, the alphabet board that Soma used might be the first place where the child could reliably locate a stable, recognizable set of symbols, symbols that *another person* could also recognize. Olga Solomon, a linguistic anthropologist at the University of Southern California, called the alphabet board that Soma used a "stable semiotic field," suggesting that this experience could be the beginning of joint attention and shared meaning—the first step toward communication.

After working together once a month for nearly a year, Soma and I struggled through describing what seemed to be the basic elements of her method.

It was 2003 and Dov had been working weekly with Soma for more than two years. He was sitting longer, attending better, and he was overall far more able to participate in learning. He had gone from a boy we thought didn't even know his numbers or the alphabet to an eleven-year-old who was completing the fourth grade. And it wasn't that he couldn't be at the correct grade level for his age—he just had a lot of catching up to do. Yet there could be no denying that the skill and accuracy of Dov's typing—of all the children's typing—had not progressed very much since they first started working with Soma.

Three teachers at Carousel School had acquired the ability to type with some of the students, and very few of the parents were able to do it. Soma had become almost like a clairvoyant, leading séances in her little booth where the children would learn and communicate as they could with no one else. *But why?*

We were treating Soma's method like a therapy; the more sessions the better. But it was not a therapy. It was a form of communication that had to be learned through use over time in order to become functional.

After two years of seeing Tito, his psychologist, Dr. Smithyman, decided to end their weekly sessions. Smithyman had been adamant in the beginning that Tito would eventually be able to communicate without his mother present, but they never succeeded in achieving this. For a time, Tito used an electronic voice output device during their sessions, which doubled his communicative output. But Soma did not like the device and when I visited them at their apartment it was usually on the shelf, without batteries. After their final session, Dr. Smithyman said: "I thought eventually we'd be able to connect. But we never really could."

As time went on, it became apparent that there were a number of things Soma and I did not see eye to eye on. One of these was Tito and Dov's futures, which I felt were integrally bound up with the issue of behavior.

I argued that no matter how intelligent and sensitive Dov and Tito were, their lives would be tragically restricted if they could not generate voluntary behavior.

But Soma didn't give a hoot about behavior, as long as they could demonstrate their cognitive ability.

There was another issue about which Soma and I held distinctly different views. Eventually this matter came to overshadow much of what we did together and even impinge upon our friendship.

If the method of communication that Soma had discovered was a kind of language for nonverbal autistic people—the equivalent of Braille or sign language—then it should be made available to everybody. About this, Soma and I were in complete agreement. How this should be accomplished was another matter. I believed that the method needed to be studied, distilled, and formalized into a standardized approach that could be learned and implemented by everyone. Soma argued that by the time this was accomplished, she would have already worked with every autistic child in the United States, which of course was impossible.

I reconciled myself to the idea that Soma was a brilliant practitioner and just because I thought her method should be widely disseminated didn't mean that Soma had to take on the role of saving the world. One child at a time was Soma's philosophy. It was what she did best and what she wanted to continue to do.

But I believed that unless this method could be understood and taught to others, there was no hope of it ever becoming accepted or widely used, and that would be a tragedy.

During the time Soma and Tito lived in Los Angeles, we flew back and forth to San Francisco many more times. The team at Merzenich's lab continued their work with Tito and began to include Dov and other children. Every few months some of the young researchers from Mike's lab would pile into a car and drive down to L.A. to do even more testing. In fact, we saw each other so often that we became friends. It was an exciting time.

One of my dreams was realized when Temple Grandin agreed to visit Merzenich's lab to undergo some of the same testing we'd done with Tito. I wanted to know if the visual and auditory subtypes of autism that I believed Temple and Tito represented would hold true under experimental investigation. It turned out that in many ways they were a mirror image of each other when it came to sensory processing—Temple was predominantly visual while Tito was predominantly auditory, although their cognitive style of information processing was very similar.

Tito had said repeatedly that he lacked a sense of his body, but, try as he might, he couldn't hold still long enough in the MEG scanner to register an image of the somatosensory maps in his brain. The term *somatosensory* is used to describe the general faculty of bodily perception while the term *somatosensory map* refers to the brain's representation of this bodily perception. I was thrilled to learn that Temple had agreed to undergo a MEG scan to look at the somatosensory map of her hand, and as it turned out the somatosensory map of Temple's hand was quite unusual. Following up on this, another one of Merzenich's protégés, Dave McGonigal, studied eight autistic children, using the MEG scanner to look at the somatosensory maps of their hands. They too exhibited abnormalities; the findings remain to be published.

As it turned out, the only thing we found that Temple and Tito shared in common was an impaired sense of proprioception. Proprioception is the sense (other than vision) that tells you where your body is in space. When Tito or Temple were blindfolded and asked to walk a straight line, they lost their balance immediately.[30]

Tito was indeed the Rosetta stone of autism, and I would have been glad if even a single case history describing Tito was published. But the reviewers at many of the journals we submitted the case history to could not believe that such a person as Tito could exist:

> "*IQ scores more typical of a child with Asperger's syndrome . . . could he belong to this subgroup? If the child is nonverbal how was the IQ test administered? And how was his verbal performance so high? On what basis is this child labeled 'low functioning'? Parent prompting during assessment is problematic.*"

I had been deeply inspired by the Russian psychologists Vygotsky and Luria whose in-depth case studies of individual patients wtih neurological disorders, done almost a century ago, had laid the foundation for our understanding of the brain today. But if nothing ever got published about a patient like Tito, even after all the questions were asked, then perhaps our struggles were for nothing. I felt discouraged and let down by the thing I believed in most: the scientific process.

Sometime after the *60 Minutes II* segment aired, and Soma and Tito's lives had been changed so radically, I could see that Soma was starting to get restless. For one thing, she began to remind me frequently that she and Tito had always moved around; they had never stayed in one place for very long.

I knew she was leaving.

I never questioned that Soma was "the best" or why. But in my heart I had resolved that I would someday learn to do what she did and I would understand it and we would be able to teach it to others.

And now that time had come. After two and a half years in Los Angeles, Soma and Tito were moving to Texas where a family was helping Soma set up her own business with an office of her own. Realizing her dreams, she would now be able to devote all of her time to working with individual children.

With Soma no longer at Carousel School or even in Los Angeles in the spring of 2004, I hired a teacher and set up a small school in our home. If I believed in the method, I had to stop saying that no one could do it like Soma. If I thought it was real, I had to stop saying that I could never be as good as she was. I had to be very good at it. If I thought it was as important as Braille or sign language, then I had to be able to teach other people to do it too. Starting a school for Dov was my first real test. Could I train a teacher on my own?

Through some combination of studying Soma and a desperate, last-ditch burst of defiant determination, I succeeded in training the teacher for Dov's new school. Since then, everyone who regularly interacts with Dov has learned how to communicate with him. Some are excellent at it, while others remain rudimentary in their skills. Much of their success seems to hinge on the sheer amount of time they spend communicating with Dov. The important thing is that Dov is connected to our world much more than he used to be. And once people learn how to use the method with Dov, they can teach it to other people.

Dov chose the name Cogwheels for his school. Today, Dov and two other students attend Cogwheels School; they are in a seventh/eighth-grade curriculum. Cogwheels has become a kind of informal lab school, developing educational methods that allow all students to remain connected to the group and participate in real time in the classroom. We videotape weekly and hope to get some examples of the Cogwheels classroom up on the Web for others to view.

In 2006 I founded a nonprofit foundation called the Descartes Institute, named after the famous philosopher Descartes, who said: "*I think therefore I am*." I established the Descartes Institute to support the documentation, study, development, and dissemination of education and communication methods for low-communicating people with autism. I use the term *low-commuunicating* because I have noticed that many people with autism who can speak still have great difficulty communicating and need bridges to communication as much as their nonverbal counterparts. I have posted information on the Descartes Institute Web site (www.descartesinstitute.org) that describes what I have learned about how to get a child started pointing.

Over the years, Dov's behavior has changed. The serious aggressive episodes and extreme rage attacks have become rare, yet tremendous frustration remains as Dov gets older and the unfairness of being autistic becomes ever more apparent to him. His motor skills remain very poor under voluntary control, and they are mobilized primarily by impulse, mainly stimming. He still needs help with almost everything.

I worry about his future. I want him to go to college one day because he is smart enough to do that and he deserves a good education. His biggest obstacle in school as far as academics is that he cannot sustain pointing or typing for more than a few sentences at a time and writing a report can take a couple of weeks instead of a couple of hours. But we are working on it. And I feel more certain than ever that we will find ways to improve things for Dov by using all that we have learned about autism since Soma and Tito entered our lives.

One night not long ago, I showed Dov a videotape of himself typing with Soma; it was one of their very first sessions. Afterward, he began to sob. I never expected the tape to affect him this way. Covering his eyes and gasping between sobs, he looked up only long enough to spell out: *"Typing is no better."* I tried to comfort him. I hugged him there on the couch and told him that his pointing was much better. I told him that his communication has improved dramatically, that he can say personal things and express complicated ideas now. We sat there for nearly an hour as I tried to comfort him, but he was inconsolable. He only looked up from crying one more time to spell out: *"Only my real voice."* I guessed that meant he still wanted to be able to talk. I wished I had a camera on, though it would be too insensitive to record this. Still, I wished I were record-ing, because anyone who saw this could not doubt that it was Dov who was feeling, and it was Dov who was communicating. Instead I just held him tightly and kept patting him and reassuring him and trying to soothe him.

What happened with Soma and Tito changed our lives, but it did not change the fact that there was still a lot of work to be done.

The sky was dark and a light rain was falling as we pulled into Dodger Stadium the morning of the annual CAN walk. But in spite of the gloomy weather, there was a feeling of excitement, a feeling of belonging—a feeling that families with autistic children rarely expe-rience. For some, this might be their only family outing of the year.

Ours was different from other movements. We didn't come out for the walk to show our pride, there was no upside to having autism unless you were the very highest functioning type. We walked to raise money for research, we walked to find treatment and a cure, we walked because our children desperately needed help, and because for many, walking was the only thing they could do. All around me there were children from every corner of the globe—African Amer-ican children, Japanese children, Indian children, Thai children, Chinese children, Hispanic children, Caucasian children; every kind of child was becoming autistic.

The crowd was dotted by cheerful expressions here and there, the flash of a smile and occasional laughter. But under the rise and fall of the voices there was another kind of sound, the eerie cries and strange noises that erupted from the autistic children who strayed, ambled, circled, and ran away, and who were reined in, pulled, car-ried, wheeled, and held up on the shoulders of exhausted parents, whose faces made me shudder because they held such a terrible sad-ness. I did my best not to see it in the mirror, and now I saw it every-where I turned.

I was glad when I finally heard the MC announce: "Okay, everybody, this is it!" The band struck up and five thousand people started walking forward in the rain.

There were no communication devices anywhere in sight. No alphabet boards, no keyboards, no voice-output devices. We still had a very long road ahead.

The CAN Walk raised nearly $1 million that day. After everyone went home, Jon and I stayed behind to fold up chairs and drag away bags of trash—anything to unwind, to come down.

One million dollars! That would fund a lot of research.

Moments later, the baby-sitter drove up with the kids in the van. They were ready to go home. But Jon and I needed just a few more minutes to let it all sink in. Gabriel and Miriam jumped out of the van, followed by Dov, who clumsily climbed out. Gabriel hugged me and Miriam sat in Jon's lap and Dov just stood there. I pulled him into our huddle and hugged him too. We were alive and together; we were living, breathing, our hearts beating together. I looked at Jon and he took my hand. Where were the answers going to come from? What would happen to Dov? These were questions for the future.

Right now, it was time to eat dinner. "Let's go," I said, untangling from everyone. The kids hopped back into the van, but not Dov. He just stood there. "Go ahead, Dov," I urged him, "get in." But Dov wouldn't budge.

"C'mon, kid!" Jon said, giving Dov a friendly push toward the van, but Dov would not move from his spot. I tried hooking my arm through Dov's the way we did when we went for a walk, but instead he dropped to the ground and just sat there, grinding his teeth. Jon shot me a look that read like a laundry list of bad behavior. Tantrum? Rage attack? Just being a jerk? What does Dov *want*?

"Mom, I'm hungry!" Gabe whined from the van. "Can't we go?" Miriam chimed in, "We wanna go home!"

I crouched down and held the letter board in front of Dov's face. "C'mon Dov," I said, urging him to point. I could feel my own irritation rising as I sat down on the asphalt beside him. "We have to go now," I insisted. "If you want to tell me something, you have to spell it out now."

"Let's just go," Jon said, ready to pick up Dov and deposit him in the van, willing or not. And then Dov started to point. "R-O-C-K," he spelled out.

"Oh, yeah," Jon said, rooting around in his sweat jacket pocket. "Here you go." Dov grinned from ear to ear and grabbed his favorite rock from Jon. "I took it away from him during the walk because he was stimming with it too much," Jon explained, a little sheepishly. But Dov had already climbed into the van and even buckled his own seat belt. He was ready to go home and he was beaming. It was good to be understood. Whether it was about wanting your favorite rock or knowing how to do algebra. It was what people craved and it was what every human being deserved.

I looked over at Jon as we pulled out of the parking lot. It *was* good to be understood. Whether it was about wanting to cure autism or needing to learn molecular biology, Jon had always stood by me and I was glad we were married.

As we drove home in the glare of the late-afternoon sun, I thought back on everything that had happened since Dov was diagnosed, since we started CAN and since we met Soma and Tito. I didn't know exactly what the next part of the journey would be for Dov, but I knew it had already begun. And most of all, we were happy that there *was* a next part of the journey for him and for that I will always be very grateful to Soma and Tito.

NOTES

1. Applied Behavioral Analysis:

The use of Applied Behavioral Analysis (ABA) to treat autistic individuals grew out of the controversial research of Lovaas and others in the early 1960s. To this day, there are extremely strong feelings and opinions on the subject. Proponents argue that ABA is the only empirically studied form of therapy for autism and that research supports the efficacy of ABA as a treatment for autism. In addition, they point out that the negative reinforcement techniques that originally caused so much outrage are no longer a part of the ABA method. Detractors argue that ABA is an unethical and inhumane approach that should not be used on humans. Still others argue that ABA therapy results in robotlike behaviors rather than naturalistic, adaptive behavior. To date, it is probably the most widely used therapy to treat autism.

There are many books about Applied Behavioral Analysis and its use in treating autism:

A moving and informative personal account of the use of ABA therapy can be found in *Let Me Hear Your Voice: A Family's Triumph over Autism*, by Catherine Maurice (Ballantine, 1994).

To learn more about Skinnerian behaviorism straight from the horse's mouth, there's *About Behaviorism*, by B. F. Skinner (Random House, 1974).

For an unbiased, very readable, informative explanation of the theories and methods underlying Skinner's original premise, there's *Don't Shoot the Dog! The*

New Art of Teaching and Training, by Karen Pryor (Bantam, 1999). This unique
book explains behavioral training in terms of training both animals and people.
This collection of early behavioral studies of autistic children provides a window
into the deeply disturbing and tragically unethical research that has taken place
in the past and sheds light on the intensely negative view of behavioral therapy
held by many autistic people and some parents of autistic children.
Library of the History of Autism Research, Behaviorism & Psychiatry:
www.neurodiversity.com/library_index.html

2. Mirror neurons:

Williams, J. H., G. D. Waiter, A. Gilchrist, D. I. Perrett, A. D. Murray, and
A. Whiten, "Neural mechanisms of imitation and 'mirror neuron' functioning
in autistic spectrum disorder." *Neuropsychologia* 44, no. 4 (2006): 610–21.

Blakeslee, Sandra, "Cells That Read Minds." *New York Times,* Science Times, January 10, 2006.

Dapretto, M., M. S. Davies, J. H. Pfeifer, A. A. Scott, M. Sigman, S. Y.
Bookheimer, and M. Iacoboni, "Understanding emotions in others: Mirror neuron dysfunction in children with autism spectrum disorders." *Nature Neuroscience* 9, no. 1 (January 2006): 28–30.

Rizzolatti, G., and L. Craighero, "The mirror-neuron system." *Annual Review of Neuroscience* 27 (2004): 169–92.

Escalona, A., T. Field, J. Nadel, and B. Lundy, "Brief report: Imitation effects on
children with autism." *J Autism Dev Disord* 32, no. 2 (April 2002): 141–42.

3. National Library of Medicine and Pubmed:

Pubmed, www.ncbi.nlm.nih.gov/entrez/query.fcgi?db=Pubmed, includes over sixteen million citations from *Medline* and other journals for biomedical articles
dating back to the 1950s. Pubmed is a service of the U.S. National Library of
Medicine, www.nlm.nih.gov, which also provides excellent search engines for
the public and health care professionals.

4. AGRE:

Contact the Autism Genetic Resource Exchange (AGRE), www.agre.org, if you
or someone you know has more than one family member affected by autism.
AGRE was created to facilitate research in autism by providing an open-access resource of genetic and phenotypic data to the entire scientific community. Partici-

pating in AGRE is a meaningful way to support this research; AGRE, in turn, provides an e-mail chat site and electronic newsletter for families.

5. 1 in 166 children:

Statistic provided by the Centers for Disease Control and Prevention, www.cdc.gov/ncbddd/autism/asd_common.htm.

6. Brain plasticity:

"Brain Plasticity—An Overview," www.faculty.washington.edu/chudler/plast.html. The Dana Brain Foundation maintains an extensive, wonderfully informative Web site about the brain and how it works, including neuroplasticity, www.dana.org.

Mapping the Mind, by Rita Carter (University of California Press, 1998), is an excellent, very accessible book about the brain, including neuroplasticity, with beautiful illustrations. Written for all reading levels, it is especially enjoyable for the armchair scientist.

7. Facilitated communication:

Rosemary Crossley is credited with pioneering the use of Facilitated Communication. Initially, she discovered that children with cerebral palsy who did not have the motor control to point accurately could sometimes communicate with physical support and often demonstrated surprising cognitive abilities that had previously gone completely undetected. Crossley first used Facilitated Communication in 1977 with one such female patient whose mental age was thought to be less than one year old; later, Crossley cowrote a book with this young woman entitled *Annie's Coming Out.* In 1986, Crossley tried using her method with an autistic child for the first time. Today, Rosemary Crossley runs a center devoted to the needs of people with severe communication needs in Melbourne, Australia (the DEAL Institute). In her 1997 book *Speechless,* Crossley describes her methods and documents a number of her cases. From the outset, she encountered resistance from those who claimed her methods were a hoax.

Related article:

Biklen, D., and C. Kliewerb, "Constructing competence: Autism, voice and the 'disordered' body." *International Journal of Inclusive Education* 10, nos. 2–3 (March–May 2006): 169–88.

Related books:

> *Speechless: Facilitating Communication for People Without Voices,* by Rosemary Crossley (Dutton, 1997).
> *Communication Unbound,* by Douglas Biklen (Teachers College Press, 1993).
> *Autism and the Myth of the Person Alone,* by Douglas Biklen, Richard Attfield, and Larry Bisonette (New York University Press, 2005).

Further reading:

An extensive list of books about Facilitated Communication can be found at: www.autismresources.com/nonfictiontopics/fc.html.

8. Handwriting:

Learning to handwrite, as I understand it from Soma and Tito, was a laborious process that took about a year. There were several stages, the first of which consisted simply of getting Tito used to holding a pencil in his hand. The next step was to learn to make a mark or line on paper. Then Tito learned to trace, though it is not clear whether learning to trace was a significant part of the process. After that, Soma prompted Tito to make a line between two dots, first a vertical line, then a horizontal line, then a curved line, and so on, until he eventually began to be able to construct block letters. Interestingly, the verbal and tactile prompting Soma used at this stage were much the same as those she used to prompt Tito to speak and point. Tito describes his experience of learning to handwrite in his book *The Mind Tree* (Arcade, 2003).

Marion Blank, Ph.D., director of the A Light on Literacy program at Columbia University, has developed a method that teaches children with autism to read and write, including handwriting. A study of Dr. Blank's method, funded by the Cure Autism Now foundation, was under way as this book was being written.

9. Hemispheric laterality and autism:

There are a handful of studies suggesting abnormalities in hemispheric laterality in autistics. Here are a few:

Boger-Megiddo, I., D. W. Shaw, S. D. Friedman, B. F. Sparks, A. A. Artru, J. N. Giedd, G. Dawson, and S. R. Dager, "Corpus callosum morphometrics in young children with autism spectrum disorder." *J Autism Dev Disord* 36, no. 6 (August 2006): 733–39.

Chugani, D. C., et al., "Significance of abnormalities in developmental trajectory and asymmetry of cortical serotonin synthesis in autism." *Int J Dev Neurosci* 23, nos. 2–3 (April–May 2005): 171–82.

Nyden, A., M. Carlsson, A. Carlsson, and C. Gillberg, "Interhemispheric transfer in high-functioning children and adolescents with autism spectrum disorders: A controlled pilot study." *Dev Med Child Neurol* 46, no. 7 (July 2004): 448–54.

Escalante-Mead, P. R., N. J. Minshew, and J. A. Sweeney, "Abnormal brain lateralization in high-functioning autism." *J Autism Dev Disord* 33, no. 5 (October 2003): 539–43.

Chiron, C., M. Leboyer, F. Leon, I. Jambaque, C. Nuttin, and A. Syrota, "SPECT of the brain in childhood autism: Evidence for a lack of normal hemispheric asymmetry." *Dev Med Child Neurol* 31, no. 10 (October 1995): 849–60.

Dawson, G., S. Warrenburg, and P. Fuller, "Hemisphere functioning and motor imitation in autistic persons." *Brain Cogn* 2, no. 4 (October 1983): 346–54.

Related books:

A very readable and thought-provoking book on the subject of hemispheric laterality is *Of Two Minds: The Revolutionary Science of Dual-Brain Psychology*, by Fredric Schiffer (Free Press, 1998). Schiffer takes the concept of the dual brain to a personal level, inviting the reader to apply the principles set forth in this book to his or her own brain and behavior.

A good layman's primer on hemispheric laterality, from a research perspective, is *Left Brain, Right Brain*, by Sally P. Springer and Georg Deutsch (Worth Publishers, 1997).

10. Others like Tito:

Over time I discovered there were a handful of other books written by so-called lower-functioning, nonverbal autistics. These books, like the one written by Birger Sellin, described sensory and perceptual experiences similar to Tito's. This, and the fact the way these nonverbal autistics described learning to communicate through pointing was so similar, suggested that perhaps the existence of an intact mind in nonverbal autistic people like Tito was not so uncommon. There are a number of books written by autistic people, a small number of which have been written by nonverbal authors. I have included some Web sites below that list such books. I strongly recommend that parents read these accounts to help them understand their child's experience of life.

Later, I met another extraordinary young man named Krishna Narayanan, who, like Tito, had little control over his body and behavior, was nonverbal, and was subject to rages but who nonetheless could type and express himself beautifully in words and demonstrated above average intelligence. Krishna also wrote a book chronicling the story of his life, *Wasted Talent: Musings of an Autistic* (Vite Publishing, 2003), and it too had much in common with Tito's accounts. Krishna, along with his mother, Jalaja, later wrote another book describing the methods she used to achieve communication with him and that allowed him to receive an education. I found it encouraging that her observations and methods bore a striking resemblance to Soma's. Remarkably, Krishna did not learn to communicate by typing until he was twenty-three years old!

Sources for books written by people with autism:

> www.neurodiversity.com/autobiography.html.
> www.nlmfoundation.org/about_autism/personal_narratives.htm.
> www.autistics.org/library/booklist.html.
> www.everything2.com/index.pl?node_id=1331484.

An interesting article about Birger Sellin and his book can be found at: www.mugsy.org/nowhere.htm.

11. Theory of mind:

Singer, T., "The neuronal basis and ontogeny of empathy and mind reading: Review of literature and implications for future research." *Neurosci Biobehav Rev* (August 2006).

12. Dyslexia and imbalance of auditory and visual processing:

It is widely thought that many forms of dyslexia are related to an imbalance between auditory and visual processing capacity. There are many research papers and books written on this subject. Here are a few papers:

Pekkola, J., M. Laasonen, V. Ojanen, T. Autti, I. P. Jaaskelainen, T. Kujala, and M. Sams, "Perception of matching and conflicting audiovisual speech in dyslexic and fluent readers: An fMRI study at 3 T." *Neuroimage* 29, no. 3 (February 2006): 797–807.

Hairston, W. D., J. H. Burdette, D. L. Flowers, F. B. Wood, and M. T. Wallace, "Altered temporal profile of visual-auditory multisensory interactions in dyslexia." *Exp Brain Res* 166, nos. 3–4 (October 2005): 474–80.

NOTES

Meyler, A., and Z. Breznitz, "Visual, auditory and cross-modal processing of linguistic and nonlinguistic temporal patterns among adult dyslexic readers." *Dyslexia* 11, no. 2 (May 2005): 93–115.

Here is a good book on the broader subject of learning styles: *A Mind at a Time*, by Mel Levine (Simon & Schuster, 2002).

13. Chorus reading:

Chorus reading is the term Soma used to describe when she and Tito read aloud together in unison. It is also sometimes referred to as *choral reading*.

Vygotsky includes chorus reading in his writing about education methods for disabled as well as typically developing children. For more, see *Scaffolding Learning: Vygotsky and Early Childhood Education*, by Laura E. Berk and Adam Winsler (National Association for the Education of Young Children, 1995).

Kalinowski, J., and T. Saltuklaroglu, "Choral speech: The amelioration of stuttering via imitation and the mirror neuronal system." *Neurosci Biobehav Rev* 27, no. 4 (September 2003): 339–47.

14. Ramachandran on synesthesia:

Hubbard, E. M., and V. S. Ramachandran, "Neurocognitive mechanisms of synesthesia." *Neuron* 48, no. 3 (November 2005): 509–20.

Ramachandran, V. S., and E. M. Hubbard, "Synaesthesia—a window into perception, thought and language." *Journal of Consciousness Studies* 8 (2001): 3–34.

15. Asperger's syndrome:

For general information, see Medline Plus Medical Encyclopedia at: www.nlm.nih.gov/medlineplus/ency/article/001549.htm.

Also see Yale Developmental Disabilities Clinic, "Asperger's Syndrome Guidelines for Assessment and Diagnosis," www.med.yale.edu/chldstdy/autism/asdiagnosis.html.

There are many books on the subject of Asperger's syndrome, as well as books written by people with Asperger's describing their experience. In addition, there are numerous Web sites dedicated to the topic that include information, resources, community discussion groups, etc. There are also Web sites created by people with Asperger's syndrome, as well as numerous Asperger's community blogs. See: www.neurodiversity.com/aspergers_general.html for comprehensive listings.

16. Galvanic Skin Response (GSR):

Critchley, H. D., "Electrodermal responses: What happens in the brain." *Neuroscientist* 8, no. 2 (April 2002): 132–42.

17. Rubber hand experiment:

Ehrsson, H. H., N. P. Holmes, and R. E. Passingham, "Touching a rubber hand: Feeling of body ownership is associated with activity in multisensory brain areas." *Neuroimage* 29, no. 1 (January 2006): 67–73.

Schaefer, M., N. Noennig, H. J. Heinze, and M. Rotte, "Fooling your feelings: Artificially induced referred sensations are linked to a modulation of the primary somatosensory cortex." *J Neurosci* 25, no. 45 (November 2005): 10564–73.

18. Hirstein, Iversen, Ramachandran study:

Hirstein, W., P. Iversen, and V. S. Ramachandran, "Autonomic responses of autistic children to people and objects." *Proceedings of the Royal Society* 268 (2001): 1883–88.

19. Autonomic arousal in autistic subjects:

Since our original study, a number of other reports have been published that also describe abnormal autonomic arousal in autistic subjects. Here are a few of them:

Kennedy, D. P., E. Redcay, and E. Courchesne, "Failing to deactivate: Resting functional abnormalities in autism." *Proc Natl Acad Sci* 103, no. 21 (May 2006): 8275–80.

Ben Shalom, D., S. H. Mostofsky, R. L. Hazlett, M. C. Goldberg, Y. Faran, D. R. McLeod, and R. Hoehn-Saric, "Normal physiological emotions but differences in expression of conscious feelings in children with high-functioning autism." *J Autism Dev Disord* 36, no. 3 (April 2006): 395–400.

Ming, X., P. O. Julu, M. Brimacombe, S. Connor, and M. L. Daniels, "Reduced cardiac parasympathetic activity in children with autism." *Brain Dev* 27, no. 7 (October 2005): 509–16.

Ming, X., P. O. Julu, J. Wark, F. Apartopoulos, and S. Hansen, "Discordant mental and physical efforts in an autistic patient." *Brain Dev* 26, no. 8 (December 2004): 519–24.

Toichi, M., and Y. Kamio, "Paradoxical autonomic response to mental tasks in autism." *J Autism Dev Disord* 33, no. 4 (August 2003): 417–26.

20. GSR and infants:

Hernes, K. G., L. Morkrid, A. Fremming, S. Odegarden, O. G. Martinsen, and H. Storm, "Skin conductance changes during the first year of life in full-term infants." *Pediatr Res* 52, no. 6 (December 2002): 837–43.

21. Sensory input vs. neural representation discussion:

If the brain had no experience, the mere ability to perceive sensory input could not impart meaning to the brain:

When cochlear implants were first invented for deaf people, researchers were surprised that these people could not suddenly hear in the same way that we do once their physical ability to hear was restored. Soon it was realized that human hearing is much more than simple physical reception of sounds. Understanding those sounds is the work of the human brain—something that can no more occur in an instant than a newborn can understand language. From the pure sensory perception of sounds, a database of meaning is constructed by the brain from which all future meaning is derived. Thus, a cochlear implant could no more facilitate the understanding of sound than a pair of speakers could. See Kral, A., and J. Tillien, "Brain plasticity under cochlear implant stimulation." *Adv Otorhinolaryngol* (2006).

Some time later, I read in the journal *Nature Neuroscience* ("Long-term deprivation affects visual perception and cortex," by D. I. MacLeod et al., September 2003) a report about a man who, at age three, lost one eye and become blind in the other. At age forty-three, he had a corneal implant in the blind eye. The surgery was a success by all physical measures, yet, in spite of his normal early visual development, his ability to see as the rest of us do remained severely impaired.

We are not born with the kind of visual and auditory representations of the world that we take to be reality. Rather these representations develop over time, they are molded and sculpted and informed by neural activity generated by our sensory systems' interaction with the environment. This is known as "activity-dependent" plasticity of the brain, and it is why a kitten with one eye patched will be blind in that otherwise physically perfectly good eye for the rest of the animal's life. It simply missed out on the period of time when vision was being shaped by environmental input. So the fact that restoring this man's vision to a physically normal state did not instantly provide him with the ability to see the way the rest of us was not unexpected. What was a surprise, however, was that he had also lost much of the visual ability he had developed prior to the loss of his sight at age three. This indicated that the activity-dependent visual development he had established by the age of three had regressed simply from nonuse.

This particular man was an expert skier as a blind person, using verbal directions from a guide, yet immediately after the operation he closed his eyes when skiing, as the visual information only served to give him a frightening sense of imminent collision. Eventually, he came to make significant use of vision in his everyday life, though after two years he made the following statement: "The difference between today and over two years ago is that I can better guess at what I am seeing. What is the same is that I am still guessing." In a real sense, we are all "guessing" at what we are seeing and hearing, all the time, or, put another way, we are constantly "constructing our reality." Some neuroscientists claim that our memory system functions in the same way; that we, in fact, construct our own memories just as we construct our own reality in the present—on the fly. Still others purport that this ongoing construction of reality is actually a form of prediction that allows our attention to focus on the new and integrate it into our ever-growing "knowledge base." Doubtless, this is the very same knowledge base that Tito has mentioned on several occasions during our interviews. I continue to be amazed at the insight into his own mental functioning that Tito demonstrates.

What *would* happen, I wondered, if Tito were suddenly able to see and hear simultaneously as we do? Tito had spent most of his life relying almost exclusively upon his hearing, to the exclusion of his vision, so it was likely that his vision had remained quite undeveloped. If he were suddenly able to use his vision and hearing simultaneously he would probably not experience the environment the way most of us do, in a seamless integration of auditory and visual information. And if this undeveloped visual system were to suddenly compete on equal ground with the auditory information, which Tito had come to rely almost entirely upon, it would doubtless interfere with his ability to derive meaning from the environment.

22. Perceptual learning:

According to the book *Perceptual Learning*, edited by Manfred Fahle and Tomaso Poggio (MIT Press, 2002), perceptual learning is the specific and relatively permanent modification of perception and behavior following sensory experience. It encompasses parts of the learning process that are independent from conscious forms of learning and involve structural and/or functional changes in primary sensory cortices.

23. Technical note:

John Houde adjusted the device once more, this time altering the frequency feedback. This was expanding the range of sound, he explained. *The frequency-altered feedback was 300 Hz sign wave carrier modulated.*

24. Autism Diagnostic Interview (ADI-R):

Lord, C., M. Rutter, and A. Le Couteur, "Autism Diagnostic Interview–Revised: A revised version of a diagnostic interview for caregivers of individuals with possible pervasive developmental disorders." *J Autism Dev Disord* 24, no. 5 (October 1994): 659–85.

25. Autism Diagnostic Observation Schedule (ADOS):

Lord, C., S. Risi, L. Lambrecht, E. H. Cook Jr., B. L. Leventhal, P. C. DiLavore, A. Pickles, and M. Rutter, "The Autism Diagnostic Observation Schedule—Generic: A standard measure of social and communication deficits associated with the spectrum of autism." *J Autism Dev Disord* 30, no. 3 (June 2000).

26. Temple Grandin:

Temple Grandin's home page: www.templegrandin.com/templehome.html.
Temple Grandin's professional Web site: www.grandin.com.
Temple Grandin's books and videos: www.templegrandin.com/templegrandin books.html.
Temple Grandin's informative article "Autism—The Way I See It": www.temple grandin.com/templegrandinart.html.
Temple Grandin's article "Thinking in Pictures": www.grandin.com/inc/visual .thinking.html.

27. Hebb:

D. O. Hebb, from his book *The Organization of Behavior* (1949), p. 70.

28. Minicolumns:

Casanova, M. F., I. A. van Kooten, A. E. Switala, H. van Engleland, H. Heinsen, H. W. Steinbusch, P. R. Hof, J. Trippe, J. Stone, and C. Schmitz, "Minicolumnar abnormalities in autism." *Acta Neuropathol* (July 2006).
M. F. Casanova, "White matter volume increase and minicolumns in autism." *Ann Neurol* 56, no. 3 (September 2004): 453; author reply, 454.
Comment on: *Ann Neurol* 55, no. 4 (April 2004): 530–40.
Casanova, M. F., D. Buxhoeveden, and J. Gomez, "Disruption in the inhibitory architecture of the cell minicolumn: Implications for autism." *Neuroscientist* 9, no. 6 (December 2003): 496–507.

Comment in: *Neuroscientist* 10, no. 3 (June 2004): 189–91.

Casanova, M. F., D. P. Buxhoeveden, and C. Brown, "Clinical and macroscopic correlates of minicolumnar pathology in autism." *J. Child Neurol* 17, no. 9 (September 2002): 692–95.

29. Autistic children become literate before they can communicate discussion:

We tend to think of literacy as the evolution of basic communication, not the road to it. By the very nature of their disorder, autistic children have missed out on the millions of opportunities to interact with other humans, which normally occur during infant development. So that by the time children like Tito and Dov are five or six years old, they may have attained literacy skills, but without possessing the most basic communicative abilities of an infant.

There has been an ongoing debate in linguistics, psychology, philosophy, and neuroscience about whether language is a uniquely human capacity. Animal intelligence has been intensively investigated, and while it has been shown that there is some overlap in the communicative abilities of humans and animals, the debate about what constitutes language rages on. The linguist Noam Chomsky (see below) argues that there are two broad and distinct categories of communication, the first being faculty for language in the broader sense (FLB), which involves the many domains of communication we have in common with other species, and the second being faculty for language in the narrower sense (FLN), which refers to spoken and written language, and is argued to be uniquely human.

Chomsky's two categories turn out to be useful for describing the most astonishing thing I have learned about Tito and Dov: they appear to possess an excellent faculty of language in the narrow sense, the uniquely human sense—yet they seem to be missing the faculty of language in the broad sense—to be devoid of the most basic communicative abilities which are shared by many species.

Hauser, M. D., N. Chomsky, and W. T. Fitch, "The faculty of language: What is it, who has it, and how did it evolve?" *Science* 298, no. 5598 (November 2002): 1569–79.

Comment in: *Science* 298, no. 5598 (November 2002): 1565–66.

30. Abnormalities in motor and somatosensory indices in autism:

Jansiewicz, E. M., M. C. Goldberg, C. J. Newschaffer, M. B. Denckla, R. Landa, and S. H. Mostofsky, "Motor signs distinguish children with high-functioning autism and Asperger's syndrome from controls." *J Autism Dev Disord* 36, no. 5 (July 2006): 613–21.

Minshew, N. J., K. Sung, B. L. Jones, and J. M. Furman, "Underdevelopment of the postural control system in autism." *Neurology* 63, no. 11 (December 2004): 2056–61.

Muller, R. A., C. Cauich, M. A. Rubio, A. Mizuno, and E. Courchesne, "Abnormal activity patterns in premotor cortex during sequence learning in autistic patients." *Biol Psychiatry* 56, no. 5 (September 2004): 323–32.

Teitelbaum, O., T. Benton, P. K. Shah, A. Prince, J. L. Kelly, and P. Teitelbaum, "Eshkol-Wachman movement notation in diagnosis: The early detection of Asperger's syndrome." *Proc Natl Acad Sci* 101, no. 32 (August 2004): 11909–14.

Mueller, R. A., N. Kleinhans, N. Kemmotsu, K. Pierce, and E. Courchesne, "Abnormal variability and distribution of functional maps in autism: An FMRI study of visuomotor learning." *Am J Psychiatry* 160, no. 10 (October 2003): 1847–62.

Erratum in: *Am J Psychiatry* 161, no. 7 (July 2004): 1320.

Schmitz, C., J. Martineau, C. Barthelemy, and C. Assaiante, "Motor control and children with autism: Deficit of anticipatory function?" *Neurosci Lett* 348, no. 1 (September 2003): 17–20.

Mari, M., U. Castiello, D. Marks, C. Marraffa, and M. Prior, "The reach-to-grasp movement in children with autism spectrum disorder." *Philos Trans R Soc Lond B Biol Sci* 358, no. 1430 (February 2003): 393–403.

Muller, R. A., K. Pierce, J. B. Ambrose, G. Allen, and E. Courchesne, "Atypical patterns of cerebral motor activation in autism: A functional magnetic resonance study." *Biol Psychiatry* 44, no. 8 (April 2001): 665–76.

Rinehart, N. J., J. L. Bradshaw, A. V. Brereton, and B. J. Tonge, "Movement preparation in high-functioning autism and Asperger disorder: A serial choice reaction time task involving motor reprogramming." *J Autism Dev Disord* 31, no. 1 (February 2001): 79–88.

Teitelbaum, P., O. Teitelbaum, J. Nye, J. Fryman, and R. G. Maurer, "Movement analysis in infancy may be useful for early diagnosis of autism." *Proc Natl Acad Sci* 95, no. 23 (November 1998): 13982–87.

Ornitz, E. M., M. B. Brown, A. Mason, and N. H. Putnam, "Effect of visual input on vestibular nystagmus in autistic children." *Arch Gen Psychiatry* 42, no. 10 (October 1985): 1018–25.

Maurer, R. G., and A. R. Damasio, "Vestibular dysfunction in autistic children." *Dev Med Child Neurol* 21, no. 5 (October 1979): 656–59.

Ornitz, E. M., C. W. Atwell, A. R. Kaplan, and J. R. Westlake, "Brain-stem dysfunction in autism: Results of vestibular stimulation." *Arch Gen Psychiatry* 31, no. 3 (September 1974): 369–75.

ACKNOWLEDGMENTS

Throughout the writing of this book I have felt an overwhelming sense of responsibility to get this story out to the world in hopes that people might look anew at children with autism who cannot speak and be inspired to build the bridge of communication into their world.

Most of all I wish to express my gratitude to my son Dov, for his patience and his perseverance through all the years when we could not communicate with each other. It is a tribute to his character and soul that in spite of all his struggles, he has remained such a kind and gentle person and so generous of spirit. I have had many wonderful teachers in my life but none so wonderful as my son.

I will forever be grateful to Soma Mukhopadhyay for her brilliant observations of her own son and the methods that she developed which enabled Tito and Dov and so many other children with autism to begin to communicate. My heartfelt thanks goes to Tito Mukhopadhyay for the many hours of discussion and interviews he participated in to make this book possible and the time and energy that he gave as he participated in research studies. More than anything, I appreciate having had the chance to get to know such a remarkable person, to begin to learn how he thinks and feels, and to have enjoyed his amazing gifts as a writer. I shall treasure the friendship I have had with Tito and Soma forever. And a special thanks to R.G. Mukhopadhyay for so graciously sharing his extraordinary family with the rest of the world.

My family deserves a gold medal for their patience and understanding during the long months that grew into years as I completed the writing of this book. My children Billy, Dov, Miriam, and Gabriel were very mature and understanding during this time and I appreciate that so very much. My husband Jon stood by me through everything, giving constant encouragement and support. I would like to acknowledge my mother Betty Jane and thank Jon's parents, Marciarose and Jerry Shestack. Their love for Dov and their support of Cure Autism Now has been unconditional and enduring.

A special thanks to Dov's favorite person in the world, my sister Sarah, without whose loving help I would not have been able to write all those long nights and weekends knowing that Dov was in good hands.

I have found scientists to be among the most generous and kind people I have ever known. I cannot begin to express the profound effect that they have had on our lives. I will always be indebted to Dan Geschwind and Bruce Miller who helped us start the Cure Autism Now foundation and guided us in the monumental undertaking of establishing the Autism Genetic Resource Exchange. A very special thanks for the moral support and tireless efforts of CAN's very first board member, Rickie Robinson, and to all the amazing CAN board members over the years, including Sallie Bernard, Nanci Fredkin, John Wilson, Elizabeth Emken, Marcia Goldman, David Baskin, Craig Snyder, Peter Bell, Janet Grillo, Magdalena Del Oelmo, Brad Whitford, Jane Kaczmarek, Anthony Edwards, Rene Russo, Maya Angelou, and so many others.

I am so grateful to the many scientists who have so generously devoted their time and energy to reviewing Cure Autism Now grants and traveling to grant review meetings. It is not possible to thank individually each of those who have contributed over the years, but only to say that if it were not for them, autism would still be in the dark ages. I will never forget those who came on board early and stayed the course, transforming the field of autism research from a desert into the flourishing field that it is today. They include John Mazziotta, Rudy Tanzi, Maja Bucan, Bill Greenough, and Pat Levitt. My deep appreciation also goes to those who have significantly contributed to the CAN Scientific Advisory Board over the years, among them: Conrad Gilliam, Ed Cook, Nancy Minshew, John Rubenstein, Ted Brown, Diane Chugani, Margaret Bauman, Geri Dawson, Sarah Spence, Michael Gershon, Ian Lipkin, and Ralph Bradshaw. I am also grateful to Dan Gillette and Skip Rizzo for their invaluable contributions to the CAN Innovative Technology for Autism program. Without the tremendous talents of Clara Lajonchere, Sophia Colamarino, and Elizabeth Kilpatrick, CAN and AGRE would not be the incredibly successful organizations they are today. I would also like to express my deep gratitude to Doug Compton, David Baskin, Carole Sprouse, and Ted Abel for all the years in the trenches with me at CAN and for all the years of service on the Scientific Review Council. Knowing that we are in this together has made it all seem possible.

I will always treasure the time I have spent with researchers who so patiently explained scientific principles and systems to me and who have greatly influenced my thinking: my sister Lenore Iversen, Mike Merzenich, Rodolfo Llinás, Bill Greenough, Pat Levitt, Michael Gazzaniga, Michael Pusner, Bill Hirstein, Yoram Bonneh, John Houde, David McGonigle, Tal Kenet, Martha Herbert, Olga Solomon, and my good friend Sharyn Walker.

I am especially grateful to all the researchers who worked directly with Tito, among them: Eric Courchesne, Karen Pierce, Natacha Akshoomoff, Guinevere Eden, V. S. Ramachandran, Matthew Belmonte, Mike Merzenich, Yoram Bonneh, David McGonigle, John Houde, Tal Kenet, Tony Norica, Helen Simon, Francesca Pei, Stefano Baldasari, Chris Moore, and Bill Hirstein. I am very appreciative of Temple Grandin for her generous participation in the research at Merzenich's lab and for sharing her valuable insights about autism with me. I will always be grateful to Dr. Samuel Smithyman for the two years of psychotherapy he so generously donated to Tito. I am indebted to the very talented Gino Campagnia, Dan Brown, Lisa Mraz, and Missy Yager for their contributions to the documentary about Soma, Tito, and Dov and I am forever thankful to Rob Lemelson for his immense generosity in supporting our documentary project.

This book would never have come into being if it were not for Sandra Blakeslee who so kindly introduced me to the kindhearted, insightful, and ever helpful James Levine, my literary agent. My humble thanks to Michele Mills and Therese Finazzo without whose extraordinary assistance I could not have managed to keep my life together while I wrote this book. A special thanks to Diana Price for the long and intense hours of editing and for the chocolate that kept me going. And to Ginny Brewer for the many hours of invaluable help with this manuscript. I cannot adequately express how much I appreciate my friends Racelle Shaeffer, Kara Lindstrom, and Sharyn Walker; I could not have survived without the hiking and the listening. And a special thanks to my dear friend Teresa Sparks who has stuck with me through everything.

My love and gratitude to all the loyal, kind, and devoted people who have worked so tirelessly with Dov, caring for him, teaching him and loving him: Maria Lopez, Karen Hudson, Jill Thompson, Lem Lem Woldemariam, Natalie Pearce, Heather Claire, Jessica Brown, Karen Spratt, Erika Karafin, and Rahel Woldemarion. A special thanks to Sonia Roman for including Dov at Emerson Academy and to Pressman Academy for including Dov in their preschool when he was still a little boy. I will always feel a great fondness for Lola Seiss, Abigail Flores, Claire Parker, and Anya Melzer for their friendship with Dov over the years. Thank you Elissa Henkin for fighting all our legal battles with the school district since Dov was a toddler. And a heartfelt thanks to Dr. Paul Fleiss and Dr. Mark Goldenberg for being the sensitive doctors that they are, and for gaining Dov's trust and meeting his many medical needs.

It all begins with the birth of a lovely child, with the dreams that never die, and with the many hearts and minds that carry those dreams into the future. Thank you for all we have received and thank you for the unknown blessings that are still on their way.

ABOUT THE AUTHOR

Portia Iversen, an Emmy Award–winning art director, has been a vigorous proponent of autism research since her son Dov was diagnosed with the condition in 1994. Together with her husband, Jon Shestack, she established the Cure Autism Now foundation (CAN), one of the largest nongovernmental funding resources for autism research worldwide. She lives in Los Angeles with her husband and their three children.